Studies in Theology and Sexuality, 1

Sex
These Days
Essays on Theology, Sexuality and Society

edited by *Jon Davies & Gerard Loughlin*

Sheffield
Academic Press

Copyright © 1997 Sheffield Academic Press

Published by Sheffield Academic Press Ltd
Mansion House
19 Kingfield Road
Sheffield S11 9AS
England

Printed on acid-free paper in Great Britain
by Bookcraft Ltd
Midsomer Norton, Bath

British Library Cataloguing in Publication Data

A catalogue record for this book is available
from the British Library

ISBN 1-85075-662-7
ISBN 1-85075-804-2 pbk

CONTENTS

INTRODUCTION

Forty or so years ago a religious or theological discussion of 'sex' would in all probability have deployed a central orthodoxy in terms of which certain sexual variations would have been only tentatively discussed. Sex would have been located firmly within the context of heterosexual (procreative) monogamy—the 'married love' to which even so radical a sexual reformer as Marie Stopes (1918) felt it necessary to defer, albeit in title rather than content, and perhaps for tactical rather than principled reasons. In 1958, Roland Bainton's *Sex, Love and Marriage: A Christian Survey* concluded with a rather coy reference to the 'very real and enriching secondary ends of delight in mutual association, companionability, and partnership in joint endeavours', but judged all such modern ideas of coupledom as less sound than the traditional view of sex and marriage: 'a union which commences alike in mutual love and loyalty to God and continues in lifelong fidelity and common labour in the work of the Lord' (Bainton 1958: 128).

Such a traditional and reticent attitude has long since ceased to be regarded as sexual orthodoxy, and the contributors to this book clearly show that the reticent tradition is now one of several competitive heresies in a world of sexual adventure and experiment. A simple correlation of the sheer amount of sex which goes on in our Western world with the number of babies produced shows very clearly that the copulation–conception ratio has shifted massively in favour of non-marital, non-procreative sex—and this with all due allowance for the vagaries of data collection in sexual matters.

What one may call the traditional-reticent view insists on seeing sex as properly and necessarily mobilized for institutional, society-serving ends. In this tradition, sex is for dutiful procreation, and sexual intercourse transforms husbands and wives into fathers and mothers, whose task is the proper socialization of the children resulting from their intercourse. The children are to be brought up, as the *Book of Common Prayer* has it, 'in the fear and nurture of the Lord, and to the praise of his holy name'—which is to say that neither the immediate happiness of the children nor the self-interest of the parents is to take precedence over the fundamental social task of nurturing a God-ward community.

As Mandell Creighton, Bishop of London, put it, 'progress is only possible if men are taught to submit their individual wishes to the common good, and to find satisfaction in curbing their desire for the immediate gratification of their impulses' (Creighton 1901: 148-49). Sexual energies are to be structured in such a way as to create permanent unions between the sexes and generations, and to establish those unions in relation to the other structures of society. The subjective self-interest, happiness or 'authenticity' of the participants is secondary—just as is, say, the subjective happiness or self-interest of a soldier or a coal-miner.

In contrast to the traditional-reticent view of sex is the liberal view, which sees the body and its sexuality as the central location of the 'self', and which sees any repression or restriction of the self and its sexual appetites as a denial of human being. This is the view that promotes and celebrates the plasticity of the body's sexual energies: an ability to form and reform an ever expanding mesh of bodily linkages. Sex is about pleasure not love; passing the time—excitedly—with a friend, acquaintance or stranger, without commitment or hurt. Sex is not an expenditure of the self toward the other, but a return to self: an investment in self-fulfilment. Its goal is not procreation—the mutual making of life in excess of the sexual partners, whether as children or as the enhancement of the human *habitus*, the enriching of common life—but self-satisfaction, the glow of successful performance. Sex is like food, a commodity, and the culture in which it is bought and sold a veritable pornotopia. It is the culture in which we live.

The essays in the first part of the book seek to explain how this pornotopic culture has come to dominate Western capitalist societies and to explore some of its consequences for their common social life—insofar as they still have one, and have not simply become collectivities of atomized consumers: lonely crowds. Jon Davies contrasts our present situation—these days—with how it was in Britain a mere forty or so years ago, when the traditional-reticent view dominated. For Davies, it was founded upon an ecclesial sexual rule—paradigmatically expressed in the 1662 *Book of Common Prayer*—which began with Augustine of Canterbury in the seventh century, and is now largely undone. The undoing of the traditional-reticent sexual rule is further explored by Norman Dennis, who identifies certain changes in law and social convention which constitute what he calls men's sexual liberation; that is their liberation from the need to make a commitment to their sexual partners and to bear a responsibility—financial and social—to any children they might father. For Dennis, these changes were fostered by certain middle-class intellectuals who today are influential in state, church and education, and who refuse to acknowledge that the social ills deplored by so many—state-dependent lone parents, social unrest, child delinquency and abuse—are the consequences of such 'liberation'. The social, physical and emotional bondage of many women and children is the price we pay for the sexual freedom of thousands of young heterosexual men.

Alan Storkey also looks to a middle-class elite for a socially dominant construction of sexuality that contrasts its fearful repression in the nineteenth century with its liberating expression in the twentieth century. With Foucault, Storkey challenges the view that sex was repressed in the nineteenth century, but unlike Foucault he argues that it was the modern tradition of sexology which sought to celebrate sexual expression/liberation in order to legitimate a pathological homosexual subculture. Storkey is concerned to challenge the easy assumption that in matters sexual, repression is bad and expression is good; but above all, he wants to return the 'having' of sex to a context of 'relationship', in particular the relationship of marriage, in which sex can be for the other rather than for the self. For Linda Woodhead also, the claims of the autonomous individual have impoverished our social life. She argues that in our day sex is increasingly confined to the 'context of the one', the individual self and his or her bodily gratification. When the *telos* of sex has become the pleasure of the one, all sex is finally masturbatory. Woodhead discusses the attempt by many Christian thinkers to locate sex in the 'context of two', of the couple, noting how such attempts often fall back into the context of one, and argues that sex should be located in the 'context of many', of children, friends and local communities. For Christians, sex is properly located in the context of the Body of Christ, and Woodhead concludes her essay with some reflections on the effect that such a location has on sex these days.

Philip Mellor and Chris Shilling also argue that our society has become increasingly atomized, with social bonds decayed and the individual rendered inviolable in the sanctity of his or her sexual appetites. They accept Anthony Giddens's (1992) analysis of contemporary sexuality in terms of contractual and confluent love, but reject his advocacy of such a sexuality in favour of a Durkheimian account of the body's 'effervescence', its erotic energies, which they associate with the 'sacred' and which, they argue, is essentially constitutive of society. Confluent love—the flowing together *and apart* of separate bodies—is appropriate to an individualistic society, where unions are increasingly subject to contract, lest the autonomy of the individual be infringed. Erotic effervescence, on the other hand, leads to *communion* rather than confluence, a mutual inflowing of self and other, a meeting of bodies that goes beyond the cognitive. Mellor and Shilling associate confluent love with Protestantism and what they call its 'cult of the dyad', and in response seek to retrieve an earlier Catholic understanding of the body. They argue that a more sensual spirituality will allow us to recognize the inherently social nature of our being, and thus resist the individualism that dominates our sexuality these days.

While Mellor and Shilling share with Davies, Dennis, Storkey and Woodhead a critique of autonomy and the forms of sexuality to which it gives rise, they are less concerned with older forms of sexual rule—such as the ecclesial order favoured by Davies—and would rather, in their advocacy of what they consider the 'effervescent foundations' of 'erotic forms of communion', direct us to uncharted waters—which are the concern of the essays in the second part of the book.

Adrian Thatcher leaves the safe haven of church pronouncements on sexuality—the new Roman Catholic *Catechism* (1994) and the Church of England's *Issues in Human Sexuality* (1991) and *Something to Celebrate* (1995)—to sail the postmodern seas of plastic sexuality, already partly charted by Anthony Giddens. Unlike some of the contributors to the book, Thatcher affirms the worth of sexual autonomy, though noting its potential for self-preoccupation. Thatcher wants free but responsible sex: chastity, or the self-ordering of a person's sexual energies for his or her own good and the good of all. Sex is for exploration, recreation, expression and procreation, and the point is to know what, when and why one is doing one or the other. There is a time to explore, to have fun, to express one self, to procreate. Thus, Thatcher outlines soft rules for good plastic seafaring: balance, patience and fidelity. Through the practice of such virtues, a person may enjoy chaste 'safe sex'.

Janette Gray explores an aspect of sexuality that is little understood in secular society: celibacy. When sexual fulfilment is thought the only form of fulfilment, celibacy—the deliberate renunciation of sexual gratification—seems like sexual deviancy. Many early Christian practitioners of celibacy, influenced by gnostic disparagement of the body as not properly God's creation, saw celibacy as a means of escaping the material, of becoming angelic; while others saw it as a way of realizing the kingdom of God now, as a foretaste of heavenly society, beyond the urges of the flesh. Against these, Gray argues for an understanding of celibacy which sees it as not so much a denial of the flesh, as a different way of being *body*, a different way of being sexual. Gray's understanding of celibacy repeats the older view of celibacy as enacting the kingdom, but now understood as an 'experimental praxis' which explores how to love without restriction, expecting nothing in return. With hope in the promises of Christ, the celibate risks lovelessness in order to enact that love which is God's—infinite expenditure without requirement of reciprocation.

For Gray, the experience of celibate women—secular and religious—is of particular importance, not least because celibacy allows women to define themselves as sexual beings without reference to the law of the *phallus*; without being the 'other' of men. Gray, who offers a bold and challenging account of how the ancient Christian practice of celibacy illuminates some darker reaches of sex these days, also shows how the practice of celibacy—so long cherished in religious women's communities—resonates with several of the dominant themes in recent French feminist thought, in particular that of Luce Irigaray. A similar concern to connect Christian and secular feminist thought is evidenced in Tina Beattie's equally challenging essay on sexual embodiment and sexual difference: the constitution of human being as *two* and not just one sex.

Tina Beattie stages a dialogue between John Paul II and Luce Irigaray, taking as her starting point their shared concern with sexual difference, that 'woman' is not simply a version of 'man'. The pope and the feminist philosopher, of course, understand sexual difference somewhat differently, for Irigaray argues that the difference that is 'woman' is unrealized in our society because women do not have a symbolic order—a 'God'—of their own, which can establish and articulate their difference. In our society women are spoken by men, their identity is framed according to a male symbolic, a male 'God'. Thus, for example, the pope identifies woman's essential character as 'mother'. Irigaray's project is to find a new language, a new symbolism, which will allow woman to be spoken by and for herself for the first time.

Neither Irigaray nor Beattie wish to deny motherhood, but nor do they wish to identify women as essentially mothers, as wombs. Beattie develops her theology of sexual difference by taking with full seriousness the church's symbolic use of the body and its organs; but rather than turning to the penis (Augustine) or the womb (John Paul II), she attends to the clitoris and its meaning of non-reproductive sexual pleasure, a site of pure *jouissance*, which is not ordered to the satisfaction of men or the production of children, but to the joy of women and the goodness of creation.

In the last part of her essay Beattie uses the pope's concern with our embodiment to challenge a certain abstraction in Irigaray's work, a flight from the physical and the social. Each can learn from the other. Beattie's essay is an example of that communion which many of the essays in this book are seeking to make possible: here a communion of discourses in which both are enriched, and thus also the men and women who are shaped by them.

Elizabeth Stuart brings yet another discourse, another voice, into play with the Christian theological tradition—the 'queer' voice of lesbians and gay men. This is not a question of homosexuality in the church, and of how homosexual people might come to be accepted as legitimate members, even as priests; for that question—Stuart argues— is really about maintaining heterosexuality: how far can homosexuals look like heterosexuals? Against such an approach—as in the idea of same-sex marriage—Stuart insists on the queerness of homosexuals; that they are *different*. Thus Stuart looks for a church that can accept and celebrate the difference that is gay and straight, just as Beattie looks for a church that can accept the difference that is woman and man: each difference being understood in terms of its own character, and not of another. The last part of Stuart's essay attempts to sketch such a possible church, by attending to the question of heaven and whether or not there is sex in it. For in contemplating how we will be, we reflect on how we are, and how much we still have to change.

Finally, at the end of the book, Gerard Loughlin reflects on how contemporary culture identifies sex not only with pleasure but with death. In the time of AIDS, when many in Western liberal societies pursue sex more maniacally the more they fear its consequences, the Hollywood film *Alien3* (1992) can be read as articulating the horror of sex, birth and motherhood. Loughlin attends to some of the religious ideas and imagery in the film—of virginal birth and Christian sacrifice—showing how even in the secular domain, theology gives voice to the bodily anxieties of a culture. At the end of his essay, Loughlin, like Stuart, turns to the contemplation of heaven, as a way of articulating the Christian hope for the body and its sex: a hope which is not voiced in the film. The essay forms not so much a conclusion to the book, as a reformulation of some of the themes in its two parts: that sex these days is a source of anxiety, of dissolution, of the violence, fear and loneliness attendant upon creating societies which are no more than lonely crowds; and the hope—present in the church and in the wider world where the theological tradition still has influence, its symbols still active—that sex tomorrow will be for us the site of a real joy and communion in difference, a society not of lone individuals but of implicated members, one of another; and that even now we might feel the presage of that new day.

Jon Davies
Gerard Loughlin
Michaelmas Term 1996

*

Several of the essays in this book began life as public lectures given at the University of Newcastle upon Tyne in Epiphany Term 1996. The lectures were organized by the two editors, who are grateful for the support of the University's Public Lectures Committee, and to Carol Smith at Sheffield Academic Press for work on the editing of the volume.

BIBLIOGRAPHY

Bainton, R.
    1958   *Sex, Love and Marriage: A Christian Survey* (London: Fontana).
Creighton, M.
    1901   *The Church and the Nation* (London: Longmans, Green).
Giddens, A.
    1992   *The Transformation of Intimacy: Sex, Love and Eroticism in Modern Societies* (Cambridge: Polity Press).
Stopes, M.
    1918   *Married Love: A New Contribution to the Solution of Sex Difficulties* (London: The Hogarth Press, 29th edn, 1956).

1994   *Catechism of the Roman Catholic Church* (London: Geoffrey Chapman).

1991   *Issues in Human Sexuality: A Statement by the House of Bishops of the General Synod of the Church of England* (London: Church House Publishing).

1995   *Something to Celebrate: Valuing Families in Church and Society* (London: Church House Publishing).

LIST OF CONTRIBUTORS

Tina Beattie is currently undertaking doctoral research at the Department of Theology and Religious Studies at the University of Bristol, where she also teaches feminist theology. She is the author of *Rediscovering Mary: Insights from the Gospels* (Burns & Oates/Dove, 1995).

Jon Davies is a Senior Lecturer in Religious Studies at the University of Newcastle upon Tyne. He has written widely on the family, war and religion and on contemporary concerns with death and burial. His most recent book is *The Christian Warrior in the Twentieth Century* (Edwin Mellen, 1995).

Norman Dennis is Leverhulme Emeritus Fellow in the Department of Religious Studies at the University of Newcastle upon Tyne. Among his many publications are *Families Without Fatherhood* (IEA, 1992), *Rising Crime and the Dismembered Family* (IEA, 1993) and *The Invention of Permanent Poverty* (IEA, 1997).

Janette Gray RSM is a Sister of Mercy currently undertaking doctoral studies at the University of Cambridge Divinity School, and is the author of *Neither Escaping nor Exploiting Sex: Women's Celibacy* (St Pauls, 1995).

Gerard Loughlin is a Senior Lecturer and Head of the Department of Religious Studies in the University of Newcastle upon Tyne. He is the author of *Telling God's Story: Bible, Church and Narrative Theology* (Cambridge University Press, 1996) and is reviews editor for the journal of *Theology and Sexuality* (Sheffield Academic Press).

Philip A. Mellor is a Lecturer in Religious Studies in the Department of Theology and Religious Studies at the University of Leeds. He is joint author with Chris Shilling of *Re-forming the Body: Religion, Community and Modernity* (Sage Press/Theory, Culture and Society, 1997).

Chris Shilling is a Senior Research Fellow in the Department of Cultural and Historical Studies at the University of Portsmouth. He is a joint author with Philip A. Mellor of *Re-forming the Body: Religion, Community and Modernity* (Sage Press/Theory, Culture and Society, 1997).

Alan Storkey teaches at Oak Hill College. He is chair of the Movement for Christian Democracy, and author of several books, including *Marriage and its Modern Crisis: Repairing Married Life* (Hodder & Stoughton, 1996).

Elizabeth Stuart is a Senior Lecturer at the University of Glamorgan. She is a Trustee of the Institute for the Study of Christianity and Sexuality, and co-editor with Alison Webster of the journal *Theology and Sexuality* (Sheffield Academic Press). She is also editor of *Daring to Speak Love's Name: A Gay and Lesbian Prayer Book* and author of *Just Good Friends: Towards a Lesbian and Gay Theology of Relationships* (Mowbray, 1995) and *Spitting at Dragons: Towards a Feminist Theology of Sainthood* (Mowbray, 1996).

Adrian Thatcher is a Professor and Director of the Centre for Christian Theology and Education at the University College of St Mark and St John, Plymouth. He is the author of *Truly a Person, Truly God* (SPCK, 1990) and *Liberating Sex: A Christian Sexual Theology* (SPCK, 1993).

Linda Woodhead is a Lecturer in Religious Studies at the University of Lancaster. She is the editor of *Christian Studies in Ethics* (T. & T. Clark) and reviews editor of *Modern Believing*.

Part I
LONELY CROWDS

SEX THESE DAYS, SEX THOSE DAYS: WILL IT EVER END?

Jon Davies

The major theme of this essay is that whereas 'sex'—historically centred in the family and in procreation—once expressed and symbolized the stability of relations between the sexes and the generations, it now—freed from both its familial and procreational purposes—expresses the individualized freedom of the sexual market. Sex has been freed from its involvement in the institutionalization of inter-generational and inter-gender relations. Conventional—originally Christian—sexual traditions are, for better or worse, breaking apart under the triumphant voracity of the sexual market, and society as a whole is embarked on a huge experiment with sexual fragmentation and sexual fission.

Five Basic Themes

Western sexual rules are changing in at least five ways. (1) Sexual transactions are going from being governed by objective rules to being grounded within the subjective expressions of 'relationships'; (2) such relationships have at their centre the single individual rather than the family; and (3) they are essentially concerned with the appetitive ambitions of adults rather than the interests and protection of children. (4) The overwhelming legitimacy of the new sexual world is the urge to sexual freedom and happiness, and a concomitant denial of any validity in the necessity of self-denial, let alone 'repression'. (5) An open sexual market has replaced the licence-issuing, licence-denying monopolistic 'command economy' of the traditional repressive sexual culture.

What Sex Was: The Sexual Rules of Catholic Europe

Fourteen hundred years ago Augustine, Pope Gregory's missionary to 'England' and the 'First Archbishop of Canterbury' found himself surrounded by what Bede calls the 'barbarous, fierce and pagan'

English (Bede 1990: 73). So dangerous were these people that Augustine and his companions had at first sought Gregory's permission to abandon the mission; but once ashore Augustine was soon writing back to the Pope asking if a man may 'enter church after relations with his wife before he has washed', or 'receive communion after a sexual illusion in a dream', or 'may a woman properly enter church at the time of menstruation?' (Bede 1990: 82).

Implicit in the Christian sexual culture that gradually spread throughout Europe was a dualism that regarded the body as problematic and the will or mind as an antidote to its carnalities: that is, the body was 'bad', and the mind (with God's help) was 'good'. Another, administrative, dualism saw the Christian sexual pilgrim as being enmeshed in two *ecclesiae*; on the one hand the *ecclesia* of the official authoritative church, which issued instructions and demanded that they be enforced, and on the other hand the *ecclesia* of the Christian community, with the task of both aiding in that enforcement by socialization and educational means, *but also* of arbitrating moderation and pastoral charity for those many Christians with failings which were all too human. Between these two *ecclesiae* there was tension, but unlike the dualism of body–mind, the two *ecclesiae* were complements, not antitheses.

Within this framework, Augustine's concerns came to exemplify what gradually became the official component of 'Eurochristian' religious sexual culture: sexual rules were authoritative—they were handed down, non-negotiable, impersonal—and indifferent to the vagaries of character or circumstance. They were implacably familial—sex, man, wife—and therefore procreational: 'lawful intercourse should be for the procreation of offspring and not for mere pleasure, to obtain children, not to satisfy lust' (Gregory to Augustine in Bede 1990: 86). To talk 'sex' was to talk 'marriage' and 'family'—nuclear family, the institution within which genders and generations transact, negotiate and elaborate their prototypical identities and moral careers.

Perhaps because of the difficulty of separating the duty of procreative copulation from its pleasure, even sex *qua* marriage was simply downgraded. Gregory quoted St Paul:

> For when the Apostle Paul said: '*If they cannot contain, let them marry*', he at once added, '*I speak this by permission, and not of commandment*'. This concession makes it lawful, yet not good; so when he spoke of permission, he indicated that it was not blameless (Bede 1990: 86).

Gregory's rules were clearly repressive, if only because they were impersonal; but for Gregory and like-minded Christian leaders, concerned precisely to repress the body, the word 'repressive' (which is now *always* pejorative, as if the test of what is being repressed no longer matters) had a positive connotation. Above all, Gregory addressed the conscience, the will. Here, said Gregory, is salvation:

> When the Evil Spirit suggests a sin, no sin is committed unless the flesh takes pleasure in it; but when the flesh begins to take pleasure, then sin is born; and if deliberate consent is given, sin is complete (Bede 1990: 88).

There was to be privacy neither of body nor mind. Christian sexual ambition sought conversion: the willing enthusiasm of the mind not the dragooned obedience of the body. The mind, the will, the conscience, had to control the body.

It was the detail that counted. On nocturnal illusions—wet/sexy dreams—Gregory commented that it was the *mental* pictures (not just physical sex) that defiled a man. If, after such a dream, a man was contemplating going to church, he must wash as if he had actually had sex, and 'unless the fire of temptation dies earlier, he should regard himself as unclean until evening'. But, Gregory continued, 'we should carefully examine the origin of such illusions in the mind of a sleeper; for sometimes they arise from overeating, sometimes from excess or lack of bodily vigour, and sometimes from impure thoughts' (Bede 1990: 87).

Over the Christian centuries, to assist in the actual application and enforcement of what must seem to us to be impractical inquiries, vastly exceeding those undertaken by the Child Support Agency and Social Services Departments, the church authorities published and promulgated manuals, confessionals and penitentials, and exerted steady influence upon a variety of laws and courts (secular and ecclesiastical), and worked both to police and 'conscientize' the sexual lives of Christian men and women. It must be stressed that these were crucially sexual rules *for married heterosexual adults*: for everyone else, there were no rules other than those subsumed under the simple and single one: 'don't'. Or, more lengthily: within marriage, chastity; for everyone else, celibacy and chastity.

The complexity of these rules must have worried many a married couple, trying to make sense of the urgencies of the flesh and the rules of the Church. Consider, for example, the Catholic theologian Sylvester, who argued that an amatory process (which he and his readers would have assumed was between husband and wife) which *began* with the intention of consummation, but where, for some reason, the man (with the consent of his wife) did not ejaculate, was a merely venial sin if there 'are not shameless touches proceeding from lust but from love, such as kisses and decent embraces... Otherwise, they are mortal sins, because every lustful action that is not conjugal coitus or ordained to it actually or potentially is illicit' (Tentler 1977: 206).

One hopes that this was as clear to both the manual-consulting marital copulators as well as to the confessor to whom they might at some point take their queries. The *Malleus Maleficarum* (c. 1486) is much clearer. In the case of male impotence the following rule applies: 'When the member is in no way stirred, and can never perform the act of coition, then it is a sign of frigidity of nature: but when it is stirred and becomes erect, but yet cannot perform, it is a sign of witchcraft' (Kramer and Sprenger 1986: 140).

External control and internalized guilt were the objects of a hier-archical legal regulation of sexual life, inside and outside of marriage. Like all legal systems, these rules were moderated by practical and pas-toral concerns. At the point where sexual activity had clearly both taken place and had broken the rules—for example, in the case of illegiti-macy—pastoral care was pretty rough, and more so for women than for men. In the Suffolk town of Bacton, during the night of 22 March 1633, Magdalen Payne secretly entered a barn belonging to Robert Cooper.

> In ye night time ye said Magdalen Payne in ye extremity of pains of childe bearing cryed out in ye night time by which ye said Robert Cooper was enforced to run and implore for aide and assistance of ye neighbouring wives by whose good assistance (God so blessing their endeavours) the said Magdalen Payne was then and there delivered of a woman child christened and named Katherine (Tate 1983: 213).

The village midwife may have been among the 'neighbouring wives' who helped and delivered Katherine. Midwives, operating at the inter-face of rules and pastoral practicalities, were licensed by the Bishop, and were in a variety of ways expected to operate within the laws relating to maternity, paternity and bastardy.

Ellen Perkin's licence, held in 1686 from the Bishop of London, has as its 'Ffirst' obligation that, 'You shall be Diligent, faithful and ready to help every woman travilling wth. Child, as well the poor as ye Rich, and shall not then forsake the poor woman and leave her, to go to the Rich' (Donnison 1988: Appendix 1).

Other books, such as Quaife's *Wanton Wenches and Wayward Wives*

(1979) and Hair's *Before the Bawdy Court* (1972), document the sexual doings and regulations of late medieval and early modern England. W.E. Tate records how in 1740 the Vestry of Gnosall in Staffordshire, agreed to pay Hannah Parton £3. 8s. 0d., 'provided she solemnizes marriage with Richd. Worrall' (Tate 1983: 218). In this case a publicly-provided subsidy dealt with the moral problem. Magdalen Payne, however was not so lucky: a month or so after her daughter was born she was up with court on a vagrancy charge (English bastardy laws were tied up with the Poor and Vagrancy Laws). Found guilty, she was 'whipped until her bodie was bloodie' and the Justice of the Peace announced that he 'Require[d] all Constables. . . to be careful in the con-veying of the sayde Magdalen Payne and Katherine her daughter from Constable to Constable by direct way to ye towne of Hitcham aforesaid there to be provided for according to his Majesties lawes on that behalf made and provided' (Tate 1983: 213).

Hard? Cruel? Very probably: but one wonders what Magdalen Payne would have made of a system like ours, so totally indifferent to the birth and life-chances of babies and children that we condone or shrug at their procreation, and at all manner of 'parenting practices' which can be shown to be, in all probability, and in both subtle and not so subtle ways, damaging to them; an indifference compounded by the insistence that it is 'simply a matter of money', as if *that* in itself was an easy matter. Recently, Britain has seen the case of parents appa-rently happy to see their 13 year old daughter go off to be 'married' to an 18 year old boy in a totally foreign culture.

We will see later on what happens when (as in our days) the rules are abandoned and there is little but a voluntary and shifting 'community', more wished for than actually existing, within which people of all sorts of age and experience have to track their own way through the sexual terrain. The error—if error it be—is to regard the existence of sexual rules as somehow incompatible with the existence of sexual community, or, to put it another way, that communities of care can be wished into existence in order to replace the despised and abolished repressive rules, as if the one can exist only when the other has gone.

The Reformation

The regulation of sex, both official and pastoral, was little affected by the Reformation. The major impact of the Reformation on sex was indirect: with the demand for and accomplishment of political freedom, conscience and political pluralism (or political 'privacy'), came the demand for a similar dispensation in sexual matters, a dispensation only very reluctantly conceded, if at all, by the sexually conservative Protestant leaders such as Luther, Calvin, Knox and Zwingli. It was absolutely clear in the minds of Protestant leaders that freedom *of* conscience was in no way freedom *from* conscience. The keeper of this conscience was the head of the household, usually the father; and it was to the household that the Reformers devolved responsibility for a proper upbringing.

'Matrimony', thundered the introductory homily to the 1662 *Anglican Solemnization of Matrimony*—the marriage service which defined the marriage ethos for near on three hundred years—'is an honourable estate, instituted of God in the time of man's innocency'.

> [It] is not by any to be enterprised, nor taken in hand, unadvisedly, lightly, or wantonly, to satisfy men's carnal lusts and appetites, like brute beasts that have no understanding; but reverently, discreetly, advisedly, soberly and in the fear of God; duly considering the causes for which Matrimony was ordained.
> First, it was ordained for the procreation of children, to be brought up in the fear and nurture of the Lord, and to the praise of his holy Name.
> Secondly, it was ordained for a remedy against sin, and to avoid fornication; that such persons as have not the gift of continency might marry, and keep themselves undefiled members of Christ's body.
> Thirdly, it was ordained for the mutual society, help, and comfort, that the one ought to have of the other, both in prosperity and adversity.

The English lived under these sexual rules until 1955. True, the first Victorians felt that they had inherited a sexual mess, and proceeded to use the power of the State—in particular the Poor Law—to reinforce and even extend the range of sexual controls. In parallel with this, as Peter Gay (1984) has shown, the Victorian bourgeoisie was, within its increasingly comfortable and confident civil culture, and through 'sweet bourgeois communions', developing an enjoyment of domestic sexuality which—if early and admittedly limited sex surveys are anything to go by—was enjoyed by women as well as by men. Peter Gay's work—unless hopelessly wrong—certainly gives the lie to the presentation by Marx and Engels of the essentially loveless nature of bourgeois marriage, just as data on the sex lives of proletarian families gives the lie to their roseate view of the sex lives of the working classes.

Whether because the sexual life of more and more families was improving, or for other and associated reasons, people in Newcastle

upon Tyne felt able to regard the century between 1832 and 1932 as a
'century of civil peace'—these being the words inscribed on Newcastle's
monument to the passing of the 1832 Reform Bill at its rededication in
1932. At that time marriage rates were high, divorce, separation and
illegitimacy rates low, as also crime rates (though at the time of rededication unemployment was high—and chronic). Geoffrey Gorer—in his
two books, *Exploring English Character* (1955 [research 1950]) and
Sex and Marriage in England Today (1971 [research 1968])—demonstrated how successfully 'christianized' English sexual life had become
by the 1950s. For better or for worse, sex was still attached to procreational monogamy and sexual life to the unification of the genders
and the generations. Gorer drew attention to the 'high seriousness with
which the great majority of English people approach and regard
marriage'.

> Whether pre-marital experience is advocated or reprobated, the effect on
> the future marriage is the preponderant consideration. Secondly, the high
> value put on virginity for both sexes is remarkable and, I should suspect,
> specifically English. Thirdly, it is interesting to note that what might be
> called the hypochondriacal attitude towards sexual activity has apparently
> achieved very little currency. This hypochondriacal view, derived from
> assorted popularisations and vulgarisations of psychology and psychiatry,
> connects sexual activity with physical and mental health, so that abstinence
> becomes, as it were, a rather more dangerous type of constipation, and
> sexual activity a kind of prophylaxis. In some other societies this view
> would appear to be widely held (Gorer 1971: 39).

It is tempting to think that the England Gorer described in 1950
would have given Augustine some grounds for satisfaction—that 1400
years of Christian proselytizing had not been altogether in vain. Gorer
and his respondents, for example, took the nuclear family for granted—
the question of what is meant by 'family', which now arises in every
discussion of sex and procreation, does not even arise. Gorer and his
respondents took for granted the 'normality' of the association of
nuclear family, welfare capitalism, and liberal democracy which was
being analysed rather more explicitly by his contemporary American
colleagues, such as Talcott Parsons and Neil Smelser. It was Parsons,
again in the 1950s, who pronounced that there would be no further
changes in family structure and sexual roles.

> The basic and irreducible functions of the (nuclear) family are two: first,
> the primary socialisation of the child. . . second, the stabilisation of the
> adult personalities of the population (Parsons 1968: 16).

Under this analysis, sex unites the genders and the generations within the institution of the family. It should be noted that in Parsons' analysis these two functions are systematically related. That is to say, the two processes of socializing the child and maturing the adult go hand in hand, and can only go hand in hand. Separate the one from the other, and neither task is performed properly: the child will be badly socialized and the adult will remain immature or even infantilized.

What Would Augustine and Parsons Make of 1996?

I had at one point thought of assembling a selection of the 'sex' magazines that are endlessly available even in a rather conservative provincial city like Newcastle upon Tyne. However, there is no need to turn to 'porn' to illustrate how far things have changed. It is in the 'ordinary' magazines, those now regarded as 'normal', that the change is most remarkable.

'Women's magazines' of the early and mid-1950s, the time of Gorer's first research, show a highly traditional sexual division of labour and very conservative depictions of the human body: a corset on a demurely posed young woman is the most risqué thing one can find; and such images are further de-eroticized by appearing on the same page as adverts for baby milk or some cooking device or recipe. Conversely, 'women's magazines' today contain the most explicit sexual material, and often carry rather impressionistic but very graphic 'sex surveys', accompanied by the most explicit advice on all manner of sexual practices, homosexual and heterosexual, marital or otherwise. 'Ordinary' daily newspapers carry nude photographs which less than fifty years ago would have been classified as hard-core pornography. I make no value judgements: merely report the absence of sexual reticence. There is now no end to sex and its variations.

Sexual Behaviour in Britain (Wellings *et al.* 1994) documents the move to a sexual market society, dominated by an ethic of appetitive individualism, and a de-institutionalized or fission society. The authors show that the age of first intercourse is getting lower; that more women are having 'underage sex' (18.7 per cent of straight women, cf. 28 per cent straight men [Wellings *et al.* 1994: 16]) and that in these as in most other sexual matters there is a convergence in the behaviour of men and women. The 'double standard' is being abolished by women adopting those male sexual practices so deplored by some feminists.

Virginity is no longer an issue. Heterosexuality has no monopoly. Marriage is on the way out. The divorce rate, which is at a historically high level, seems to be levelling off only because people no longer bother to get married. Marriage has lost both its sexual and procreational monopoly. The average age of first sexual intercourse of those aged 16 to 19, is 17 and declining. The majority of people co-habit before marriage, and marry late. The average age at which a woman has her first child is 29, and 33 per cent of all births, and 60 per cent of all conceptions, take place outside marriage. Abortions are fairly readily available, and contraceptives are no longer on sale only in Gentlemen's Hairdressers and are no longer only the responsibility of men. The vast bulk of all heterosexual sex clearly takes place outside of procreation and marriage. A Conservative government abolished the legal concept of 'illegitimacy'. The prediction of 70 per cent of births outside 'marriage' moves us steadily to a society of subsidized matriarchy: 75 per cent of women aged 16 to 24 believe that a single parent can bring up children as well as a couple (Wilkinson and Mulgan 1995: 74).

Late twentieth-century capitalism appears not to need the nuclear family. The 'individual' which was the icon of liberal economics *was generally the nuclear family*, subsumed under the (usually male) head of the family. The 'individual' is now a 'person' on his or her own. Neither does late twentieth-century capitalism need the exclusive sexual (heterosexual) monopoly historically claimed for the 'nuclear family'. Our households get smaller and smaller, and fragment more frequently.

In the sexual market the genders and generations are separating from one another, relying on 'contract' and 'self-sufficiency' rather than on 'sentiment' and 'covenant' as the prime form of sociation. The latest round of discussion about pensions has been about the pension rights of divorcing couples and the necessity for one generation, in its lifetime, to pay for its own retirement and death arrangements. This is a historical first. Perhaps the major departure from traditional sexual discourse has been the elimination of children and childbearing from the adult realm of sex. Alistair McFadyen's influential *The Call to Personhood* (1990), has no index entry for 'children' and no discussion of them. 'Relations between the sexes', he states, 'are of primary importance': the 'sexes' clearly being adult, the 'relations' sexual. There is no longer a Council to guide people in the ways of marriage, but rather Relate: like 'have a nice day'. There is a huge significance in the change in name of The Marriage Guidance Council to Relate. There is only one Marriage Guidance Council: the word 'guidance' implies the existence of rules to which this authoritative body (the Council) will guide people. 'Relate', on the other hand, is an objectless verb masquerading as a noun, a cross between a small hope and a mere description.

Our culture is profoundly child-indifferent—or at least pro-adult, because only adults can play the contract-game. One in four children will see their parents divorce before they are 16 (Wilkinson and Mulgan 1995: 73). Nearly all the data available shows that at the level of probability children flourish or suffer in direct relationship to their proximity to their monogamous biological parents: the closer to that entity, the less they suffer. In some inchoate way our society is beginning to realize this: we are either stopping having children, or nationalizing them, or, in the most subtle way of 'solving' the child problem, pretending that they can and indeed should be treated as adults. Children are being treated as an indivisible public good, everyone's responsibility, and therefore no one's. Children have simply ceased to be regarded as part of the culture of sex.

The Church (of England) in the Sexual Market

The sexual disunions of the market are breaking up the synthesis of the two *ecclesiae*, the *ecclesia* of rules and the *ecclesia* of community. Christian sexual culture—the two *ecclesiae*—has actually split into two: the tensions have indeed become antitheses. The extent to which 'what the church says' will have much consequence in the broader society is hard to predict: but it seems reasonably certain that the irruption of the sexual market into the church itself will cause more schism and fission than anything caused by the dispute over women priests, a dispute which at heart was a highly old-fashioned and even reactionary gender quarrel. Sexual, not gender, tensions, will carry the real force of the market into the church, and will in all probability see it abandoned by the vast majority of people, who will see in a sexually 'liberated' church nothing to distinguish it from the general sexual market of a secular, permissive culture, less ludicrously handled by the efficient exploitative competence of capitalism than by our increasingly ludicrous, if endearing, church leaders.

Already, on the one hand, we see the theological tradition-insisters— a sect adamantly insisting on the continued primacy of the rules of church or Bible or both—forced, by the radicalness of the sexual changes we have made, 'not to know' the second *ecclesia*, the *ecclesia* of tolerance and concession. Equally, the second *ecclesia* now knows *nothing but* tolerance and concession, in which any rule or restriction is suspect simply because it exists. The end result of this set of attitudes is that the sexual behaviour of Britain is now set to be as resolutely 'pagan' as it was in Augustine's day.

To this excess of tolerance the sexual liberals have some kind of answer. The limit of tolerance is found in the body! The once bad body has now become good. The body is proclaimed to be the incarnated community, a community of the body, with 'a new erotic body spirituality' (Nelson 1995: 58). The body is Christ and the body is sexual.

The body-indifferent sexual agenda of the 1970s and 1980s, in which all was gender, endlessly plastic, unrestricted by dismal anatomy, proved a little too radical, too fleeting for an ethic of sex, too claimable by the market and money—as indeed it has been claimed by the endless bisexualities, multi-sexualities and androgynies of the likes of David Bowie, Madonna, Boy George, Freddy Mercury, making all too obvious the huge inexperience of Christian ecclesiology and theology when confronted with the ruthless, ceaseless radicality of the market in which sex, like everything else, is merely a wallet.

In liberal theology, body/sex has replaced gender. The *ecclesia* of rules which Augustine so anxiously sought to establish has to go—these rules come from an 'austere, repressed old man doling out his moralisms from the sky' (Walton 1994: 37-39). The second ecclesia is now seen as separable from the despised and rejected first ecclesia: it stands alone, locating a new community in the body! The body in question is Jesus.

The incarnation, the embodying of God, demonstrates the legitimation of the body as a moral order, a moral community. James Nelson, at the launch of *Theology and Sexuality*—the journal of the Centre for the Study of Christianity and Sexuality—stated that:

> Sexual theology. . . invites us to listen to the body's own speech, to think theologically *with* and *through* our bodies. It is convinced that the sexuality that has such power in our lives—the source of such anxiety, such joy, such yearning, such shame, such woundedness, such curiosity, such fulfilment—must be very close to the center of things. . . As Nikos Kazantakis wrote, 'Within me even the most metaphysical problem takes on a warm physical body which smells of sea, soil and human sweat. The Word, in order to touch me, must become warm flesh' (Nelson 1995: 46-47).

The body of Christ, crucified and risen, transcends 'one time, and becomes for all times, one community for all communities, one sex for both sexes' (Ward and Wild 1995: 4). The body, the incarnate, is all: 'Becoming "one flesh" denotes neither sexual intercourse nor its product (Seth), but human existence as a whole under the aspect of corporeality' (McFadyen 1990: 37).

There is one very major qualification of this body-based sexual theology: the penis or, more precisely, the phallus—the erect penis— has to go. The phallus, for Nelson, symbolizes the first *ecclesia*, the hierarchical church:

> Ideally, the phallus is big, hard and up. So we have accented those values in the divine. God, too, must be big, hard and up: sovereign in power, righteous in judgement, the transcendent Wholly Other. It is hardly an erotic or incarnational understanding of the divine (Nelson 1995: 49).

Reviewing Nelson's book, *The Intimate Connection* (1992), the Rt Revd Professor Peter Selby also felt it necessary to remove the phallus from the repertoire of the Body-Community:

> The legacy of male domination is a concentration on the male sexual organ in its aroused state, as phallus, with all its connotations of imperiousness and penetration, and a resultant competitiveness and seeking after power. To reflect also on the male organ as penis, as unaroused, includes within masculinity the sense also of rest and vulnerability (Selby 1992: 455-56).

This is rather a radical diminution of the body. No doubt the flaccid penis has much to commend it, though I have some suspicion that we see in this distaste for the erect penis, another, if indirect, version of the diminution of children which is so central to liberal 'post-modern' promotions of sex. More importantly, perhaps, is a doubt about whether the body really is a proper basis for a moral community? The body is surely a very fallible little thing—mine is anyway—not capable of being either a moral agent or the basis for a new community—a community of everyone's bodies is likely to be a community caring for no one's body—except as objects of exploitation and abuse, as objects of disunion.

The really endearing thing about theologians is the zeal with which they get on yesterday's about-to crash bandwagon from which every one else is rapidly jumping. Do we have to learn, again, that a community which is, or promises to be, a community for everyone tends to turn out to be a community for no one—other than the most unpleasant manipulators of the dedicatedly and determinedly naive and vulnerable?

The Times (27 November 1995) reported the case of an Anglican priest, Christopher Brain, who was 'kicked out' (made to resign) after a predatory sexual career pursued, it would seem, through new forms of worship. 'He would talk', said one of his female partners, 'about how we were discovering a post-modern definition of sexuality within the Church. But it is language covering up what was going on—one bloke getting his rocks off with about 40 women'. A repentant [*sic*] Brain said: 'Most of the time I was involved sexually it was after a long period of developing a close relationship with that person. I did get gratification. The gratification I was after was not sexual although there was sexual gratification.'

The Lonely Crowd

In the amazingly optimistic era of the 1950s and 1960s, the world that went to Woodstock, the era that some theologians are now catching up with, people like David Cooper in *The Death of the Family*, called for the dissolution of the ontological restrictions of family and procreative sex and extolled the liberating power of liberated sex.

Among these optimists was David Riesman, whose subtle and evocative book, *The Lonely Crowd* (1950), is still the finest, if most wrong-headed of all the summons to joy produced by the decades of Woodstock. Riesman (generally much more perceptive and ironic than people like Cooper) used a sexually reticent language, as was the practice in those days, but like Cooper also looked forward to the end of 'the provinciality of being born to a particular family in a particular place [and to the desired time] when ties based on *conscious relatedness* [would replace] those of blood and soil' (Riesman 1950: xlvii). There was, he wrote, no point in 'any effort by the neo-traditionalists to close the sexual frontier (though this might restore the glamour that sex had in the earlier era) as this would be irrelevant to the problems created by the greater demands a leisure-oriented people put upon their choice in companionship, sexual or otherwise' (Riesman 1950: 331-32).

Riesman was discussing the sexual anxieties, sexual preoccupations and the rising divorce rate of what he called 'the self-exploiting peer-groups' of middle-class America (Riesman 1950: 35). Riesman saw modern society as having solved the historical problems of humanity. He was convinced that all the material problems of society had been solved and that wealth creation was no longer *the* human problem. Neither did society (especially American society) face a security problem: all military or political threats to the liberal-democratic way of life had been seen off (Riesman 1950: 35). The only problem remaining, said Riesman, is other people! 'Increasingly, *other people are the problem, not the material environment*' (Riesman 1950: 18-19).

Riesman, in one of a flow of excoriating and almost unconscious throw-way lines, refers to 'self-exploiting adult peer-groups' who are preoccupied with attending to sexual matters in this leisure-world. In discussing the growing problem of divorce (then at about ten per cent of what it is now) the only problem, he felt, quoting Margaret Mead, was that 'new demands for sociability and leisure freedom for sensitive middle class couples include the dynamic that each partner to a marriage *expects the other to grow and develop at approximately the same rate as himself*' (Riesman 1950: 18-19; my emphasis).

There, surely, is the rub—especially for a body-based sociability. Without rules, and with maximum legitimacy for all expressions of carnal subjectivism, in which every transient itch is happiness and every happiness an imperative, but an imperative only for the itcher, there is no possibility of relationship beyond a whim. Body-driven sociability is a contradiction in terms.

In twentieth-century capitalism there is a flesh and sexual market of such voracity as to require all the experience and wisdom of the two *ecclesiae*. There is no limit to the empire of the appetite, especially when the appetite, as body, my body, is made the moral arbiter of everything. Apart, even, from that, there is the evident fact that—and here, yes, I speak for myself as well as for millions of others—as bodies, we are an anarchy of bungling and decay, lonely and unsure in all the various 'ages' of human life, requiring the most steadfast altruism and sure attachment from known and anchored others, the 'mutual society, help, and comfort, that the one ought to have of the other[s], in prosperity and adversity'. Our contemporary sexual–erotic culture, endlessly asserting the primacy of subjectivity and difference, is separating the sexes and generations from each other.

Sex as Disunion

This essay was originally given as a public lecture on the day before St Valentine's Day, 1996. Valentine's Day is, of course, the day of romance and true love. The Valentine's Day issue of *Cosmopolitan* magazine gave us this:

> If I had my way Valentine's Day would be a national holiday for everyone
> to stay in bed with the lover of their choice. And wouldn't *that* get
> complicated (*Cosmopolitan*, February 1996: 89).

Last year's Valentine's Day issue of the *Journal for the Independent
Parent* gave us Tracey Greenwood's thoughts on how to 'cope alone'
on Valentine's Day—a genuine comment on how 'complicated' such a
cosmopolitan pseudo-*gemeinschaft* is likely to be:

> Coping with being alone on Valentine's Day? Judging by my past record
> of picking up totally unromantic gits, I think I'd rather be alone. This year
> I'm going to send myself a card and proudly display my self-love on my
> shelf. Then in the evening I'm going to curl up on the settee with my cat,
> a box of chocolates and a sloppy video, and have a good old boo hoo
> about how unloved, unwanted and unnoticed I am. I want to sulk, and
> it'll certainly make me feel better. I hope to have romance in my life one
> day. I'm not going to look for it, it'll just. . . come to me.

If 'Tracey' is the girl illustrated by the accompanying photograph,
she has also a child to consider, presumably on her own, as her musings
conclude with an expression of gratitude for having lost her lover:
'I'm grateful to be in control of my life now that I'm finally free'.
Tracey is, of course, likely to live in a world increasingly composed
of free single people like her, as the birth rate falls and more and more
people live in single person households, generally (ironically, given
the readily deployed vocabulary of 'independence') very dependent
on the 'public' (i.e. other people's) purse. In such a world, the non-
existence of Richey Edwards makes sense. Richey Edwards, lyricist,
spokesman and guitarist of The Manic Street Preachers, just 'stepped
off the edge' one day, and his memoriam, as sung by ex-porn star
Traci Lords, tells us why:

> No God reached me
> Faded films and loving books
> Black and white TV
> All the world does not exist for me
> (*The Independent Colour Magazine*, 20 January 1996).

The lonely crowd indeed—terribly lonely bodies, with the Tracey
of *The Magazine for the Independent Parent* being, in her photograph,
a young and attractive body, but apparently neither generously expan-
sive nor happily narcissistic: merely beleaguered, as Christopher Lasch
might put it (Lasch 1985: 16).

Without clear rules—the sort which do not have to be 'reflexively retransacted', to use the jargon, at every new human encounter—we will get only—what we are getting—a sexually self-exploiting pseudo-community, ceaselessly eating its own inflated hopes, rapidly coming to ground itself in that most desolating of all sexual convictions, sexual cynicism: expect nothing, get nothing, give nothing. We will be a lonely crowd, kept apart by sex.

BIBLIOGRAPHY

Bede
  [1955] 1990   *Ecclesiastical History of the English People* (trans. Leo Sherley-Price and R.E. Latham; Harmondsworth: Penguin Books).
Cooper, D.
  1971   *The Death of the Family* (Harmondsworth: Penguin Books).
Donnison, J.
  1988   *Midwives and Medical Men* (London: Historical Publications).
Gay, P.
  1984   *Education of the Senses*, I (Oxford: Oxford University Press).
Gorer, G.
  1955   *Exploring English Character* (London: Cresset Press).
  1971   *Sex and Marriage in England Today* (London: Nelson).
Hair, P.E.
  1972   *Before the Bawdy Court* (London: Elek).
Kramer, H., and J. Sprenger
  1971   *Maleus Maleficarum* (London: Arrow).
Lasch, C.
  1985   *The Minimal Self* (London: Picador).
McFadyen, A.
  1990   *The Call to Personhood: A Christian Theory of the Individual in Social Relation* (Cambridge: Cambridge University Press).
Nelson, J.
  [1988] 1992   *The Intimate Connection: Male Sexuality, Masculine Spirituality* (London: SPCK).
  1995   'On Doing Body Theology', *Theology and Sexuality* 2: 38-60.
Parsons. T.
  [1956] 1968   *Family Socialisation and Interaction Process* (London: Routledge & Kegan Paul).
Quaife, G.R.
  1979   *Wanton Wenches and Wayward Wives* (London: Croom Helm).
Riesman, D.
  1950   *The Lonely Crowd* (New Haven: Yale University Press).
Selby, P.
  1992   Review of *The Intimate Connection* by J. Nelson, *Theology* 95: 455-56.
Tate, W.E.
  1983   *The Parish Chest* (Chichester: Phillimore).

Tentler, T.
    1977   *Sin and Confession on the Eve of the Reformation* (Princeton, NJ:
                 Princeton University Press).
Walton, H.
    1994   'Theology of Desire', *Theology and Sexuality* 1: 31-41.
Ward, H. and J. Wild
    1995   *Human Rites: Worship Resources for an Age of Change* (London:
                 Mowbray).
Wellings, K., *et al.*
    1994   *Sexual Behaviour in Britain* (Harmondsworth: Penguin Books).
Wilkinson, H. and G. Mulgan
    1995   *Freedom's Children* (London: DEMOS).

MEN'S SEXUAL LIBERATION

Norman Dennis

The progressive release of men from *sociological* fatherhood, as Malinowski called it, is one of the most important expressions of the general movement, in urban-industrial societies that are at least nominally Christian, from cultural control to self-regarding hedonism. It is the most striking and important change of the past forty years.

What, first, of the matter of a man becoming a father without accepting, or being made to accept, the responsibilities of spousehood and fatherhood, and without having to live under the same roof as the mother and child so long as he is not kept away by work or war? If the question of the change in the cultural conditions of boys and young men is addressed to the period since 1836, when the record of births and marriages first begins to become reliable, and becomes increasingly reliable, the picture is quite clear. From 1836 up to the early 1960s in this country, even in wartime, the ratio of men not marrying the mother of their child by the time the baby was born had fluctuated only two or three percentage points above and below 7 per cent. But between 1960 and 1984 the rate had suddenly risen from this century-long norm of well under 10 per cent to 17 per cent. In the mere twelve years after 1984 it doubled again.[1] If we consider men occasioning a conception outside marriage (as distinct from a birth outside marriage) the figure rose from 40 per cent to just under 60 per cent from the early 1980s to the early 1990s.[2]

That significant changes have taken place in the tightness with which men's sexual activities were confined within the family is denied in influential circles. 'Cohabitation, births outside marriage, lone-parent

1. Office of Population Census and Surveys, OPCS Monitor, 28 June 1995.
2. OPCS, *OPCS Updates* (7 July 1995). The figures are for 1982 and 1992 (England and Wales). In 1992, 58 per cent of conceptions outside marriage led to a birth outside marriage, and only 8 per cent to a birth within marriage. Thirty-four per cent of the conceptions outside marriage led to a legal abortion.

families, repartnering and reconstituted families, were common in earlier centuries', said a major Church of England report on the family in 1995. The difference between today and the past is not in male conduct, the report says, but in the fact that 'previously these things were hidden'.[3]

Exponents of the 'nothing much has changed' school of family thought refer vaguely to 'previous centuries'. Lawrence Stone is a writer whose work on the family is authoritatively used by many academic, church and media commentators to justify the proposition that men's sexual and family situation has not changed over the centuries. Yet in the Elizabethan period, according to Stone himself, the ratio of children whose fathers were not married to their mother when the child was born, ran at the level of under 4 per cent. During the period of Puritan control, Stone tells us, the ratio fell steadily to a low point of one-half of 1 per cent in the 1650s. It was still under 2.5 per cent in the 1720s. There was then what he calls a 'remarkable rise', a 'striking increase', to 4.5 per cent in the 1760s and to 6 per cent after 1780.[4] That these are underestimates I do not for one moment doubt. But these are the figures that he supplies.

Stone, therefore, writing as he was before 1977 (that is, in the early years of the dramatic transformation in the conditions under which men could engage in sexual intercourse which could have the consequences of procreation) still saw a rise of 2 per cent in the figures from 4.5 per cent to 6.5 per cent, a rise of 2 per cent over a period of *forty* years as being 'remarkable' and 'striking'. While he was writing his book he was in the midst of a rise from 7 per cent in 1964 to 32 per cent in 1994, a rise of *25 percentage points* over a period of *thirty* years.

The social effort aimed at attaching the man to his children and the mother of his children through (if necessary) 'shotgun' marriages and disadvantages in law, as well as the shame *suffered by his child* if he did not marry the mother, has been gradually relaxed. The effect on the man of stigmatizing the child gradually disappeared. In 1972 Lord Hodson was able to say that 'the legal incidents of being born a bastard are now almost non-existent'. The Family Law Reform Act 1987 in

3. Working Party of the General Synod Board for Social Responsibility, *Something to Celebrate: Valuing Families in Church and Society* (London: Church House Publishing, 1995), p. 205.

4. L. Stone, *The Family, Sex and Marriage in England 1500–1800* (London: Weidenfeld & Nicolson, 1977), pp. 612-13.

effect abolished the legal category of 'illegitimate child'. A child's relationship to other people was now to be construed without regard to whether or not the father or mother had ever been married to one another.[5] It removed the 'separate and disadvantageous' treatment that had been accorded to children born outside marriage under all previous legislation.[6] The terms 'legitimate' and 'illegitimate' were banned from government publications from 1988.

I am not, of course, recommending in any way the restoration of a social device so cruel and unjust as to make the child pay for his father's freedom from responsibility for it. I am only saying, as a matter of fact, that *as a control on men's conduct* it (like his own social disgrace in 'letting the girl down' or the insistence that if he was the father, he had to marry the mother) has almost ceased to operate.

The Children Act 1989 is quite clear on the unmarried man's liberation from the consequences of his begetting a child. 'Where the child's father and mother were not married to each other at the time of his birth, the mother shall have parental responsibility for the child; the father shall not have parental responsibility for the child...'[7]

Stone's figures refer to a time when contraceptive technology was poorly developed. The conception–fornication ratio must have therefore been very high compared with today. We have had the modern sheath since 1928. We have had the contraceptive pill since 1961. There was never much restriction on knowledge about or use of the pill. The taboos that surrounded discussion about and the sale and use of the sheath were dissipated from the late 1970s onwards. In 1995 many of Newcastle upon Tyne's buses were embellished with the picture of a

5.   Family Law Reform Act 1987, Section 1.-(1).

6.   J. Cooper, 'Births Outside Marriage: Recent Trends and Associated Demographic and Social Changes', *Population Trends 63* (London: HMSO, 1991).

7.   Children Act 1989, Sections 2.-(1) and 2.-(2). 'Parental responsibility' means 'all the rights, duties, powers, responsibilities and authority which by law a parent has in relation to the child and his property'. The fact that the father does not have 'responsibility' does not affect any 'obligation' he might have, such as the statutory 'duty' to maintain the child (Section 3.-[1], [2] and [4]). The Child Support Act 1991 lays upon the absent father his share of both parents' duty of maintenance. The court can grant a father parental responsibility if it approves an application for him, or if it approves a 'parental responsibility agreement' made between the father and mother (Section 4.-[1]). The rule of law that the father is the natural guardian of his *legitimate* child was abolished under section 2.-(4), another considerable liberation from a legal burden.

giant sheath, and the slogan, 'If you want to get it off, get it on'. The dramatic reduction in the conception–fornication ratio therefore makes the current figures on fathers not marrying the mother before the birth of his child an index also of the increase in men's freedom to fornicate.

Men's sexual liberation from the late 1950s onwards was largely a demand made upon British society, not by the products of the mines and factories, or the secondary modern and grammar schools, but by establishment figures in the higher civil service, ex-public-school boy entertainers at and from the elite universities, and senior politicians who came from the same social background (or those from puritan working-class backgrounds who had assimilated themselves to the *mores* of the sexually enlightened upper-middle class and aristocracy). The attacks on the public notion of 'obscenity' in the *Lady Chatterley's Lover* trial was part of the middle-class spirit of the times, which owed to 'the working-class' nothing but the absurd middle-class fantasy that the working-class was already sexually libertine.

By one historical accident television was on the scene to celebrate and disseminate the shedding of men's heterosexual inhibitions and controls. By another, a vast constituency receptive to such ideas was contemporaneously created. The expansion of the universities after the 1963 Robbins report put unprecedentedly large numbers of sexually mature young men with other unmarried young people, away from their own homes, kinship networks, neighbourhoods and towns.

The exponents of men's sexual liberation had the satisfaction of hearing the Archbishop of Canterbury himself say that the Church had been *guilty of* treating pre-marital, extra-marital and self-indulgent sex too seriously as a sin.[8] For a short time fornication without conception did not matter so much in one respect. Gradually since 1928 penicillin had greatly reduced the danger from venereal disease. But venereal disease has clearly come to matter again.

The consequences for the man of making a woman pregnant were also much reduced by the greater ease with which the option of abortion could be chosen. Before 1967 nearly all abortion was illegal. By 1995 20 per cent of all conceptions were being aborted. In Greater London

---

8.   The Church was 'just as guilty as any other section of the community in thinking sexual sins more significant than other sins' (*The Independent*, 20 March 1992). In 1992 which other section of the community thought any but very few sexual acts were 'sins' at all?

the proportion was 25 per cent. In inner London it was 35 per cent.[9]

Men have been progressively released since the mid-1950s from social pressures and institutional arrangements that required them to channel their sexual energies into reproduction within the family. Public opinion, the law, and the tax structure formerly favoured the man who had done so. By the mid-1990s this was no longer the case.

By then, taking all benefits, taxes and rents into account, a married couple with two small children earning £150.00 gross ended up with £136.11. A single parent with two small children claiming her £40.00, with a gross wage of £150.00, ended up with £170.62. Even on a part-time gross wage of £75.00 a week she got £163.31.[10]

Except for the handful of cases of divorce by Private Act of Parliament, divorce in this country was allowed only from 1857. After 1857 divorce was possible if one of the spouses committed a grave matrimonial offence. This was for long perceived primarily as the offence of throwing the issue of paternity into confusion within marriage—the offence of one man possibly being betrayed into the care and maintenance of another man's child.

As late as the 1950s the figures stabilized at about 13,000 men a year applying for a divorce. When the law was changed under the 1969 Divorce Reform Act the number of men seeking a divorce rapidly rose fourfold to 50,000 a year.

By the mid-1990s there were 95,000 divorces a year of married couples *with a family*, affecting 176,000 children.[11] One hundred years before, by contrast, the average annual divorce rate was about 300 *in total*, of couples without children as well as those with children.

In 1988 a discussion paper from the Law Commission suggested that there was no need for the legal system to support marriage any more than 'any other living arrangement'.[12] The subsequent Green Paper,

9.   Office of National Statistics (ONS), *Population Studies 84* (London: HMSO, 1996).

10.   P. Morgan, *Farewell to the Family? Public Policy and Family Breakdown in Britain and the USA* (Choice in Welfare Series, 21; London: IEA Health and Welfare Unit, 1995), p. 18.

11.   OPCS, *Marriage and Divorce Statistics 1993* (London: HMSO, 1995). In 1993, 95,000 couples divorced who had one or more children under 16, the total number of children under 16 being 176,000.

12.   *Facing the Future: A Discussion Paper on the Grounds for Divorce* (Law Commission Discussion Paper, 170; London: HMSO, 1988). Eight years before one of the Law Commissioners had already written that 'logically we have already reached

and the Family Law Bill of 1996 that followed it, in effect announced that spousehood was no longer the business of the public.[13] The Foreword to the Green Paper contained the statement that the law can never 'prescribe the expectations' with which people enter marriage 'and so cannot enforce them'. Thus was the sociologically exceptional opinion of Britain's social-affairs elite of the previous thirty years presented to the softened-up public as a universally valid generalization.

Those who expressed the view that the law made no difference, and had made no difference, to the stability of the average marriage based themselves on the implausible proposition that although there were only 32,000 actual divorces in 1961, there were in addition 160,000 couples in that year, and another 160,000 in 1962, another 160,000 in 1963, and so on, who were actually married still, but were only together because the law did not allow them to divorce. They were 'divorce equivalents'. They were 'virtually' divorced couples. According to this view, the law did not affect the determination of married people to make theirs a lifelong relationship which, if it could not be loving, fruitful or fulfilling, then at least it could be tolerable. Changes in the law, the experts on the family in the legal profession were now saying, had simply made visible what previously existed. According to this proposition, the fact that the law did not enable them to divorce except on the grounds of a serious matrimonial offence (or by their elaborately faking one) had no or little effect on how they related to each other and to other people from day to day.

By the mid-1990s, of course, that *was* the situation. The situation had been brought about by a series of small movements. Seen from the point of view of the population it was a process of drift. From the point of view of most of the senior guardians of the culture in the church, the law, the universities and the responsible media it was the result of their apathy, naiveté or misjudgement. From the point of view of those actively encouraging those changes, it was the population's shunted progress down a 'betrayal funnel'.

a point at which. . . we should be considering whether the *legal institution of marriage continues to serve any useful purpose*' (B. Hoggett, 'Ends and Means: The Utility of Marriage as a Legal Institution', in J.M. Ekalaar and S.N. Katz [eds.], *Marriage and Cohabitation in Contemporary Society* [London: Butterworth, 1980], emphasis added).

13. Lord Chancellor's Department, *Looking to the Future: Mediation and the Grounds for Divorce* (Cm 2424; London: HMSO, 1993).

By the 1990s, it *was* true that the law could neither prescribe nor enforce controls on men's heterosexual activities that public opinion would not *by then* accept. But in Britain for centuries the law and public opinion did together most strongly define and effectively enforce through marriage (and the endless array of rewards and penalties that supported marriage) the social obligations of the man for his own children, within the household of his children and his children's mother.

From 1999, then (when the Family Law Act 1996 would come into operation), a husband even blatantly at fault would be free to terminate the relationship with much less legal difficulty than the *defaulting* party in almost any commercial situation. Marriage thus became almost unique among relationships in so far as one's own delinquency was sufficient grounds for dissolving it. The amendments proposed in Parliament by MPs who wished to support the institution of marriage, even where they were accepted, did not touch on this basic point. The privatization of marriage had already gone so far that the amendments concerning 'mediation' periods of eighteen or twenty-one months instead of twelve could only be of symbolic significance to any but those professionals and semi-professionals who had a financial stake in mediation themselves.

A principal concern of the BBC's social affairs editor appointed in 1988 (a highly representative figure of the cultural elite in a key cultural position) had been to 'take the shame out of divorce', and she was one of the first to celebrate. The Marriage Guidance Council had changed its name to Relate, and its Chief Executive also publicly welcomed the 'no-fault' essence and the 'mediation' auxiliaries of the 1996 Family Law Act. Her *credo* was that individuals be given the opportunity to 'talk through their feelings' so that the 'relationship is stronger in the end'.[14]

The Lord Chancellor, whose Bill it had been, said that the criterion of the Act's success would be that it 'strengthened marriage'. But these innocent sentiments from the most senior legal official in the land, who was himself an adherent of a strict Scottish Christian sect, were an effective demonstration of how thoroughly the social affairs elite had been impregnated by anti-family propaganda (where they were not already active disseminators of it). Since *Putting Asunder* in the mid-1960s, first the appeal *to* the churches, and then the case *from* the churches, has been that weaker divorce laws will strengthen the

14. 'Yesterday in Parliament' and 'Call Nick Ross', 18 June 1996.

institution of marriage. Senior clerical figures were on hand to make the same Panglossian claim for the Family Law Bill 1996:

> I hope that opponents of the present Bill will not go on repeating unsubstantiated charges that it will 'undermine the strength of the marriage contract'. It is far more likely to have the reverse effect.[15]

Lord Habgood must be right that the charges were unsubstantiated in the sense that the results of the new Act lay in the future. In the nature of things, therefore, they could not be 'substantiated' at the present time. But the observation that similar measures had hitherto weakened the institution of marriage was substantiated on the basis of all past experience. Lord Habgood's claim, then, that the Family Law Bill was 'far more likely' to strengthen the institution of marriage, was doubly unsubstantiated. For like anybody else's claims it can have no 'substantiated' support from the unknown future, and is directly contradicted by the lessons from the known past, which is the only guide to policy that we can ever have.

Why were there so many fewer divorces before the 1960s? It was because the system before the 1960s was a child-centred one. As it takes fifteen or twenty years to raise a child in the home, for all practical purposes the two adults had to settle down from the beginning to make their own relationship a lifelong one. If they subjected their children either to marital quarrels or to their parents' separation, then they were the subjects of public censure. However much it would have suited the husband, or the wife, or both of them, to part, they had to find a *modus vivendi* and stay in the same home. That was because it was generally believed (even before research showed the old intuitive public opinion to be probably correct) that on the average children of divorced parents did worse even than the children of quarrelling parents. Parents stuck together, and most of them did their best, even if their own adult situations were unhappy, 'for the sake of the children'.

Spousehood (as distinct from parenthood), from being up to the late 1960s the most binding of contracts, by the mid-1990s has become one of the least binding. By mid-1996, therefore, Dutschke's 'long march through the institutions' had been almost entirely completed so far as the traditional family was concerned.

'Some commentators have argued that the relative proportion of children affected by "broken marriages" was at least as high in the

---

15. Lord Habgood, former Archbishop of York, *The Times*, 6 April 1996.

past as it is today'.[16] 'It looks very much as if modern divorce is little more than a functional substitute for death'.[17] Two comments must be made on this very popular and influential view of the matter.

The first is that losing a parent through death is in its consequences very different from losing a resident parent by divorce. Certainly, on today's evidence, being made a widow or widower, or having a widowed mother, are quite different in their effects from having divorced a spouse or having a divorced parent.[18]

The second is that the argument that families were broken as quickly by death in the past as they are by divorce today, and therefore the man (and the woman) were as free from the bonds of marriage then as they are today—that men's situation has not changed significantly—depends upon an elementary demographic error. It is true that the expectation of life at *birth* was much lower in the past than it is today. In the 1870s the expectation of life for a man at birth was only 41 and for a woman only 45. At the end of the nineteenth century a man's expectation of life at birth was still only 44. It is now 73.[19] But the relevant figure is not the expectation of life at *birth*. It is the expectation of life at *marriage*. The first reliable figure for the expectation of life at the age of 20 in this country is that for 1871. A man aged 20 could expect to live not until he was 41 (his expectation of life at birth), but until he was 59.[20]

Marriage is increasingly being preceded by the freer association of cohabitation. Whatever may be the true picture for times for which we have no reliable data, the much more reliable data of the past thirty years shows a great expansion in men's freedom to live with a woman without marrying her first. Of those women under 30 years who first married in the years 1965–69, only 3 per cent had cohabited with their future husband. Among those marrying for the first time in 1970–74 the rate had suddenly quadrupled to 12 per cent, and by 1985–89 it

16. A. Giddens, *Sociology: A Brief but Critical Introduction* (London: Macmillan, 2nd edn, 1986 [1982]), p. 128.

17. Stone, *The Family, Sex and Marriage*, p. 56.

18. M. Cockett and J. Tripp, *The Exeter Family Study* (Exeter: University of Exeter Press, 1994). On divorce in the United States see J.S. Wallerstein and S. Blakesee, *Second Chances: Men, Women and Children after Divorce* (London: Bantam, 1989).

19. OPCS, *Mortality Statistics General 1992*, 27 (London: HMSO, 1994); and OPCS, *Annual Abstract of Statistics 1995* (London: HMSO, 1995).

20. *Statistical Abstract for the UK 1912–26* (London: HMSO, 1928).

had more than quadrupled again to 51 per cent.[21]

A sense of the extreme rapidity of men's liberation from marriage as a condition of living with a woman, and an indication of future trends, is provided by the figures on 16–19 year olds. Among 16–19 year old women living in 'unions' in Great Britain in 1980, 13 per cent were cohabiting. This proportion *tripled* between 1980 and 1986 (1986 = 42 per cent), and increased almost *fivefold* between 1980 and 1989 (1989 = 62 per cent).[22]

For some time those who attribute the rise in social disorder to low income and a widening gap between those high and low in the income scale propagated the view that cohabitation was marriage, but simply without the meaningless piece of civil paper or a meaningless church ritual. The instability of cohabitation is now clearly established, and the break-up of cohabiting couples is making its due contribution to the rise in the number of fatherless households.[23]

In 1976 there were 90,000 households in Great Britain with dependent children where the father had not married the mother and was not a member of the household of the mother and child or children. By 1991 there were 430,000. In 1976, 290,000 households with dependent children did not have the father as part of the household due to divorce or separation. By 1991 there were 680,000.[24] That is how rapidly and how greatly the cultural position of men in our society has been transformed.

All these trends have mattered to all of us in our capacity as consumers with an interest in a buoyant economy. To most of us who are not in the category of the low-income, lone-parent household, it has been diffusely highly beneficial. With a stable population and therefore potentially a stagnant size of market for consumer goods, the break-up of the population into ever smaller units came as a godsend to industry and services. A never-married mother and her non-cohabiting boy

21. A. Bridgwood and D. Savage, *General Household Survey No. 22 1991* (London: HMSO, 1993).

22. K. Kiernan and V. Estaugh, *Cohabitation, Extramarital Child-bearing and Social Policy* (London: Family Policy Studies Centre, 1993).

23. Hoem and Hoem show that in Sweden, for so long the spiritual homeland of anti-family theorists, Swedish cohabitation is far from being as stable as Swedish marriage; see B. Hoem and J. Hoem, 'The Disruption of Marital and Non-Marital Unions in Contemporary Sweden', in J. Trussel (ed.), *Demographic Applications of Event History Analysis* (Oxford: Clarendon Press, 1992).

24. Figures from the General Household Survey data.

friend require not one but two dwellings. Even if they are cohabiting, the technicalities of state benefit provisions very often mean that he has to have a council house or other accommodation as well as the mother to make sure that they jointly receive as much state benefit as is obtainable.

A divorced couple need a house each, a refrigerator each, their own carpets, curtains and TV. Few of those planning and supporting the Divorce Reform Act 1969 or the Family Law Act 1996 had that in mind. The predominantly stated, and no doubt in many cases genuinely meant, intention and expected result was to stabilize the institution of marriage, to strengthen and solidify it, by ridding it of several thousand accumulated, and few thousand future, failed ones.

But from the *economy's* point of view, the hardships at the bottom of the income scale are a matter of indifference. In the short run the economies of certain cities depend very heavily on incomes from state benefits, state grants, or state salaries of one kind or another, including the benefits generated by lone parenthood.

Similarly, the successive international campaigns for 'children's rights', as currently exemplified by the European Convention,[25] by weakening the control of parents over their children generally, make children *economically* a more powerful force, as consumers making claims on their parents' income. The intention is to protect children from slavery and sexual abuse, not to boost the market in Morphin Power Rangers' spin-offs. But that is the desirable macroeconomic effect. The advantage to the economy of this attack on the authority of the adult is that it is effective whether the child is at home with both his married parents or in a home without his father being part of the household. It is probably more effective, indeed, in the latter instance than the former.

No capitalist plotted the downfall of the family. But you can be sure that if the economic consequences had been as severely detrimental to the economy as they have been in practice beneficial to it, a lot more attention would have been paid to any adverse effects in other directions.

This includes the greater attention that would have been paid to the long-term adverse effects on the economy itself. With the erosion of the obligation on men to take responsibility for their children within the context of a permanent common home, the motivation for men to

25. Council of Europe, *Draft European Convention on the Exercise of Children's Rights*, Directorate of Legal Affairs, Strasbourg, 18 July 1995.

improve their skills and adjust to the requirements of efficiency comes
to depend more on themselves as self-regarding individuals, and less on
their responsibilities as husbands and fathers for the long-term
wellbeing of their family.

This is already quite apparent in schools. From being about equally
successful in O-level days, by 1994 48 per cent of girls achieved five
A–C grade GCSE passes, but only 36 per cent of boys. Boys had clung
on in 1994 to a slight lead at A-level overall, but by the mid-1990s male
students made worse use than female students of the opportunities of
sixth-form colleges and colleges of further education.[26] At the top end
of the scale, among the schools where selection on ability takes place,
all the leading five schools in 1995's GCSE results were girls' schools,
seven of the top ten and 35 of the top 50.

It is because they have been deprived of the context of firm social
expectations directing them to family responsibilities that boys and
youths have become much more prone to deal with their frustrations
by turning to crime, to riotous destructiveness, and—a problem that
could and is likely to overshadow all other economic and social problems in the near future—to drugs.

It is interesting to turn to an old standard sociological text-book such
as Ross's *The Foundations of Sociology*, and read about the 'unusually
low criminality of the British population'.[27] Britain was still renowned
internationally for, and the British population itself was proud of, its
low crime during and after the First World War, during the years of
mass unemployment, poverty and appalling housing conditions of the
inter-war period, and during and after the Second World War.

In 1955, just before the rapid increase in crime began, there was a
total of 460,000 recorded indictable offences in England and Wales. By
contrast, when the *increase* of 310,000 *in the single year* 1991–92 was
reported, officials of the Home Office described this as an encouraging
slowdown.[28] As compared with the total 460,000 of *all* indictable offences in 1955, in 1993 there were 1,370,000 *burglaries* alone. There was
satisfaction when the official figures showed a fall of about half-a-
million a year or two later. If there had been a fall of that magnitude

26. 'GCSE and GCSE A-level in England 1994', *Statistics of Education*
(London: HMSO, 1995).

27. A.E. Ross, *The Foundations of Sociology* (New York: Macmillan, 5th edn,
1912 [1905]), p. 338.

28. *The Guardian*, 29 April 1993.

only forty years before, there would have been no recorded crime at all.

Since the days of *Putting Asunder* and the 1966 Law Commission report on marriage and divorce[29] crime and drug addition have escalated, and civic safety plummeted. At twenty past eight on a Spring morning in 1996 a 74 year old man who was simply asking the way in Chapeltown, Leeds, was murdered for the few possessions he had on him.

In recent years the consumption of legal and illicit drugs has amplified and coalesced with crime. In the mid-1950s the excise returns showed that the per capita consumption of alcohol had fallen continuously since the First World War, and in terms of alcohol intake from beer the per capita consumption had fallen more steeply still. The same was true of spirits. Wine consumption had risen somewhat, but from small beginnings and was still at a very low level.

In 1955, as the annual Home Office reports show, narcotic addicts numbered a few hundred people in special groups such as musicians and doctors. By the prosperous, low-unemployment mid-1960s the system of treatment suited to the small scale of the phenomenon in the 1950s, allowing doctors to prescribe heroin to addicts, had broken down as it became the prey of widespread abuse.

Addicts today run into tens of thousands. In the small Northumberland town of Blyth eleven drug-related fatalities were reported in three years in the early to mid-1990s.[30]

On the morning after the passage of the Family Law Bill through the House of Commons, the reporter giving an account of the proceedings

29. A Group Appointed by the Archbishop of Canterbury, *Putting Asunder: A Divorce Law for Contemporary Society* (London: SPCK, 1966). Law Commission, *Reform of the Grounds for Divorce: The Field of Choice* (Cmnd. 3123; London: HMSO, 1966).

30. In the meantime I use a University lift. On the walls and door are scrawled 'I love you all! Like a blow job. Bill and Bob not Ted. LFC. Shite! Rape!' Is this anger? If it is, it will be explained, I expect, in terms of the cuts in student grants (if students put the graffiti there) or the poor employment expectations of interlopers. I then walk down the corridor. Notices on the wall pour scorn on what they describe as the 'moral panic' about drugs; they protest at the attempts to stop 'us' consuming them as our inclination takes us. Perhaps University premises were always festooned with such sentiments and they had hitherto escaped my notice: nothing had changed in the real world; all this 'change' was an illusion created by my own 'phenomenological transformation'.

for the BBC said that the opposition to it had been the work of 'right-wing Tory MPs'. In the programme that followed a highly skilful—and, in his consistently unbiased chairmanship, exemplary—BBC presenter, Nick Ross, said that opposition had been the work 'if I can paraphrase it, of the Religious Right'. Marriage as the *private* affair of the couple, on the other hand, had been successfully defined, not, of course, as 'left wing', but as normal, sensible, pragmatic.

'Right wing' covers views as diverse as free-market economics and religious beliefs other than New Age paganism. It covers a pro-victim stance in cases of crime. It is right wing to disapprove of private violence in parliamentary democracies. It is right wing to prefer *High Noon* to *Reservoir Dogs*. It is right wing to disdain pornography and to use the term 'prostitute' instead of 'worker in the sex industry'. It is right wing to be a racist and to approve apartheid. 'Right wing' is therefore a very handy cudgel with which to belabour one's opponents. For the term invites the implication that to conclude from the evidence that marriage is good for children and bad for crime is to endorse every right-wing position on the list.

So far as sexual matters were concerned, the procreation and care of children, and the relationship between their parents and other relatives, 'right' and 'left' were labels that had been switched round since the 1960s. There has always been in modern times a meeting of the extreme left and right in anarchism and nihilism. In both, each separate individual should do just what he or she wants to do. The anarchism of the left has said that if people do as they like, all acting in accordance with to their own unique moral judgements, the result will be harmony, peace, energetic activity and altruism. That is what true human nature leads us to. The anarchism of the right has said that if people do as they like, the weakest will go to the wall. But in their case the conclusion is, 'and a good thing too'.[31]

31. Just as it has been a remarkable propaganda coup by individuals and interest groups hostile to the family or lifelong monogamy to identify 'the left', including the Labour party, with anti-monogamous-family sentiment, so was it a remarkable propaganda coup to identify the Labour party with pro-criminal sentiment. In reporting the 'confession' (authentic or not) in the *Melody Maker* of a prominent and successful songwriter to burglary and breaking into cars, *The Times* casually remarks, 'Cue outrage from *Tory* MPs': as if *Labour* MPs are supposed to look with sophisticated indifference on residents who come home to find that their houses have been burgled or come back from the shops to find that their cars have been broken into by thieves (*The Times*, 6 April 1996).

In practice, self-styled anarchists, whether in principle altruistic anarchists or in principle egoistic anarchists, often claimed complete freedom for themselves, but demanded strict adherence to rules by others. If they ruined themselves they demanded to be rescued by formally or informally socially-provided welfare measures. 'You must be a stodgy, conformist husband, grandfather, parent, neighbour or citizen, vulnerable to feelings of guilt if you don't behave decently, so that I can be a free spirit. You must do your duty towards me so that I don't have to consider my duty towards anyone'. As the parish priest said, 'The egoist does not tolerate egoism'.[32]

But the overwhelmingly most important body of the non-anarchist and non-nihilist left in this country, the Labour party in this century and its predecessors, envisaged that the characteristics of the *well-functioning* family of the permanently married couple and their own children—love, loyalty, duty, and service to the family's common good—should be spread into all other parts of society. In particular, public service and unselfishness on a small scale, as evidenced in the ordinary British working-class families of the time, should replace on the large scale the self-centred mentality of the market economy.

The division of labour within the working-class family in the first half of this century was not a matter of principle, but a function of the hard and dangerous demands of work outside the home, and the time-consuming and arduous work within the home. At the time no reasonable person argued—it could hardly occur to him or her—that working-class work outside the home was a privilege retained by men and perversely and selfishly withheld from women. The Labour party was the party of male and female equality, not least in its demand that as high a standard of fidelity, continence, sobriety and refinement should be required of fathers as was already the ideal and, as compared with men, the practice of working-class mothers.[33]

The upsurge in crime and drug consumption among young men cannot be attributed to increasing poverty in either the everyday

---

32. J. Roux, *Meditations of a Parish Priest* (Boston, MA: Crowell, 1986), p. 9.

33. How did it happen that some time around 1970 it became radical chic for first middle-class Labour, and then working-class Labour, to slander these men—in the working-class case, their own fathers, grandfathers and great-grandfathers—and to jeer for the next twenty years, as if he was a barmy Gulliver making up tales about impossible lands, at anyone who cited their indispensable fatherly merits within the realities of their lives at the time? The proletarian male: from universal hero to incestuous and adulterous brute at the flick of a switch!

meaning of the word or in its refined sense of relative poverty. In the first twenty years of the upsurge in crime among young men, unemployment among them was extremely low. Before the upsurge in crime there was a widespread problem of 'dead-end jobs' for the young and mass unemployment for men in general—at the time apparently permanent unemployment.

What has been true of the whole forty-year period of increasing crime, violence and drug abuse has been the rapid weakening of the public opinion (in which the weakening of the law has played its not inconsiderable role) that had previously required men to get married to, stay married to, and live in the same home as the woman who would be the mother of their children. Over the past forty years both upbringing and social control had largely ceased to take seriously even the possibility that it would be the normal experience of the child to have a married mother and father when it was born, and a home with the same mother and father until it reached adulthood. When it had these things, then it also had a lifelong array of clear and certain grandparents, great-uncles, and great-aunts, uncles, aunts and cousins which was rich in potential providers of unconditional services and sentiments.

The steep rise in the crime rate, the drug-addiction rate and the frequency of riots in the period 1955–77 coincided with a long period of *low* unemployment, the construction of new towns and new housing estates, and *rising* standards of living for working people absolutely and *declining* income inequality.

What *has* marked the whole period of the rise in crime, riot, drug abuse and the loss of male motivation in education and employment has been the progressive emancipation of the boy from socialization, and the youth and man from social control, that formerly required him to be a father to his children in one home for the duration of his adult life.

Clearly the choice in this country is now heavily skewed in the direction of men's sexual liberation. By and large, adult men, especially young men, have reaped self-regarding benefits in improved sexual access to females, and in increased freedom from the extremely onerous responsibilities of monogamous spousehood and fatherhood. These moral choices having been made by the beneficiaries, then children, drug addicts, struggling lone mothers on housing estates, directionless young men, and eventually the economy have paid and will continue to pay the diverse and heavy price.

CONFLUENT LOVE AND THE CULT OF THE DYAD: THE PRE-CONTRACTUAL FOUNDATIONS OF CONTRACTARIAN SEXUAL RELATIONSHIPS

Philip A. Mellor and Chris Shilling

Introduction

Although there is a great deal of debate about the precise nature and importance of love, sex and intimacy in contemporary society (Jackson 1993; Dunscombe and Marsden 1993; O'Connor 1995), Anthony Giddens's (1992) discussion of 'pure relationships', or 'confluent love', has provided an influential and widely read account of the dominant characteristics of contemporary sexual relationships. Giddens (1992) views these contractarian and democratically structured forms of intimate relationship as being reflexively constructed, formed as a result of individual choices, and developed on the basis of conversation. Within this view, there is the assumption that sexual relationships no longer involve the collective transformation of individual needsand desires into transpersonal social forms, with all the moral obligations this involves, but instead that they rest merely on the reflexive construction of a mutually beneficial confluence of interests and needs (see Sorokin 1943: 167; 1947: 100).

We suggest that the value of Giddens's analysis rests on its capacity to highlight real tendencies in how many contemporary persons are inclined to understand their sexual relationships, rather than in its capacity to shed light upon the question of whether such an understanding is a sociologically supportable one. What we shall argue, in fact, is that the very notion of 'confluent love' rests on an egoistic and cognitive misconception of the thoroughly social and embodied nature of sexual relationships. This misconception arises from a lack of attention to the socially creative role of effervescent emotions and passions, which, following Emile Durkheim (1995 [1912]), we associate with the creation, maintenance and development of various forms of human society.

We also follow Durkheim in seeing this effervescence, immanent within bodies, as the social source of the self-transcending experience of the sacred. This means that all sexual relationships have a potentially sacred character. In Giddens's view, the self-referentiality of 'confluent love' rules out any relationship with the sacred: his vision of modern societies as the products of, and arenas for, reflexively applied knowledge is underpinned by a strong secularization thesis (Giddens 1990; Mellor 1993). We shall argue, however, that the embodied basis of the social experience of the sacred is especially evident in the effervescent passions and emotions of human eroticism. 'Pure relationships' may sublimate this eroticism, and its sacred potentialities, but they are only viable in so far as it underpins them. In other words, it is an effervescent eroticism, expressed ritually as a 'cult of the dyad', that provides the pre-contractual foundations of modern contractarian sexual relationships. In spite of concerns for reflexive planning, talking through problems, and the careful regulation of contractual demands and obligations, pure relationships are only viable in so far as they are sustained by social forces they ignore or theoretically preclude.

In developing this argument we draw principally from the French sociological tradition associated with Emile Durkheim. In particular, we seek to apply to the specific issue of sexual relationships Durkheim's general point that the pre-contractual foundations of contract rest in the collective effervescence through which both religion and society are able to emerge (Durkheim 1995 [1912]: 9; Nisbet, 1993 [1966]: 245). In the course of our discussion we shall pursue this issue through a consideration of the specific character of 'confluent love', which we shall contrast with various concepts of erotic communion. We shall also touch upon certain aspects of Protestant and Catholic models of confluence and communion, which manifest divergent theological accounts of sexual relationships and provide important cultural sources for more contemporary conceptualizations. Initially, however, we shall discuss the nature and role of the sacred in Durkheim's analysis of society, as this is the basis upon which we consider the inherently social nature of eroticism, and its relationship with the more individualized and cognitive dimensions of sexual relationships.

Sensual Solidarity

A central component of Durkheim's (1995 [1912], 1951 [1897], 1984 [1893], 1973 [1914]) sociological studies, and that of his followers in

the Année Sociologique group, such as Robert Hertz (1960 [1907–
1909], 1996 [1922]), was the analysis of the intimate relationship
between social life and various collective experiences and representations of the sacred. This Durkheimian focus also underpinned much of
the work of the later Collège de Sociologie, especially that of Georges
Bataille (1987 [1962], 1992 [1973]), as well as becoming one of the
most important components of the modern sociological tradition. For
Durkheim, religion was *le clef de voûte*, the keystone of society
(Pickering 1984: 516). The very possibility of society was contingent
upon the experience of an effervescent stimulation of emotion and
energy which gave rise to an immanent-transcendent experience of
solidarity. This collective effervescence, and the sense of solidarity
associated with it, was the very essence of the sacred and of society
itself. Society would die along with the sacred, in fact, and individuals
would succumb to an egoistic self-absorption, if this effervescent
sociality was not experienced (Durkheim 1995 [1912]: 349; Richman,
1995: 72).

The experience of the sacred, 'something added to and above the
real', is therefore always at some level a *sensual* experience because it
rests on the collective stimulation of powerful passions and emotions
which individuals experience as a form of self-transcendence, and
which allows them to be integrated into either a large social whole or
into smaller collective bodies (Collins 1988: 110; Durkheim 1995
[1912]: 422-25). As Célestin Bouglé (1926) recognized, for Durkheim
society was a 'fiery furnace' which forged new identities and transformed relationships in the sacred fires of collective effervescence.
Society may substitute 'for the world revealed to us by our senses a
different world that is the projection of ideals created by society itself'
(Richman 1995: 62), but this new world also arises from the thoroughly
sensual energy and magnetism of collective effervescence. Moral
obligations, ritual orders of practice and meaning, and the development of particular conceptual frameworks to make sense of the world,
all arise from this basis.

The Cult of the Dyad

In Durkheimian terms, sexual relationships can be viewed as a form
of effervescent sociality because they manifest a stimulation of emotions
and passions immanent within bodies yet transcendent of each individual involved, and because they give rise to ritual practices and moral

obligations which help define and consolidate a sense of solidarity between the sexual partners. Although Durkheim did not discuss sexual relationships in detail, they can be considered within his analytical framework because they 'connect us with something that surpasses us' (Durkheim 1973 [1914]: 161). A recent study of *friendship*, for example, has sought to draw upon Durkheim's theory of religion to argue that intimate friendships contain elements of ritual, moral obligation, experiences of self-transcendence and self-sacrifice (Wallace and Hartley 1988). *Sexual* relationships, however, are more powerful examples of Durkheim's concern with the immanence of the sacred within social relationships because of their *embodied basis*, as Bataille (1987 [1962]) made clear in his analysis of the close relationship between the religious and the erotic. A sexual relationship can be viewed as a *society of two*, centred on this embodied experience of 'collective effervescence'.

Randall Collins's (1981, 1988) conflict theory of the family is developed from precisely this Durkheimian basis. He argues that modern love can best be understood through an analysis of the interrelationships between ritual and the stimulation of bodily passions (Collins 1981). He suggests that in modern societies there is an evident idealization of the couple, a 'cult of the dyad', which encourages patterns of courtship where couples are structurally isolated, becoming intensely focussed on each other, so that whatever emotions they feel for each other are intensified through the ritual mechanism of the cult and attached to symbols of the relationship itself (Collins 1988: 120). This leads to the development of 'a substratum of moral sentiment' ordinarily manifest in positive bonds, such as tenderness and self-sacrifice, but can be expressed as violence, jealousy and hatred when the ritually constituted moral bond is violated through sexual or affectional infidelity (Collins 1988: 121). Implicit in this understanding of relationships is a recognition that phenomena such as spouse abuse cannot be dealt with very easily through *talk*, 'because they rest upon ritual foundations which operate with moral sentiments, below the level of ordinary reflection' (Collins 1988: 121; see Dobash and Dobash 1979).

If 'negative bonds' are only understandable through an attention to the ritual, moral and effervescent foundations which rest below conscious reflection, then the same point is valid with regard to 'positive bonds'. Durkheim was attentive to the fact that the collective stirring of passions could give rise to a 'bloody barbarism' as well as a

'superhuman heroism', but also argued that effervescence was not confined to exceptional circumstances alone: 'There is virtually no instant
of our lives in which a certain rush of energy fails to come to us from
outside ourselves' (Durkheim, 1995 [1912]: 213). Certain forms of
sociality, however, clearly stimulate and channel this energy in
particular ways. Despite Erving Goffman's (1967: 95) suggestion that
the individual self is the pre-eminent sacred object in modern societies,
the cult of the dyad is an especially powerful and important form for
the contemporary experience of the immanent-transcendence of the
sacred (Collins 1988: 120).

In the light of this, we can question the thoroughly secular character
that modern sexual relationships appear to have, and the implicit
assumption by writers such as Giddens that the embodied potentialities
of human sexuality *can* be so thoroughly colonized by the cognitive,
interpersonal emphasis upon democratic and contractarian forms of
intimacy which are defining features of 'confluent love'. We can also
contextualize notions of confluence alongside the apparent resurgence
of an eroticism which promotes a more transcendent, *transpersonal* and
thoroughly sensual form of intimacy which has a strongly effervescent
character.

Confluent Love and Erotic Communion

The differences between the interpersonal and transpersonal characteristics of sexual relationships can, to some extent, be captured through
the metaphors of 'confluence' and 'communion'. These two metaphors
imply very different things, not only about sexual relationships, but
also the experience of embodiment and the construction of meaning in
all social relationships. Before looking briefly at Georges Bataille's
(1987 [1962]) discussion of eroticism, which has a broadly Durkheimian
character, it is worthwhile considering the nature of 'confluent love'
in more detail. As already suggested, it is Giddens (1992) who has
crystallized many contemporary views about sexual relationships
through his notions of 'confluent love' or 'pure relationships', though
similar concerns are evident in a much broader literature. Implicit in
the notion of 'confluence' are two important assumptions about the
social character of modern sexual relationships.

First, the notion of confluence presupposes the essential *separateness*
of sexual partners, in the sense that these relationships do not involve
some sort of merging or transformation into a transpersonal whole.

These relationships are entered into as the result of individual judgements in terms of a person's own life plans. The fear of economic
hardship, and the pressure exerted by a society marked by sacred
communities and what Durkheim (1984 [1893]) termed 'mechanical
solidarities', are no longer understood to exert the influence on relationships they once did. As a consequence, a thoroughgoing individualism is not only an apparent precondition for the possibility of such
relationships, but a major constituent feature of their continuance.
Thus, sexual relationships cease to be 'pure', and therefore 'authentic',
when elements which defy the reflexive, cognitive management of
individuals are introduced into them.

Secondly, the notion of confluence also implies the inherent *transience*
of modern relationships, in the sense that lives can run parallel only
for a time before they diverge again as the individuals concerned
pursue new life-courses and seek to fulfil new needs. Thus, *choice* plays
a central role in pure relationships: while the importance of external
anchors diminishes, so the value attached to ongoing (and potentially
revocable) decisions to continue and invest in this 'intimate contract'
increases. In view of this, it is not surprising that married couples who
understand their relationships in these terms tend to have a high rate
of divorce since the idea of an irrevocable bond is alien to them (Hall
1996). Johnson and Johnson (1980: 146), for example, have noted how
some individuals 'cycle in and out of marriages'. Such relationships
recall Ferdinand Tönnies's (1957 [1887]: 64) characterization of
Gesellschaft forms of sociality: relationships which are associational
rather than communal, and where human beings 'are essentially separated in spite of all uniting factors'.

These forms of sexual relationship are thoroughly *contractarian*:
individuals enter into them on the basis of a highly reflexive assess-
ment of benefits and needs, and remain in them only as long as these
are met. As Carole Pateman (1988) has discussed, the idea of 'intimate
contracts', developed in certain sections of the American feminist
movement, is only an extreme form of a thoroughgoing contractarian
mentality which has had a defining influence on modern sexual relationships. This mentality encourages an ideology of egalitarianism, the
recognition and maintenance of difference, and an unwillingness to
submit to bonds which have not been freely chosen and subject to continuing critical review: in short, it implies all of the characteristics
which underpin Giddens's notion of confluent love. Where the inherent

transiency of such relationships is resisted, there is a tendency for ever-larger areas of contact between couples to become carefully regulated according to the individual needs and requirement of each partner. A common response to the pressures faced by 'dual career couples', for example, has been the emergence of an increasing number of 'commuter relationships' (Zinn and Eitsen 1987); a relational form which highlights the more general importance of *talk* in modern intimate relationships where so much—from careers, leisure, children, shopping and even sex—has to be negotiated and scheduled.

Pure relationships can be seen as the latest flowering of the ideology of 'companionate marriage' (Cate and Lloyd 1992; Stone 1987). They are centred on the 'mutual growth' of partners though what Lawson (1988) terms the 'talking revolution'; a revolution in which 'knowledge has become the new commodity of exchange between intimate partners' (Lawson 1988: 29; see also Gray 1992; Berger and Kellner 1964). In this context, 'confluent love' requires self-revelation and a capacity to share, and there is a tendency for *authentic* intimacy to be achieved less through the sensual potentialities of eroticism, and much more through the revelation of 'secrets' and the knowing of the intellect (Giddens 1992; Lawson 1988). Here, the breaking of sexual fidelity within a marriage, for example, is important not only, or even primarily, in terms of physical action, but because of the lying and other *betrayals of discursive trust* it represents (Askham 1984; Lawson 1988). The *erotic* dimensions of human experience are, theoretically at least, thoroughly colonized by a cognitive and contractarian mentality: the form, number and nature of the sexual activities people engage in have to be ceaselessly subject to negotiation and reflexive scrutiny with regard to the physical, emotional and cognitive satisfaction of each partner.

The Effervescence of the Erotic

This attempt to colonize the erotic through the reflexive demands of a thoroughgoing contractarianism raises the question of how sufficient the idea of confluent love is with regard to human embodiment. Despite the presence of the word 'eroticism' in the subtitle of Giddens's (1992) book, the erotic potentialities of bodies occupy an insubstantial place in his analysis of sexual relationships. Pure relationships are clearly unable to cope with sweaty, heaving and breathless bodies, animalistic urges and sexual fluids which might colonize the mind and interfere, however temporarily, with the reflexive and democratic processes of 'talk work' central to 'confluent love'. Defined in terms of a relentless, cognitive reflexivity they cannot account for the pre-contractual, effervescent, and transcendent dimensions of embodied experience, or what Collins (1988: 121) calls those ritual foundations of the cult of the dyad lurking 'below the level of ordinary reflection'.

In contrast, Bataille's writings on eroticism provide us with a view of 'intimacy' that is centred on a notion of *communion* rather than confluence, is sensually rather than cognitively based, and is imbued with a sacred character on account of the immanent-transcendent experience of the solidarity that eroticism can give rise to. Bataille (1987 [1962]: 18) draws our attention to the capacities of the erotic to bring about a 'fusion of beings with a world beyond everyday reality'. In contrast to Giddens's emphasis upon the individualistic character of modern sexual relationships, Bataille (1987 [1962]: 15) sees in eroticism a route towards transcendence and away from 'our random and ephemeral individuality'. This balance between the transcendent experience of solidarity and the immanence of meaning within the sensual capacities of bodies is expressed in his comment that 'all eroticism has a sacramental character' (Bataille 1987 [1962]: 15-16).

The notion of sexual intimacy as a form of 'communion' has a long history and finds various forms of expression. In the Roman Catholic Church (1994), for example, religiously sanctioned forms of sexual intimacy are understood in terms of a transpersonal form of communion rather than as merely interpersonal, contractual arrangements. More broadly, James B. Nelson (1983: 34) has interpreted the deepest meanings of human sexuality in terms of a religious communion. In Bataille's work, an erotic communion refers to a heightened experience which transgresses the self, wipes away the discontinuities which separate individuals, and accomplishes a temporary fusion of selves. As Bataille (1987 [1962]: 15) notes, eroticism can be physical, emotional or religious, but the intensity and attractions of each lies in their ability to substitute for the individual's isolated discontinuity a feeling of profound continuity: 'the unity of the domain of eroticism opens to us through a conscious refusal to limit ourselves within our individual personalities' (Bataille 1987 [1962]: 24).

Eroticism can never be reduced to talk and it exists apart from purposive reason and productive work. While reason is bound up with work and relationships which threaten to turn us into 'mere things', erotic pleasure 'mocks at toil' (Bataille, 1987 [1962]: 168). While eroti-cism provides us with a sensual intimation of how the world could be, the talk-based mentalism of 'pure relationships' encourages people to 'lose touch' with any pre-contractual foundations for their relations with others. For Bataille, it is our erotic, effervescent sexual exuber-ance which can rupture us from the profane 'world of things' and put us back in contact with an experience and dissolution which allows us to regain touch with the sacred. The sacred potentialities of eroticism are thus analogous to the sacred self-transcendence stimulated through the effervescence of social life described by Durkheim (1995 [1912]).

The Homo Duplex

Echoing Bataille, Paul Ricoeur (1994 [1964]: 83) has discussed how the erotic dimensions of human experience are 'perhaps basically impermeable to reflection and inaccessible to human mastery'. If we accept this view then Giddens's (1992) proposition that modern sexual relationships can be defined in terms of their thoroughgoing reflexivity, their contractarianism, and their emphasis upon cognitive management of the erotic looks manifestly unworkable. On the other hand, however, it is also unrealistic to imagine that erotically-based relationships do not have cognitive and contractual components as well. Durkheim (1984 [1893]) argued that it is an error to believe that all social relationships can be reduced to contracts. Nevertheless, this did not lead him to dismiss the importance of contracts completely, but to an attempt to clarify the social circumstances under which contracts appeared to become more important in Western societies, and the pre-contractual bonds of solidarity which made these contracts sustainable.

Giddens's (1992) account of confluent love is insufficient with regard to human embodiment in the sense that it precludes even the possi-bility of a consideration of these pre-contractual bonds. Furthermore, Giddens himself clearly approves of this sexual contractarianism which he views as being appropriate to a modern egalitarian and democratic society, though from a Durkheimian point of view this contractarianism tends to conceal the true nature of social relationships. Giddens's analy-sis does have the merit, however, of drawing our attention to the fact that many people *do* increasingly understand their sexual relationships in contractarian terms, and so the trends he discusses need to be taken seriously, however mistaken they may be in their own terms.

Sexuality is, obviously, an enduring feature of what it means to be human, but it can be experienced and thought about in different ways. Given Durkheim's emphasis on the enduring significance of the social experience of the sacred for how humanity understands itself, it is to be expected that, within this analytical framework, changing experiences of the sacred and changing accounts of human sexuality overlap and impact upon each other. Durkheim (1995 [1912]) emphasized that the sacred persists in a variety of societal contexts, but was attentive to the fact that the sacred and profane spheres of life not only change their social expression as Thompson (1993) argues, but can expand or contract in relation to each other (Luckmann 1967; Girard 1977). The contradiction between the banal self-referentiality of pure relationships and a consciousness of the sacred potentialities of the erotic can thus be contextualized within these patterns of the expansion and contraction of the sacred and profane spheres of life in relation to each other.

The tension between an emphasis on the persistence of the sacred and tendencies towards the profanation of modern life have an embodied basis in what Durkheim understood to be the *homo duplex* nature of humanity; the 'double centre of gravity', which finds expression in changing forms of sociality (Durkheim 1973 [1914]: 152). In other words, beneath Durkheim's theories of the sacred and the nature and historical development of human societies, is a theory of humanity. Durkheim's essay, 'The Dualism of Human Nature and its Social Conditions' (1973 [1914]) was written as a further illumination of the concept of the *homo duplex* which he regarded as the fundamental principle underlying *The Elementary Forms of the Religious Life* (1995 [1912]). This 'double centre of gravity' of human beings was manifest in two ways: first, the enduring tension between irrational passions and rational thought; and second, the tension between individuals and society (Durkheim 1973 [1914]: 152). Thus, to be human meant being subject to recurring tensions between the individual and collective poles of social life, covering 'sensory and sensual appetites', intellectual and rational criteria, and the moral obligations arising from membership of a society (Durkheim 1973 [1914]: 162).

Meštrovic´ (1993: 186) has drawn attention to the importance of the *homo duplex* for the whole of Durkheim's thought, and stressed its centrality to his sociology of religion, emphasizing the precariousness and volatility of achieving a balance between the different poles of the *homo duplex*. It was Durkheim's view, in fact, that the incorporation of individuals into the sacred experience of effervescent sociality was a highly contingent and fragile phenomenon (Collins 1988: 110; Richman 1995: 72; Durkheim 1995 [1912]: 422-25). Bataille has developed Durkheim's concern with this contingency and fragility. For Bataille (1992 [1973]: 36), the sacred is inherently ambiguous. Following Durkheim he understands it to be a source of attraction possessing an incomparable value, and which is rooted in an embodied, 'animal sense' of transcendent meaning immanent within human communities and their natural environments. He also suggests that the sacred can be dangerous, however, as it constantly threatens the profane world of human projects, designs and goals.

There is thus a tension between the sacred and the profane which is manifest in a number of ways. In broad terms it is apparent in conflicts between the collective and the individual. With regard to the specific issue of embodiment, it is evident in the conflict between accepting the immanence of transcendence within the sensual capacities of bodies, and tendencies towards a prioritization of all that is cognitive and individual. Thus, in the work of both Durkheim and Bataille being human means being drawn in two different directions, and in each case the sacred has a crucial role in overcoming tendencies towards a profane individualism through the magnetism and energy of collective effervescence. Consequently, Bataille's (1987 [1962]) theory of eroticism is intimately related to his broader theory of religion (Bataille 1992 [1973]), just as Durkheim's (1973 [1914]) theory of the *homo duplex* is central to his own theory of religion (Durkheim 1995 [1912]).

The modern concern to contain the erotic within the discursive and cognitive sphere of a contractarian mentality can be contextualized within this analytical framework. The denial of the effervescent basis for sexual relationships reflects a sense of the dangerous unpredictability of humanity's embodied potentiality which is constantly threatening to break through the rational barriers constructed around humanity (Bataille 1992 [1973]: 52). In view of this, we could even say that pure relationships operate on the basis of a *fear* of the sacred potentialities of the erotic, rather than on a simple assumption of secularity. The notion of confluent love can thus be understood as a cognitive strategy to sublimate the social and religious implications flowing from the cult of the dyad. In a modern world which places considerable emphasis on individual freedom and autonomy, the pre-contractual foundations of contractarian sexual relationships have to be denied because acknowledging them would mean accepting the immanence of transcendent moral obligations within embodied experience, with all the negative implications this would involve for relationships ostensibly constructed around democratic and individualistic criteria.

Nevertheless, given that this contractarian mentality is currently of considerable influence in shaping how people conduct their sexual relationships, we need to be able to account for how it arose to such prominence. In this respect, a Durkheimian analysis points towards a further irony: despite the apparent secularity of confluent love, it has a particular *religious* source. Although Giddens associates confluent love with the specific context of advanced modern societies, many of its characteristics first came to prominence in the Protestant Reformation. Consequently, in seeking to explain how it is that the modern experience of sexuality has developed in the way it has we can look back, briefly, to the social impact of the Protestant Reformation of the sixteenth century as this helps clarify more contemporary issues. We shall suggest that in making marriage more of an interpersonal relationship rather than a sacred form of transpersonal communion, the Protestant Reformation prepared the ground for modern notions of 'pure relationships', 'confluent love' and 'companionate marriage'.

The Protestant Cult of the Dyad

As part of a broader deconstruction of the ritual and sacramental dimensions of religion in favour of an emphasis on the interior commitments and beliefs of the individual (Dumont 1982: 117; Berger 1990 [1967]: 126), the Protestant Reformation removed sex from the sacramental economy of Catholic Christianity while simultaneously investing sexual intimacy with a high moral seriousness centred on the cognitive commitment of the individuals involved. This movement away from sacrament and ritual to the cognitive realm of individual interiority was symbolized by the dismissal of the confessor from his traditional position of authority within the family and, symbolically, the marital bed. While domesticity itself became highly valued, this removal from the marital bed of a representative of the ritual community of Christianity could therefore be understood to signal the beginning of the reduction of the transcendent social significance of sexual activity to the interpersonal concerns of two individuals (Davies 1993; Zaretsky 1976; Turner 1984).

In Collins's (1988) terms, however, the Protestant reconstruction of sexual relationships can also be understood as the point at which the modern 'cult of the dyad' emerges, and Colin Campbell (1987) has, in fact, discussed how Protestantism gave enormous impetus to the emergence and spread of modern notions of romantic love, despite the life-denying fatalism of the Puritans. In other words, the removal of marriage from the sacraments, and the elimination of the church's representative from his position of symbolic authority in the marriage bed, signal the disengagement of sexual relationships from the broader ritual community, but do not necessarily imply the removal of ritual elements from the 'society of two' constituted by sexual intimates. Protestantism's hostility to Catholic ritualism, however, and its own focus upon the importance of cognitive clarity and commitment in all areas of life (Levine 1985), encouraged the *sublimation* of this ritual dimension and the emergence of a self-conscious voluntarism. Thus, Protestantism may mark the emergence of the cult of the dyad, but it also marks the emergence of the significantly different view of sexual relationships central to the notion of confluent love.

This is not to say that the notion of confluent love emerged fully formed from the Reformation. The increasingly interpersonal and voluntaristic conceptualization of sexual relationships was to some extent obscured, for example, by the emergence of a modern patriarchy which limited the opportunities for women to participate in sexual relationships on an egalitarian basis. The early Protestant attitude towards women can be summarized as one of men seeking to regulate and control women's lives rather than to elevate their importance. According to one scholar, Luther said that the narrow shoulders and wide hips of women were signs from God that 'he intended them to limit their activity to the home' (Ozment 1993: 152); that women were created to conceive and bear children, which is why cloistered virginity was understood to be an offence against God (Ozment 1993: 155); and that wives should be constantly pregnant even if they wore themselves out in the process because 'this is the purpose for which they exist' (Ozment 1993: 164-65).

Nevertheless, despite the effective denial of women's opportunities to participate in sexual relationships on the same terms as men, the Reformation progressively emphasized the idea that marriage was a *voluntary* contract between man and woman. Marriage was a relationship entered into by individuals as a result of free choice. This inevitably stimulated those processes of introspection and reflexivity which characterize the individual and cognitive dimensions of the *homo duplex*, and which would find their extreme form in the 'pure relationships' of late modernity. Because marriage had become an individual decision, people were encouraged to ask themselves questions regarding their love for their proposed partner, and the extent to which their motives and feelings were authentically Christian. Luther opposed the Catholic Church's acceptance of 'secret' marriages, for example, arguing that 'mature' marriages should be striven for, and that the secret marriages of youth 'indicated a cavalier approach to the most serious of life's decisions and the most important of human institutions' (Ozment 1993: 156). Instead of being a mainly impersonal, identity *giving* institution, marriage began to become *personalized*, a relationship in which identity was constructed. People became more readily aware of themselves as individuals with individual responsibilities and needs, rather than the subjects of passions, emotions, obligations and duties within ritual communities (Berger 1990 [1967]). Viewed within this context, the Protestant prioritization of words over unwritten traditions (Cameron 1991; McGrath 1993) must also have encouraged the importance of talk in the construction and maintenance of relationships.

As the Protestant promotion of marriage as a voluntary relationship increased, so the status of marriage as a sacred 'social fact', standing over and above its participants, declined. Furthermore, the Protestant stress on freedom of conscience brought to the foreground not only the importance of the individual in *forming* a marriage, but also raised the issue of the *dissolubility* of marriage. Divorce remained unacceptable as a solution to an unhappy marriage for a long time (Turner 1984: 134). However, as the focus on marriage as a relationship was accompanied by its removal from the sacraments, theological reasoning against divorce became increasingly problematic and difficult to maintain. With the ultimate acceptance of divorce, the importance of marriage was reduced to what was practically, emotionally and psychologically sustainable between two consenting adults: a psychological orientation was created in which the importance of purely interpersonal emotional ties could flourish in a relational structure with an inherent tendency towards transience.

The Catholic Cult of the Body

The Protestant prioritization of the cognitive dimensions of human experience, manifest in its emphasis on words (Cameron 1991; McGrath 1993) and the importance of clear and cogent understanding and communication (Levine 1985), together with its attack on ritual (Burke 1987), can be associated with a general tendency to associate evil with bodies (Delumeau 1990; Mellor and Shilling 1997). The fear of the body this attitude implies co-existed easily with the cognitive bias of an increasingly contractarian voluntarism which followed the Protestant reconstruction of sexual relationships, and is still manifest in the sublimation of eroticism in modern confluent love. If Protestantism prefigures the emergence of modern pure relationships, however, Catholicism has, on the whole, historically promoted a view of sexual relationships that takes seriously the effervescent dimensions of the *homo duplex*. Catholicism has not only tended to recognize the pre-contractual bodily foundations for sexual relationships, but has sought to integrate them into its ritual and dogmatic systems of religious meaning.

Looking back to before the Reformation, medieval Catholic attitudes to sexuality have to be understood in the context of a religiosity where, in broad terms, religious meaning was often to be found *through* the body, not in spite of it (Bynum 1987). Medieval self-identities had much less to do with individualized, reflexive narratives of the self, and much more to do with a form of embodiment in which the fleshy body and its senses were experienced as integral to the gaining of knowledge about oneself and one's world. As Euan Cameron (1991: 16) notes, 'all the most popular activities of late medieval religion were based on doing something, on participation, activity, movement, essentially on experiencing an event more than on learning or understanding a message'. The Church promoted, in Durkheim's (1995 [1912]) terms, an effervescent form of sociality: it bound individuals through the ritual incorporation of the immanent potentialities of bodies into the transcendent moral orders of Catholicism. What medieval persons understood to be the truth of God in Christ was not just a *message*, but a particular experience of *embodiment*: the church was the incarnation of Christ continuing in sacramental form, and individuals were united with this incarnate God through their incorporation into this religious body (Martin 1980: 74). This strong 'sense-contact' with religious knowledge meant that sexual relationships were not essentially private matters, but had a strong societal and sacred dimension: the cult of the dyad was a sub-cult of the broader cult of the embodied community of Christians.

In social and economic terms, medieval marriage had been based on economic and kinship considerations that always involved more than an agreement between two individuals. Families and sometimes entire communities were involved in an agreement that imposed strong sanctions against the break up of any wedded couple, and which assigned very different roles to women and men (Klapisch-Zuber 1990: 287). In this system of the exchange of women, their sexual fidelity was a source of great concern since the children of an adulterous wife might 'pollute' the blood lineages at the heart of family alliances. The moral substratum of sexual relationships was thus based on ritual foundations which took human embodiment very seriously. It was a common view that during conception and pregnancy paternal 'blood' was merely 'baked' in the mother, and it was therefore essential that there was absolutely no doubt that a pregnant wife was carrying only her husband's child, so that women's bodies required unflagging surveillance (Turner 1984: 118; Klapisch-Zuber 1990: 292).

In this system of property transfer, Catholicism did much to assist the male control of female sexuality. The discipline of confession, and the requirement of priestly control over it, provided a powerful, some would say 'panoptic' (Foucault 1981), apparatus of control over women's actions (Turner 1984: 127). Catholic doctrine on sexuality, as well as the existence of convents and monasteries, also helped 'siphon off' those 'surplus' daughters and sons who were an inevitable product of this system of primogeniture. On the other hand, the church's not uncritical interaction with this social milieu was evident in its growing number of attempts to regulate the use of women in family alliances by insisting, especially firmly from the late eleventh-century onwards, that women had to give their free assent to any marriage, and that women should not be forced into marriage at such an early age that this consent would be meaningless (Klapisch-Zuber 1990: 292). The betrothal of couples also became subject to the church's control. In Normandy, for example, the ceremony of the transfer of the bride from the father to the husband, which had been a private ceremony, was moved from the home into the church where the priest welcomed the couple and they exchanged their statements of consent in a ritual context (Klapisch-Zuber 1990: 293).

In contrast to later Protestant developments, the church was engaged in an attempt to regulate sexual relationships through sacred, communal rituals, not through the interior reflexivity of individual partners. Durkheim (1977 [1938]: 25) noted that the Catholic Church had, for centuries, attempted to operate a 'one-sided syncretism' which drew alternative accounts of reality, meaning and experience into its own systems of practice and belief (Archer 1988: 200). This syncretism may have operated at the level of dogma, but it also involved a corporeal syncretism. Medieval religion made all sorts of associations between the natural, the social and the supernatural. These linkages encouraged people to direct their emotions into particular activities and to treat their bodies, and the bodies of others, with reference to certain sacred practices. In this context, the power of the church to forge particular links with persons can be understood best with regard to its privileged role as the creator and maintainer of a community which engaged all the body's senses.

Spiritual and Sensual Communion

The development of the Counter-Reformation and modern Catholicism brought about significant changes in the church's engagement with the sacred potentialities of human sensuality which are beyond the scope of the present discussion (see Mellor and Shilling 1997). Nevertheless, in broad terms, Catholicism continued, and continues, to offer a view of human sexuality which challenges the cognitive and individualized perspectives of Protestant and modern conceptualizations. In the recently revised *Catechism of the Catholic Church* (1994), for example, the broader dimensions of the *homo duplex* are implicitly recognized in the emphasis on the idea that human persons are both spiritual and corporeal, and that the body is a good which must not be despised but honoured, because it is only through the union of body and soul that human nature comes into being (*Catechism* 1994: 83). Sexuality, while particularly associated with human affectivity, involves all aspects of this union of body and soul, and is therefore an integral component of what it means to be a human being (*Catechism* 1994: 500). Sexual unions between men and women add another dimension to this unity of body and soul because the individual persons become 'one flesh', manifesting a transcendent spiritual and corporeal *communion* (*Catechism* 1994: 84, 500). The religious significance of this communion, which is understood to signify the union of Christ and the Church, is represented by marriage's status as one of the seven sacraments (*Catechism* 1994: 372).

The demanding moral obligations the church seeks to encourage in relation to sexual partners are not in contradiction to this positive attitude towards human embodiment, but a direct consequence of it.

Durkheim (1984 [1893]: 331) defines morality with reference to the solidarity which takes individuals beyond their own egoism and forces them to recognize their obligations towards others. The Catholic *Catechism*'s (1994: 512) condemnation of what it calls 'free unions' and 'trial marriages' reflects a strong sense of the importance of these obligations: 'carnal union is morally legitimate only when a definitive community of life between a man and a woman has been established'. The church's (*Catechism* 1994: 512) condemnation of the 'inability to make long-term commitments' and tendencies towards 'inconstancy', which arise from a failure to establish pre-contractual foundations for sexual relationships in the public sphere of the ritual and sacramental orders of the church, show how far away Catholicism's concern with the ritual foundations of sexual 'communion' is from modern notions of 'confluent love'.

Although many theologians would no doubt be uncomfortable with parts of Bataille's (1987 [1962]) account of the transcendent potentialities of eroticism, the Catholic theology of sexual relationships is similarly built upon what might be called a 'Durkheimian' recognition of the sacred dimensions of human solidarity and the moral obligations which flow from them. Thus, Hans Urs Von Balthasar's (1982) emphasis on the objective, overarching significance of sacramental marriage in the face of subjectivist interpretations includes a strong sense of the self-transcendence and sacrifice necessary for such relationships to be religiously meaningful. He argues that in such marriages individuals do not merely commit themselves to each other, in an interpersonal sense, but to a transpersonal form which transcends two selves and integrates biological, social and religious dimensions of human experience through the sacramentally-mediated grace of God (Von Balthasar 1982: 57; Mellor 1990). The same theological vision of sexual relations underpins the Second Vatican Council's assertion that 'sexual activity within marriage should be guided by objective criteria' (Lawler 1985: 63). As it is expressed in *Gaudium et Spes*, the intentions and motives of individuals are inadequate for judging the morality or immorality of sexual actions and such individuals must necessarily defer to the authority of the Church (Abbott 1966: 256).

Working within the Durkheimian tradition, Robert Hertz's (1996 [1922]: 75) study of sin and expiation reflects a similar understanding of the importance of yielding to transpersonal authority, since it is the encounter with a transcendent representation of collective life which enables the individual to realize the potentialities of religious meaning immanent within human relationships. To deny the essentially collective character of religious ideas and emotions and reduce them to the 'banal' self-referentiality of individual feelings is, in fact, to risk destroying society itself (Hertz 1996 [1922]: 71). This helps explain Durkheim's (1951 [1897]) association of Protestant forms of religion with greater tendencies towards suicide: Protestantism's religious individualism encourages patterns of individual reflection, critical scrutiny, and reflexively-defined forms of relationships with others which abstract individuals from society, and thereby renders it an alien 'other' rather than the route to the sacred.

The Spirituality of the Body

Many modern sexual relationships may continue to be shaped by notions such as that of 'confluent love', where it is assumed that 'authentic' intimacy is established through a basically contractarian pattern of mutual self-revelation and a commitment to *talk*, rather than through the sensual potentialities of a self-transcendent eroticism (Giddens 1992; Lawson 1988). Despite the Protestant religious sources of this banal self-referentiality, however, a number of Protestant theologians have increasingly begun to challenge the denial of the sacred potentialities of erotic communion which has been a significant feature of their religious tradition.

Elisabeth Moltmann-Wendel (1994: 36), for example, singles out the Protestant tradition as having placed an excessive emphasis upon the word and preaching in its understanding of Christianity, and has consequently separated the truth of Christianity from the human body. Explicitly repudiating the disenchanting rationalism of the Reformation, she emphasises the centrality of the embodied immanence of the sacred to the Christian story: 'God is there in bodies and their energies, alive and active. Though the story may smack of magic to some enlightened people, it is a physical story, the story of our bodies' (Moltmann-Wendel 1994: x). Similarly, James Nelson (1992: 36-37) criticizes the Protestant Reformation's transformation of the relationship with the sacred from an embodied immanence to a radical transcendence which encouraged 'analysis, criticism, distinction, and rationality', and devalued all that was 'material, bodily, emotional'. In contrast, Nelson emphasizes the sensual and collective dimensions of the *homo duplex* through a focus on the incarnational character of Christianity.

It is Nelson's (1992: 8) belief that 'men are hungering for a more erotic spirituality', which leads him to offer an imaginative account of the spiritual meanings of men's genitals: the erect phallus, with its 'sweaty, hairy, throbbing, wet, animal sexuality', represents life-giving spiritual energy (Nelson 1992: 92), while the flaccid penis, a state of *being* rather than doing, represents yielding, trusting to the power of God (Nelson 1992: 96). The purpose of this spiritualization is to establish a theological basis for an embodied transcendence of self through the immanence of the sacred. This recalls Bataille's (1992 [1973]: 57) suggestion that the essence of religion is the search for a lost undifferentiated intimacy. The separate, individual human exists in a profane world of differentiated things in contrast to the animal which is 'in the world like water in water': the animal part of humanity, however, which manifests the magnetism and the horror of all that is sacred, offers a route through to this intimacy (Bataille 1992 [1973]: 19, 51). Echoing Bataille, Nelson (1992: 130) says that 'Eros is a passion for connection, the enemy of dichotomy and disconnection'. In other words, sexual activity can offer a religious route to a sense of connectedness with everything else in the universe (Nelson 1992: 131).

Beyond Individualism

This renewed sense of the potentialities for a sense of embodied connectedness also underpins Michel Maffesoli's (1996) Durkheimian account of the decline of modern individualism and the emergence of 'postmodern tribes'. In contrast to Giddens's (1992) emphasis upon voluntaristic and contractarian forms of sociality, Maffesoli (1996: 18) is attentive to the increasing emergence of passionate and emotional forms of commonality centred on an effervescent *puissance*, or vital energy, of the community. He declares that in contemporary Western societies, the accent is no longer on that which separates but on that which unites, signalling the end of modern individualism: 'No longer is my personal history based on a contractual arrangement with other rational individuals' (Maffesoli 1996: 10).

Such sensual forms of solidarity are based on the feelings, emotions and the effervescence which can derive from *being with* others, as opposed to simply discursively communicating with them (Mellor and Shilling 1997). Simmel (1971 [1903]: 324) has suggested that the deepest existential problems of modern life flow 'from the attempt of the individual to maintain the independence and individuality of his existence', but the emergence of sensual solidarities signals a carnal challenge to this cognitive experience of self and others. Thus, certain strands of radical feminism are able to emphasize a solidarity amongst women based on blood and birth, rather than an egalitarian contractarianism (see Hunt 1991; Pateman 1988).

Part of the appeal of such forms of solidarity for many feminists rests on a recognition that contractarianism has rested on highly problematic assumptions about male and female bodies. As Carole Pateman (1988) has suggested, the emergence of modern contractarian understandings of social relationships was based upon a conception of the unequal distribution of rationality. While men's rational minds were meant to be able to control and direct their physical bodies (even if male rules of bodily conduct were long observed more in the breaking than in the making) (Roper 1994: 145-67), women's relationships to blood and birth meant their 'fragile minds' were ruled by their demanding, unpredictable bodies. Men no longer had 'body-obsessed-bodies' but lived more in their minds, while women suffered from an incapacity to absent themselves from their bodies (Starobinski 1970). Women were unable to exert individual control over bodies suffused with what Rousseau called 'unlimited desires' (Pateman 1988: 55; 97).

It is in recognition of this marginalization of women upon the basis of their incapacity to absent themselves from their bodies that the series of 'apparitions' by the Virgin Mary in the nineteenth and twentieth centuries has been understood as 'anti-modernist' eruptions of female power, and the power of the sacred, within the predominantly male, Protestant culture of modernity (Meštrovic´ 1991: 147-48). It is also the case, nevertheless, that many forms of feminism have sought to facilitate the equal participation of women within this contractarian mentality. As Lerner (1993) suggests, those features of Protestantism concerned with introspection, reflexivity, and the importance of achieving 'good works' on earth, have increasingly permeated women's consciousness and experiences in a manner which has been understood to be highly liberating. Alternatively, as Meštrovic´ (1991: 161) expresses it, feminism has often sought only to make both sexes 'equal in relation to Protestant, abstract, subjectivist values'. It is these abstract, subjectivist values which underpin notions of confluent love, and which preclude both the immanence of the sacred and the possibility of self-transcendence.

Conclusion

Pitirim Sorokin (1943: 167; 1947: 100) has suggested that the essence of friendship is not a mutually beneficial confluence of interests and needs, but a merging of selves into a single 'we' (Wallace and Hartley 1988). In the work of Durkheim (1995 [1912]), the emergence of this 'we' always has a religious dimension because it signals the encounter with a collective life which transcends the egoistic concerns of the individual, and is the source of the moral values and obligations which give shape and meaning to human life. In sexual relationships, the effervescent passions and emotions which facilitate the emergence of this 'we' possess a specifically erotic character which makes the embodied basis of human sociality especially clear. Thus, to return to Durkheim's point about the possibility of society being contingent upon the experience of an effervescent stimulation of emotion and energy which gives rise to an immanent-transcendent experience of solidarity (Durkheim 1995 [1912]: 349; Richman 1995: 72), we can say that the denial or sublimation of the sacred potentialities of the erotic is likely to have very serious consequences for the continued existence of society itself.

In this respect, it is worth touching upon Cameron and Fraser's (1987) study of sexual murder: one of the most anti-social acts imaginable. Defining sexual murder as a distinctively modern phenomenon, they associate it with the sexual objectification of women and an extreme individualism which refuses any moral obligations that limit the possibilities of other people being used to satisfy the desires of the individual (Cameron and Fraser 1987: 22). Seeking out the roots of this mentality in Western culture, they detect in the literary works of writers such as the Marquis de Sade, Jean Paul-Sartre, Simon de Beauvoir and André Gide an individualism that sets the desires of the individual against the body and society: freedom and transcendence are realized not through an embodied communion, but through an individualized rebellion against the limitations of embodiment and the conventions of society (Cameron and Fraser 1987: 58-59).

This individualized transcendence is thoroughly *metaphysical*, in the sense that it rests on a rejection of the embodied bonds of human society, and reflects a prioritization of the cognitive and individual poles of the *homo duplex*. Cameron and Fraser (1987: 173) also associate this individualism with the discourse of 'sexual liberation', but in Durkheimian terms such individualism surely signals the death of the erotic rather than its extension. Although Cameron and Fraser (1987: 169) comment on the explicit eroticization of transcendence in the writings of Sade and his followers, such transcendence is not erotic but *pornographic*: the individualized rebellion against society for the sake of pursuing egoistic sexual desires is the exact opposite of transcendence immanent within human solidarity as envisaged by Durkheim.

In view of the above, it would not be going too far to say that the notion of confluent love, or the 'pure relationship', is not entirely free of a pornographic element as well. The contractarian negotiation of sexual and emotional satisfactions, although contained within a discourse of 'mutual growth', ultimately has a recognizably egoistic basis: moral obligations do not extend beyond the contract, and if individuals do not feel their needs are being met adequately then the contract will be terminated. The erotic potentialities of such relationships are therefore seriously constrained by the reflexive contractarianism which shapes them: the effervescent capacities of bodies, and the sensual solidarities which can arise from them, are subject to the cognitive control of the individuals concerned. Consequently, we could say that pure relationships are inherently anti social, in the sense that they preclude the possibility of individuals sacrificing their egoistic desires for the sake of collective obligations. It is not surprising, therefore, that relationships structured by such a mentality tend to break down more easily than those of a less egoistic character: the more people commit themselves to the notion of the pure relationship, the less viable their relationships are likely to be (Hall 1996).

On the other hand, however, the insufficiency of this conceptualization of sexual relationships with regard to human embodiment also suggests that even where relationships of this sort endure, they do so for reasons contrary to the reflexive contractarianism which gives them their apparent character. The increasing number of popular self-help guides on improving understanding and verbal communication within relationships may encourage couples to believe that their intimacy is founded on the reflexive negotiation of a mutually beneficial confluence of interests and needs, but Durkheim directs our attention to those effervescent emotions and passions, below the level of conscious reflection, which provide the embodied basis for human solidarity, including the modern 'cult of the dyad'. In other words, the pre-contractual foundations of contractarian sexual relationships rest in the same effervescent solidarity that underpins erotic forms of communion.

This solidarity may often not extend beyond the sexual partners, in contrast to the broader effervescent bonds of Catholicism and the world-transforming eroticism envisaged by Bataille and Nelson. Nevertheless, if we are to establish an adequate understanding of the specific character of modern sexual relationships it is to these effervescent foundations we must look.

BIBLIOGRAPHY

Abbott, W.M.
    1966   *The Documents of Vatican II* (London: Geoffrey Chapman).
Archer, M.
    1988   *Culture and Agency* (Cambridge: Cambridge University Press).
Askham, J.
    1984   *Identity and Stability in Marriage* (Cambridge: Cambridge University Press).
Bataille, G.
    1987 [1962] *Eroticism* (New York: Marion Boyars).
    1992 [1973] *Theory of Religion* (translated by R. Hurley; New York: Zone Books).
Berger, P.
    1990 [1967] *The Sacred Canopy: Elements of a Sociological Theory of Religion* (New York: Anchor Books).
Berger, P., and H. Kellner
    1964   'Marriage and the Construction of Reality', *Diogenes* 1-23.
Bouglé, C.
    1926   *The Evolution of Values* (trans. Helen Sellars; New York: Henry Holt).
Burke, P.
    1987   *The Renaissance* (London: Macmillan).
Bynum, C.W.
    1987   *Holy Feast and Holy Fast: The Religious Significance of Food to Medieval Women* (Berkeley: University of California Press).
Cameron, D. and E. Fraser
    1987   *The Lust to Kill: A Feminist Investigation of Sexual Murder* (Cambridge: Polity Press).
Cameron, E.
    1991   *The European Reformation* (Oxford: Oxford University Press).
Campbell, C.
    1987   *The Romantic Ethic and the Spirit of Modern Consumerism* (Oxford: Basil Blackwell).
Cate, R., and S. Lloyd
    1992   *Courtship* (London: Sage).
    1994   *Catechism of the Catholic Church* (London: Geoffrey Chapman).
Collins, R.
    1981   'Love and Property', in R. Collins, *Sociological Insight: An Introduction to Non-Obvious Sociology* (New York: Oxford University Press).

1988   'The Durkheimian Tradition in Conflict Sociology', in J.C. Alexander (ed.), *Durkheimian Sociology: Cultural Studies* (Cambridge: Cambridge University Press).

Davies, J.
1993   'From Household to Family to Individualism', in J. Davies (ed.), *The Family: Is it Just Another Lifestyle Choice?* (London: IEA Health and Welfare Unit).

Delumeau, J.
1990   *Sin and Fear: The Emergence of a Western Guilt Culture 13th–18th Centuries* (New York: St Martin's Press).

Dobash, R.E., and R. Dobash
1979   *Violence against Wives* (New York: Free Press).

Dumont, L.
1982   'The Christian Origins of Modern Individualism', *Religion* 12.1: 1-28.

Dunscombe, J., and D. Marsden
1993   'Love and Intimacy: The Gender Division of Emotion Work', *Sociology* 27.2: 221-41.

Durkheim, E.
1951 [1897]   *Suicide* (London: Routledge).
1973 [1914]   'The Dualism of Human Nature and its Social Conditions', in R.N. Bellah (ed.), *Emile Durkheim on Morality and Society* (Chicago: University of Chicago Press).
1977 [1938]   *The Evolution of Educational Thought* (trans. Peter Collins; London: Routledge & Kegan Paul).
1984 [1893]   *The Division of Labour in Society* (London: Macmillan).
1995 [1912]   *The Elementary Forms of Religious Life* (trans. Karen E. Fields; New York: Free Press).

Foucault, M.
1981   *The History of Sexuality*. I. *An Introduction* (Harmondsworth: Penguin Books).

Giddens, A.
1990   *The Consequences of Modernity* (Cambridge: Polity Press).
1992   *The Transformation of Intimacy* (Cambridge: Polity Press).

Girard, R.
1977 [1972]   *Violence and the Sacred* (Baltimore: The Johns Hopkins University Press).

Goffman, E.
1967   *The Presentation of Self In Everyday Life* (Harmondsworth: Penguin Books).

Gray, J.
1992   *Men Are From Mars, Women Are From Venus* (New York: HarperCollins).

Hall, D.R.
1996   'Marriage as a Pure Relationship: Exploring the Link between Premarital Cohabitation and Divorce in Canada', *Journal of Comparative Family Studies* 27.1: 1-12.

Hertz, R.
1960   *Death and the Right Hand* (New York: Cohen and West).

[1907–1909]
1996 [1922]   *Robert Hertz: Sin and Expiation in Primitive Societies* (trans. and ed. Robert Parkin with a preface by W.S.F. Pickering; Oxford: British Centre for Durkheimian Studies).

Hunt, L. (ed.)
1991   *Eroticism and the Body Politic* (Baltimore: The Johns Hopkins University Press).

Jackson, S.
1993   'Even Sociologists Fall in Love: An Exploration of the Sociology of Emotions', *Sociology* 27.2: 201-20.

Johnson, C.L., and F.A. Johnson
1980   'Parenthood, Marriage and Careers: Situational Constraints and Role Strain', in F. Pepitone-Rockwell (ed.), *Dual-Career Couples* (Beverly Hills: Sage).

Klapisch-Zuber, M.
1990   'Women and the Family', in Jacques Le Goff (ed.), *The Medieval World* (London: Collins and Brown).

Lawler, R.
1985   *Catholic Sexual Ethics* (Indiana: O.S.V).

Lawson, A.
1988   *Adultery: An Analysis of Love and Betrayal* (New York: Basic Books).

Lerner, G.
1993   *The Creation of Feminist Consciousness* (Oxford: Oxford University Press).

Levine, D.
1985   *The Flight from Ambiguity: Essays in Social and Cultural Theory* (Chicago: University of Chicago Press).

Luckmann, T.
1967   *The Invisible Religion* (New York: Macmillan).

Maffesoli, M.
1996   *The Time of the Tribes: The Decline of Individualism in Mass Society* (London: Sage).

Martin, D.
1980   *The Breaking of the Image: A Sociology of Christian Theory and Practice* (Oxford: Basil Blackwell).

McGrath, A.
1993   *Reformation Thought* (Oxford: Basil Blackwell).

Mellor, P.A.
1990   'Objective Form and Subjective Content: Marriage and the Transcendence of Self in Roman Catholic Theology', *The Irish Theological Quarterly* 56.2: 136-49.
1993   'Reflexive Traditions: Anthony Giddens, High Modernity and the Contours of Contemporary Religiosity', *Religious Studies* 29: 111-27.

Mellor, P.A., and C. Shilling
1997   *Re-forming the Body: Religion, Community and Modernity* (London: Sage).

Meštrovic´, S.G.

    1991   *The Coming Fin de Siècle: An Application of Durkheim's Sociology to Modernity and Postmodernity* (London: Routledge).

    1993   *The Barbarian Temperament: Toward a Postmodern Critical Theory* (London: Routledge).

Moltmann-Wendel, E.

    1994   *I am My Body: New Ways of Embodiment* (London: SCM Press).

Nelson, J.B.

    1983   *Between Two Gardens: Reflections on Sexuality and Religious Experience* (New York: Pilgrim Press).

    1992   *The Intimate Connection: Male Sexuality, Masculine Spirituality* (London: SPCK).

Nisbet, R.A.

    1993 [1966]   *The Sociological Tradition* (New York: Beacon Press).

O'Connor, P.

    1995   'Understanding Variation in Marital Sexual Pleasure: An Impossible Task?', *The Sociological Review* 43.2: 342-62.

Ozment, S.

    1993   *Protestants* (London: Fontana).

Pateman, C.

    1988   *The Sexual Contract* (Cambridge: Polity Press).

Pickering, W.S.F.

    1984   *Durkheim's Sociology of Religion* (London: Routledge & Kegan Paul).

Richman, M.

    1995   'The Sacred Group: A Durkheimian Perspective on the College de Sociologie (1937–39)', in C. Bailey Gill (ed.), *Bataille: Writing the Sacred* (London: Routledge).

Ricoeur, P.

    1994 [1964]   'Wonder, Eroticism and Enigma' in James B. Nelson and S.P. Longfellow (eds.), *Sexuality and the Sacred: Sources for Theological Reflection* (London: Mowbray).

Roper, L.

    1994   *Oedipus and the Devil: Witchcraft, Sexuality and Religion in Early Modern Europe* (London: Routledge).

Simmel, G.

    1971 [1903]   'The Metropolis and Mental Life', in D. Levine (ed.), *Georg Simmel: On Individuality and Social Forms* (Chicago: University of Chicago Press).

Sorokin, P.

    1943   *The Crisis of Our Age* (New York: E.P. Dutton).

    1947   *Society, Culture and Personality* (New York: Harper & Row).

Starobinski, J.

    1970   *Portrait de l'artiste en Saltimbanque* (Paris: Champs-Flammarion).

Stone, L.

    1987   *The Past and the Present Revisited* (London: Routledge & Kegan Paul).

Thompson, K.

    1993   'Durkheim, Ideology and the Sacred', *Social Compass* 40.3: 451-61.

Tönnies, F.
  1957 [1887]   *Community and Association* (Michigan: Michigan State University Press).
Turner, B.S.
  1984   *The Body and Society* (Oxford: Basil Blackwell).
Von Balthasar, H.U.
  1982   *The Glory of the Lord. A Theological Aesthetics*. I. *Seeing the Form*
                (trans. Erasmo Leiva-Merikakis; Edinburgh: T. & T. Clark).
Wallace, R.A., and S.F. Hartley
  1988   'Religious Elements in Friendship: Durkheimian Theory in an Empirical
                Context', in J.C. Alexander (ed.), *Durkheimian Sociology: Cultural
                Studies* (Cambridge: Cambridge University Press).
Zaretsky, A.
  1976   *Capitalism, the Family and Personal Life* (New York: Harper & Row).
Zinn, M.B., and D.S. Eitsen
  1987   *Diversity in American Families* (New York: Harper & Row).

THE RISE AND FALL OF 'SEX'

Alan Storkey

Introduction

Throughout modern times the prevailing orthodoxy has been of 'the dark ages' of sexual repression from which we have been rescued by a liberal and scientific sexual revolution which has constituted the era of sexual progress in which we now live. This understanding has been challenged by a number of postmodern theorists, who have recognized patterns of special pleading in the interpretation. They have noted that the 'success' of sex claimed by modernism when measured by broken and exploitative relationships does not seem all that great. Foucault goes a stage further and suggests that a great modern orthodoxy has settled on the idea of sex in Westernism which is largely formed around the idea of 'repression' and a *scientia sexualis* which defines what sexuality has to be (Foucault 1981). This chapter carries Foucault's challenge to this modern metannarrative further and locates it in England. It looks at the process of the reification of 'sex' and suggests that what is interpreted as progress has actually been myth creation, the blowing of a bubble which will grow thin and collapse. It shows the orthodox history of 'sex' to be a subcultural approach which needs deconstructing, and it fundamentally questions the idea of 'sex' (Storkey 1994: 118-28). Sex no more exists in and for itself than walking, toothache or letter writing, and it suggests that the prior Christian relational meaning of sexual intercourse is inescapable.

Deconstructing this orthodox tradition involves showing how this artifice has been constructed on a partial and biassed reading of history. In this chapter, which is just a sketch, the detailed historical evidence is not marshalled and assessed. Indeed, in this area much of it is unavailable or indirect. Nevertheless, in my view, the particular modern 'spin' that has been given to the history of sexuality ignores so much social history, that the case easily holds, with room for revisions, in Britain and possibly elsewhere (but see Copley 1989: 79-107). The Emperor has actually been fully clothed for most of history and did not think of taking his clothes off until very recently. Although this study draws on Foucault and other postmodern patterns of deconstruction, the approach is not postmodern, because it depends on the one great untried metannarrative. The Christian insights on marriage, life and our relationship with God remain largely implicit, but being implicit is different from being ignored. The subculture that I am examining has largely labelled Christianity as repressive and has marginalized it. Here I consider on what insubstantial and shaky grounds this has been done. Nor is this just an academic issue, for this orthodoxy is spoiling the lives of millions and causing inestimable hurt and harm. It is an evil lie. Millions of young people especially are lonely and without peace because of the failure that I am about to chart. It is, to state the obvious, the biggest 'cock up' of the times.

Repression

One of the interesting phenomena of the history of ideas is the way nuanced concepts become thought hammers. Such is the history of the word 'repression'. For Freud it was a delicate concept involving wanting to forget, growing up, dreams and unconscious energy (Freud 1976 [1900]: 745-69; 1975 [1901]: 40-42; 1973 [1915–1917]: 327-43), but in later use it often reduces to the Animal Farm idea, *expression good–repression bad*, the philosophy that human sexual expression can be thwarted only at some dreadful cost. The orthodoxy is not difficult to discover. The seers are Havelock-Ellis, Krafft-Ebing, Freud, Kinsey and Masters and Johnson, who have written texts like *Human Sexuality* (Masters, Johnson and Colodny 1992) that convey the enlightened orthodoxy (Brecher: 1970). This is roughly as follows. There are varieties of forms of sexual expression which we can experience, and which it is our right to explore. The point is that we should explore them in a rewarding and technically-aware way, free from the inhibitions and judgements of the past. Bringing this about is one of the greatest forms of human fulfilment. The path through to this stage is marked by a number of pioneers: Algernon Swinburne, Oscar Wilde, Annie Besant, Marie Stopes, Bertrand and Dora Russell, D.H. Lawrence and Theo van der Velde, before the stream widens into the post-war flood of orthodoxy. These people were the heroes of sexual expression, sometimes persecuted and suffering for their faith. The repressive forces against which the battle had to be waged were the churches, a vague group of establishment moralists, and patterns of personal ignorance and folk religion. This neat history has often been, and will often be, told. It has some elements to commend it, but, in a broader sense, is it true?

Foucault questioned whether it was. He looked at the idea of 'repression' and questioned its authenticity. He looked at the idea of the 'repressive hypothesis', whereby the whole of normal Victorian and post-Victorian society was supposed to engage in this conspiracy of repressive censorship, except for a few liberated souls who became the constructors of a new science (Foucault 1981: 1-73). He suggested that those who proposed that repression reigned until the breakthrough which liberated our culture were myth generators. Moreover, they were priests, theologians, gurus demanding that *their* liberation reign. They conveyed and now publish the *scientia sexualis* in glossy texts, by imposing their discourse and by creating research agendas and empires. Foucault, of course, often put the judges in prison, and this dialectical reversal is not necessarily good history. But is the history of sexual repression as it is often portrayed?

The view taken in this study of sexuality in the mid-nineteenth century in Britain is substantially different from the 'repression' orthodoxy. It is that couples were primarily orientated not to sex, but to marriage, faith, family and work. If we ask whether millions of married couples, working, living together, looking after families and going to bed every night were engaging, or refraining to engage in, repressed 'sex', the question is misconceived. They were often tired. They often loved one another and had a deep sense of commitment. They wore thicker clothes in winter because they had no central heating. They made love, presumably, with the normal senses of marital commitment that are present today. Marital sex was usually firmly dissociated from adultery into a different category of relationship. Celibacy was often quite normal and, without a public pornography industry, not a difficult aspect of life, and norms of privacy kept sexual relationships firmly within marriage. There were sexual issues. Intercourse, birth control and family size were a point of concern for many women, but children were often rightly seen as a blessing and not a curse. Getting a man who was reliable and would not leave the woman unsupported was key, and so men were expected to show their 'respectability', their ability to hold a marriage and family together.

Researchers today could conclude that the fatigue of work for both men and women, poorer diet and childbearing led to less frequent 'sex', but that would not be repression, but fatigue. *Marrying* a person for life was the focus of domestic life, and a sexual relationship, along with childbearing, heavy domestic housework, bringing up children, earning a wage and coping with illness was part of that package. Reified 'sex' was not what they were 'having', as we often say today, but marriage with sexual intercourse was a normal part of life. Far from living under a cloud of sexual repression, sex occurred as part of a complex set of social relationships which were rich and problematic. Marriage, family, class relationships, were usually prior to and more fundamental than having sex. This is the story which was the dominant one throughout the Victorian era. Football crowds who are told they are really missing baseball can correctly disagree.

This position needs to be qualified, and this can be done partly in class terms. There were people from all groups (for this is a personal choice), who at certain times were committed to sexual expression. Often this attitude was linked, as it is now, to social power, that is, the ability to control other people's lives in the service of one's own. This certainly had a class basis. The abuse of servants, mistresses and prostitutes grew out of a pattern of aristocratic control that is already reflected in the earlier novels of Richardson and many others. There was also working-class drunkenness, wife abuse and promiscuity. There was a massive increase in the birth rate associated with the movement to the Lancashire cotton towns and 'bundling' as a form of premarital sex was quite common. But this pattern was not so culturally powerful and often reflected patterns of poverty involving large numbers sleeping together. The sexually focussed attitude was thus primarily identified with the landed/wealthy elite, and through them with a wider social ethos.

It was an ethos. This group, through the Grand Tour and English landed culture, often drew its inspiration from classical and Renaissance sources, rather than Christian ones. It thus had an alternative view of sexuality which remained strong, but contested, throughout the late nineteenth century. There were actually two competing cultures of love and sexuality. One was Romantic–Classical and the other was Christian. Romanticism was a reaction against eighteenth-century Classicism, and in many ways they are different. Romantic passion is different from duty. Precept does not fit with an idealized relationship.

Yet the landed gentry often drew on Classical, Renaissance, Enlightenment and Romantic sources through the Grand Tour, imported art and sculpture, education and the available literature. True, Classicism was of the head and Romanticism of the heart, but for both, either human understanding or human passion became the crucible of love and marriage. Oft quoted lines by Tennyson in *In Memoriam* (1850) reflect this synthesis:

> Let knowledge grow from more to more,
> But more of reverence in us dwell;
> That mind and soul, according well,
> May make one music as before,
> But vaster.

Nude Greek and Roman statues were carted in by the boatload. Greek and Latin literature became public school staple diet and a vast Classical culture, together with its views of love, sex and gender, became a massive formative influence on those who often regarded the Classically unlearned as uncivilized. Christianity, which had concentrated on elementary education, was often looked down on and God was, it was supposed, marginalized.

This Classical–Romantic amalgam generated a new approach. Already Romanticism had made the break with Christianity. If the muse of love and sex called, then this was a higher calling than marriage. Love was not a way of obeying God through care and patience towards others, but an inspiration of the soul which swept you up. It was inspiration, duty, an ideal, the search for happiness or a quest of the subject. There was much handwringing associated with this pattern: 'La belle dame sans merci hath thee in thrall'. The great romantic tragedy of Abélard and Héloïse was given another twist as their six hundred year old bodies were buried together in one grave in 1917. De Rougemont, Praz and Pearsall draw the shape of this European and English cultural movement (De Rougemont 1983; Praz 1970; Pearsall 1971; Storkey 1994). It started out with ideals, hope, vision, but ends in disillusionment, tragedy, imprisonment. As Pearsall brilliantly portrays, *The Worm in the Bud* eats through, and the worm is the self-centred human inspiration which becomes subjective and loses the Christian meaning of love. There were many variants in the outcome. Sometimes love was transmuted into an erotic search which created problems for those who pursued it. Otherwise, it became sentiment, a feeling which came and went, often with music hall songs. Or else it became tragic: the love of Romeo and Juliet, Anthony and Cleopatra was recycled as maudlin tragedy. Or it drifted into sado-masochistic forms. But it is here that the cultural meaning of repression is really to be found, because it is really posited on the imperative that the inner drive towards the expression of sexual love must find fulfillment. Only a minority had reached this conclusion at the end of the nineteenth century, but they were an insistent and influential minority. Indeed, here we face one of the questions associated with the construction of the sexological tradition. Were Havelock-Ellis, Krafft-Ebing and others the great founding fathers of a new tradition, as they are frequently portrayed, or were they merely people with weaknesses trapped in the later obsessions of romanticism? The latter conclusion seems the better one.

Often the cultural conflict between Christian and Classical–Romantic views of love, sex and marriage was obscured. Partly this was because Christian teaching was mixed up with idealism, romanticism and a Roman sense of duty. But it was also because the establishment orthodoxy became so dominant. Earlier, Byron, Shelley and other Romantics had been radical, with a strong sense of their antichristian stance. Now they were part of the sacred tradition, enshrined by Palgrave into the civilized orthodoxy. But the real antithesis was still there. Christian teaching said and says firmly, 'Thou shalt not commit adultery' and those who did became antagonistic to the faith. It is probable that much late Victorian turning from faith has more to do with personal romantic quest and sexual compromise than with intellectual challenge, as perhaps it still has.

An important part of this picture, explored further below, is the limited and specific nature of the group which developed these views. As in much history, the idiom of part of the elite is posited as the orthodox interpretation. Because the establishment largely monopolized the written word, it has allowed the creation of a general history of repression from a minority experience. But even here our own modes of interpretation weigh heavily. The thesis would be, for example, that George Eliot, Charles Darwin, John Stuart Mill, John Ruskin, Charles Dickens and Lord Tennyson did not write 'bonkbusters' because they, or their reading public, were sexually repressed. Actually, they seem to be interested in different things—brother–sister love, natural history, the Wages Fund theory, aesthetics, social life, death—and genuinely interested in these things. The conclusion which seems to follow, although it is always subject to detailed historical qualification, is that outside, and even among, the Victorian literati the history of 'repression' is largely invented by a late twentieth century culture obsessed by reified sex. What actually concerned them much more was marriage, faith, work, love and family.

Victorian Reform

The theme of Victorian rectitude is part of an academic folk-lore. Many texts cite the fact that table legs often had to be covered to keep young imaginations sober, and unmarried male and female authors could not touch covers on the bookshelves. But this is not quite what was going on throughout a substantial part of English culture. Mayhew gives a conservative figure of 80,000 prostitutes in London in 1862 and describes the troops of courtesans on Holborn, Oxford Street, the Strand and Regent Street among other areas. They were part of the London scene among all classes, although particularly among the gentry and nobility, or what could be called 'high life'—almost all the men in Kate Hamilton's Night House or at the Haymarket wore top hats (Mayhew, 38-39). But Mayhew sees it as a wider urban problem as well. Certainly, money always flowed. Money bought prostitutes and mistresses, and money came from a middle-class and capitalist establishment which wanted things done their way, including these sexual services. Often, of course, there was secrecy and deception towards wife and family, but this was not 'repression', but just what is more normally called cheating and lying. Interpreting the meaning of this prostitution for Victorian life is complex, and several possibilities must be reviewed.

Certainly, one interpretation is that perceived sexual needs among the wider population were repressed in their immediate social context and expressed in the Haymarket. It fits the repression hypothesis. But there is another, which sees prostitution not as part of general repression, but as a minority lifestyle among some of the population. The former case is quite strong. The demand for this number of prostitutes must have involved a substantial proportion of the population. If we guess that there were five male customers from Greater London to each prostitute annually, we are talking about nearly a quarter of the male London population of 1.75 million or so. Initially, this seems a conservative estimate. But is it the right conclusion? First, London was the great drawing city, fed by the railways and port, and attracting much wider custom for prostitution. Secondly, as Mayhew makes clear, some of the prostitutes were mistresses and prima donnas, kept by one man. But thirdly, the picture drawn by Mayhew is of quite circumscribed groups—sailors, soldiers, members of the underworld and overseas visitors—who provide the clientele for many of these women. Taking these factors into account, the place of prostitution in English social life is likely to be much more circumscribed and dependent on a limited clientele. Indeed, rather than most people being sexually repressed, a substantial majority probably felt that prostitution was wrong, as Mayhew did. It is possible to believe that prostitution is wrong without being sexually repressed.

Why was prostitution wrong? Again, the repressive thesis response is: because others who are repressed want to stop people enjoying sex. But this was not the attitude of the time. Prostitution was brutalizing; it involved women being used and abused by bawds, pimps and clients; it destroyed people. It was the opposite of a career, usually involving sudden or gradual degradation from the Haymarket to Shadwell. But the actual response was more immediate. The concern among the establishment was not moral or repressive, but with venereal disease. Prostitutes were given and spread venereal disease. Calculations were made and the health of the British Army and Navy and the wider population was held to be at risk. As a result the Contagious Diseases Acts were passed between 1864 and 1869. These involved humiliating medical examinations and 'cleaning' of prostitutes; that is, the problem was the transmission of disease, not the degradation of prostitution and its association with poverty.

But here another myth in the sexologists' view of history must be recognized. Religion is entirely associated with repression. Although the Christian faith is concerned about God, the creation of the universe, the meaning of history, the teaching and life of Jesus, and what is greater than our own destiny, the sole significance of the faith in sexological history is that religion is sexually repressive. Not only is there more to life than this, but it is also not true, or at least not true in the terms of the interpretation it is given. For here we must face the fact that there is a confrontation of world-views. For the sexologists' history, sex is the point. In Christian history and faith the whole of life is involved, and the meaning of sex is relativized in the context of married love and celibacy. Here the point is marriage and even this point occurs in the wider context of our relationship with God. So the orthodox history does not even see the point. Indeed, the extent to which historical and current interpretations fail even to be basically aware of Christian meanings and perspectives is amazing. They see but do not perceive; listen but do not hear.

This is evident in the characteristic response to prostitution. Among Evangelicals and wider groups within the church the response was not repression, but to rescue the people involved. Whether it was Baptist Noel and his midnight meetings for prostitutes or Mr and Mrs Gladstone helping women and girls off the streets, the response was to help those who were otherwise heading for personal disaster. Poverty was seen to be the large part of the problem. Nor was the response just personal; it was also structural. Josephine Butler fought for the repeal of the Contagious Diseases Acts, because she did not want a prostitute to be turned into a vessel periodically cleaned for public use. This struggle undertaken by an Evangelical against the obvious moral response should awaken us to how different the perspective was. The crucial point of reference was personal, direct concern for persons in the light of God's relationship with us. It was not sexually focussed. The question now becomes quite direct. Is it 'repressive' to end prostitution, or a great reform for the women and their clients? In this area, in the fight against alcohol, in educational expansion, the care of orphans, in the fight for Sunday rest, in the reform of working hours and conditions, the underlying motivation lay with a Christian understanding of the person and marriage.

The best word to convey this tradition is 'reformist', growing out of the Evangelical tradition of Wilberforce and Shaftesbury. This reformist tradition had a distinct character. Information about social ills or problems was gathered directly. The problem was addressed in terms of personal reformation—conversion or spiritual change—and through structural and legal change. Often, voluntary agencies were formed to open up new social possibilities. Laws were enforced to make sure that wrongs were righted. The key was always to be love. Much of this perspective was carried throughout the West into the twentieth century in a broad social philosophy. Lloyd George and the Nonconformist Conscience gave us Social Insurance. Destructive pressures were pushed back from marriage and family life to give them the room and resources (but for War) to flourish in an unprecedented way. But this Christian tradition of reform had by the twentieth century lost its moorings; it was often being expressed in socialist, liberal or conservative terms. Nevertheless, this great cultural trend should not be obscured by the obsessive subculture of emerging sexualism.

But this may be to move too quickly. Repression is still an issue and Gladstone is an interesting test case, because his diaries give clear evidence of his fight with sexual issues. Himmelfarb gives her interpretation.

> Gladstone's diaries are titillating; one's eyes are inevitably drawn to those whip symbols and the little x's that signified encounters with prostitutes or impure thoughts. But the diaries are also (like Carlyle's memoirs, or Mill's autobiography, or Eliot's letters) sobering. For they remind us that the eminent Victorians were not only eminently human, with all the failings and frailties of the species, but also eminently moral, they did not take sin lightly—their own sins or anyone else's. If they were censorious of others, they were also guilt-ridden about themselves. They were not hypocrites in the sense of pretending to be more virtuous than they were. On the contrary, they deliberately, even obsessively, confessed to their sins. If they did not all punish themselves quite in the manner of Gladstone, they did suffer in private and behave as best they could in public. They affirmed, in effect, the principles of morality even if they could not always act in accordance with those principles (Himmelfarb 1995: 26).

Clearly Gladstone had some problems in the way he understood and dealt with his sexuality, but not those of cheating on his spouse or engaging in dishonest relationships. The idea of repression as obsessive behaviour is evident in his case, but there is also the straightforward biblical understanding of saying 'no' to temptations to think and do things that harm others. Gladstone can be understood. As Himmelfarb says, 'If Gladstone gave way to masturbation, it was perhaps because of the periods of abstinence resulting from the nine pregnancies of his wife in fifteen years. (The convention of the time was to abstain from sexual intercourse during pregnancy and nursing)' (Himmelfarb 1995: 25). The sexual struggles of Gladstone were carried out in terms of faithfulness to his wife. Perhaps he should not have had to struggle so much, but the outcome was for the good, and not the harm of others. The underlying issue can be pushed a stage further. The false polarity which is created by the Animal Farm slogan 'Repression–bad, Expression–good' does not address the issues of life realistically. Many forms of sexual *expression* are obsessive and destructive, both of oneself and also of others, and some forms of sexual repression are similarly obsessive and destructive. The real polarity in which we are all involved, as part of our relationship with God, is between sexual relationships which are destructive or dishonest and those which are holy and healthy. This involves respect for marriage, family and the personal integrity of others. Gladstone did not get it all right, but drifting into another marriage or taking advantage of a teenage girl is getting it a great deal more wrong.

We have actually now travelled quite a long way. The defining fissure has moved from expression/repression to good marriage, family, single life/destructive and degenerate relationships, and we have seen that perhaps the self-defined orthodoxy of much Victorian life was marital and not sexual. Now I shall consider the subcultural nature of many of these attitudes.

Class and Sexual Fixation

It is easy to ignore the massive change in sexual culture that occurred within the nineteenth-century working class, the overwhelming English majority. The fight to reduce poverty, homelessness, death, over-crowding, drunkenness, filth, cruelty and incest was a long one that people undertook on their own behalf and with help. Yet this ameliora-tion of family life did occur, partly through reform, and partly through church, chapel and schooling. Industrialization had often created new urban jungles, and gradually the possibility of good families and marriages was re-established. In this context the agenda of establishing a more formal pattern of courtship and marriage—engagement, banns, wedding, and so on—was a way of giving the woman greater respect and protecting her against the predatory and unreliable male. However, there was another element to the picture which was eloquently brought out by Marx and Engels. It was the *bourgeoisie* who destroyed many working-class marriages and families. Prostitution, the abuse of ser-vants, overwork, pressured seduction were widespread reasons for working-class women's defeat. There was widespread bourgeois sexual exploitation. Marx rails: 'Our bourgeois, not content with having the wives and daughters of their proletarians at their disposal, not to speak of common prostitutes, take the greatest pleasure in seducing each other's wives' (Marx and Engels 1967: 101). Against this background the effect of Methodism, Evangelical piety and established church prac-tices was to uphold and defend the position of women, and although the churches remained patriarchal in many of their practices and structures, this was one of the great strengths of mid-Victorian Britain. Women were given a sense of their integrity before God, their right to respect and love, and their right to choose to marry or stay single. This again is one of the great hidden histories of Victorianism. *Jane Eyre* or *Little Women*, although middle class, convey well the ethos of the steady climb of many women in personal stature before God, and it was a fight. Hodder records in the 1880s how the dying Shaftesbury was in prayer and continual work for a Bill to protect young girls, saying, 'I hope it is not wrong to say it—but I cannot bear to leave the world with all the misery in it' (Hodder 1887: 771). The real battle, as Shaftesbury clearly saw, was for good working-class marital and family life. It involved housing, male (especially) sexual faithfulness, good parenting, education, protection of children from overwork and abuse, and a clear doctrine of marriage. Crucial to this change was the conversion of men and women into personal integrity before God through knowing Jesus as Saviour.

Among middle-class groups Christianity had some of the same kind of leaven. But other social changes were also formative. One involved the segregation of the sexes in the armed forces (obviously), in politics, business, civil service, church, sport, school, family, clubs and university. Why this gender segregation occurred so fully is a difficult historical question. Certainly, Arnold's idea of 'muscular Christianity' was part of the picture, but probably more significant was the earlier contribution of John Keate at Eton, who subjected generations of boys to manic floggings that were public events seen as essential to their upbringing. It was here at Eton that Gladstone's problems probably began, not with his faith. Basically, bullying and brutality were the norm, and during these earlier years women became an alien species. Even deeper was the loss of family intimacy with father and mother (also increased by servant-run households), which left these boys without the close, unconditional love which is the birthright of each of us. This was where the real repression occurred. Men came to marriage as strangers for they knew little of their parents' relationship. Same-gender school sexual experience and the yearning associated with loss of parental love created homosexual pathologies which dominated school, university and other male institutions for decades, and the system produced generations with enormous sexual difficulties to work through. It was from this subculture that much of the subsequent sexological tradition emerged.

Thus, the particular group which engendered this doctrine of repression had itself experienced an atypical and even rather bizarre pattern of gender relationships. They were especially the group which had lost a lot of the intimacies of parental and sibling relationships, who had been subjected often to cruelty, and who had been deprived of most normal experience of the other, or opposite, sex, for most of their formative years. It is ironic that out of this experience a cry to end repression should come to the wider population whose experience of marriage and family life was much more normal.

Reification: This Thing Called 'Sex'

The underlying question which this study raises is how the transition occurs from living in intimate relationships of trust, care and love to a culture where 'having sex' is the main definition of 'being intimate'. This is, of course, no simple or automatic historical regression. There are incredible complexities in the quality of our personal relationships. Having sex, the reified activity, must go through processes of dissociation from the self and from relationships. Paul highlights the way our bodies are to honour God, so that we cannot distantiate our body acts from ourselves (1 Cor. 6.12-20). He also identifies a number of attitudes which must characterize love and respect of the other—patience, kindness, no self-seeking and no anger (1 Cor. 13.4-7). The good relationship comes out of integrity and wholeness before God—holiness—and it addresses with love the integrity of the other person before God. It cannot extract *something* from the other that it would have, whether money, sex or work. Marriage as a lifetime giving to the other retains this sense even in the union.

The breakdown of both respect for the other and self respect is thus primarily rooted in turning away from our relationship with God. Then we are prepared to live in dualisms of action, motivation, thinking and relationship and treat others in the same terms. Thus, the process we are tracing is fundamentally linked to the secularization, the turning from God, which has marked our culture and our intimate relationships. The triumph of the sexological tradition, apart from some physiological insights, is actually a deep loss to our culture. Going 'through' relationships, pornography, broken marriages, public eroticism and deserted children show the stupidity of sex as a human imperative. Although the idiom is now buttressed by massive, mammonic industries, that cannot disguise the rotten fruit of this extended cultural myth. It has risen, but it can fall in favour of relationships which are tender, unmanipulative and peaceful.

The Development of Secular Love

The historical decline of Christianity in Britain is too big a subject to take up here. There were good (i.e., bad) reasons for it in a retreat to a sacred and privatized faith, dilution with romanticism, historicism, nationalism and liberalism, weak educational and political engagement and a tendency to synthesize the Christian faith with any passing philosophical or cultural fad. Christianity, in short, lost the transforming power of response to God and educated obedience to Christ. Thus, although all kinds of Christian piety continued in families, schools, churches and other institutions, the cultural orthodoxy tended to become and be that which grew out of the liberal establishment I have already partly discussed. Here again it is important not to overstate the transition.

For example, Marie Stopes's *Married Love*, first published in 1918 and running through to sales of a million between the Wars, was what its title proclaimed. Its focus was on happy marriages and homes, a search for the joy of marriage, and Stopes was critical of prostitution, drunkenness, self-indulgence, selfishness, or seeing the solution in terms of walking out of marriage (Stopes 1918: 9-17). Sometimes the view of romance is quaint: 'So far as possible ensure that you allow your husband to come upon you only when there is delight in the meeting. Whenever the finances allow, the husband and wife should have separate bedrooms, failing that they should have a curtain which can at will be drawn to divide the room they share' (Stopes 1918: 95). Similarly, Van de Velde's *Ideal Marriage* (1928–47), the standard text on the physiology of intercourse, is premissed on the sacred covenant and passion of married love. Thus we see that the institution of marriage remains that structure within which sexual love is expressed (Brecher 1970: 82-103).

Another figure of note, D.H. Lawrence, became one of the high priests of sexuality. But here again we find a person whose marriage to Frieda was rich and firm. At the same time he was engaged in a sexual quest which led him to the pagan gods of Mexico, but few would say that this quest reached any resolution, and the overwhelming message in Lawrence's work is that honesty in sex involves honesty and integrity in relationships. Lawrence's Lawrence remains very different from the Lawrence used in the *Lady Chatterley's Lover* pornography trial.

Thus, the interwar years were largely marked by two counterpoised trends. First, there was the slow ebbing of Christian faith in which the Christian meaning of love and marriage was gradually transposed into humanist forms like romantic, ideal, moral and duty-centred love. Although these changes were going on they were not much evident in structural terms. At the same time the building of marriages and families was a strong part of public policy, especially against the background of marital and family disruption caused by the Wars. No-one can appreciate the depths of intimate destruction and tragedy caused by those Wars. Yet smaller families, the fight for livelihood in the Depression and a strong understanding of communal welfare opened the way for good postwar family development. The resources available to marriages and families—homes, leisure, mobility and income—have been unprecedented. In one sense the vision of the Garden City visionaries has been realized for many. Even after the Second World War this agenda retained its integrity. The emphasis was on providing state support for homes that would give the next generation the ability to form flourishing units. But when the weighty matters of defeating Fascism, postwar reconstruction and the welfare state receded, what was left?

It is here that we face a largely unwritten history. For by this time many people had moved thoroughly out of living Christian faith. Their relationship with God was dormant. Their education was a-Christian. Their parents may have retained elements of Christian 'behaviour', but these were unsupported by Christian conviction or thought. The great integrating truths of Christianity—God's relationship with us, the creation, the centrality of neighbour love have been lost—precisely at that point English and Western marriage has suffered an unprecedented historical crisis. Surely, we can now blame this crisis, involving the collapse of a third or more marriages and the failure of many other intimate relationships, on sex, or at least on the cultural forces which have pushed sex at generations of emerging adults?

Modern and Postmodern Sex

In part I think we can. Largely this process has occurred through the media. Most people, but especially the young, are exposed to twenty or thirty hours of media a week, and here they learn relationships. Girls' magazines set out to replace mothers and even sneer at them. Soaps define relationships, usually in terms of attractiveness, sex, compatibility and subjective rewards. Sexual myths and obsessions are exploited on a scale which makes it impossible to believe we are still ordinary men and women. Obsessions with pornography, figure, appearance, and sexual experiment cramp the lives of millions. In one sense the sexual tradition that I have examined has become a great modern metanarrative, reinterpreting history, shaping persons, defining success and focussing art. Its claim to be a form of modern salvation and liberation, whether through the prophets like Masters and Johnson, or through pin-ups, seems to be rampant. But that is not really the case. The old certainties, when Marilyn Monroe and Bridget Bardot were sex symbols, are gone. But what is sex now? Presumably, it is often subjective and lonely, the product of a screen or a magazine plus a person's supposed need for this kind of sex. Often it is bought, and the real meaning of the product will be that someone is making money out of someone else. Often it has ended in failure as a sexual relationship, promising intimacy, care and warmth, has been followed by rejection and hurt, and the understanding that even this was not enough to sustain a relationship. For some, 'page three' and a cup of tea are habit, middle-aged rituals. For others, odd sexual quests lead to obscure outcomes. Postmodern sex is fragmented. It is not big enough to be a god, but becomes a number of Bodhisattvas to which people pay occasional devotion.

Self-Justification, Profit, Individualism and Lust

It is wrong to take false gods on their own terms. The myth is without real power and is held in place by cultural supports which are themselves suspect. I shall briefly examine three of these.

One of the crucial dynamics in this whole process is the business of self-justification. Sexual expression is often undertaken in relationships and ways which are wrong. Sexual sin, like economic and political sin, is extremely common. There are two possible responses to this situation. The first is to face it as wrong—normal Christian repentance—but the second is to justify it, to change the criteria of judgement. If Racine drinks the love potion, then all responsibility is gone. I couldn't help myself, could I? If I am really in love with this other person, why should I stay with my husband or wife? Surely an affair could improve my sex life? In order to justify their own sexual attitudes a whole range of people create and collude in self-justifying myths which then validate the behaviour they have chosen. The compulsive power of the need to avoid repression and engage in sexual expression, we agree, don't we, makes any sexual career 'OK'. In the construction of these modes of self-justification it is useful to construct sex as an irresistible force, as that which must be obeyed. Moreover, this process often has a social dimension. Those who have pushed back the boundaries in their own sexual lives, may well feel led to invite others to collude. They, and not those who believe in private marital tenderness, will generate the sexual avante-garde, the new films, books, pornography. Thus, the motive of self-justification, or at least the more subdued theme of 'it-is-all-right-isn't-it', drives the culture on to the reification of sex. Because self-justification is a subjectively biassed process, which will always tend to ignore the wrongs done to others and allow my failures to be unchallenged, it leads to degenerate solutions. But always the question remains: Is my attitude, action, motive justified before God? Hundreds of thousands of men who know it is wrong to leave their wife for a younger woman have found a gloss which paints it white.

The second cultural support is making money. Those who run the sex industries of modern Britain are probably more keenly motivated by money than sex. They have recognized that sometimes sex can be used as a short cut to money. Murdoch exemplifies the fact that more profit can be made in the *Sun* through some sex plus cheap journalism than through journalism alone. Sadly, enough people are taken in by this package to encourage others to feed off the same formula. We have already reached the stage where the market is saturated, even allowing for the dulling effect of continually feeding off garbage, but still the situation remains that the commercial pressures towards sexually focussed communication are very strong. It is supply-side economics driving on a tired idiom.

But neither of these is the nub of the issue. The deepest appeal is always to the self. The point about much sex is not sex, but sex for the self. This underlying motive of self-gratification is part of the individualism of the twentieth century, and it is here that the sexual culture stops. Much of the culture has the structure of self-gratification—buy this and you will receive this reward, it will offer you sexual fulfilment. The ego-focus of sexuality is frightening. It makes celibacy seem impossible. It validates anger and rapacity in sex. It justifies unfaithfulness. It abuses the young. It destroys trust and even the possibility of trust. It uses and then scraps other people. So we find that often sex is not the god, but sex in the service of the self. And the inevitable consequence is deep levels of alienation between those who suppose that they are being intimate. Thus the sexual tradition which in many ways seems so dominant today is actually rather ephemeral, propped up by other supports and hoping that its mythical foundations do not collapse.

The Real Issues

The real calamity of myths is that they do not allow people to address the issues of life in real biblical terms. Thus, the young woman with anorexia who believes she is struggling with her figure and appearance is really struggling with recognizing her glory and integrity before God and within her family. When she truly knows where she is, her problems are solved. Escaping from myths has this shape. It involves moving out of the cultural construct, because it is not true. We have seen how the myth has cast religion and even marriage in the role of the repressor and constructed a triumphant history for the liberating power of sexual knowledge. Not only is this inaccurate history, because it ignores the dominant historical experience and elevates a (mixed-up) subculture to orthodoxy, but it also fundamentally misstates both the problem and the solution. The problem is the reification of sex, and the solution, in the nineteenth century, as now and throughout history, is truthful, honest relationships before God. We must also question whether the substance of good or unhappy marriages lies with 'the quality of sex' or with issues like love, work, tenderness, temper, drink, communication, stress, housing and parenting.

BIBLIOGRAPHY

Brecher, E.
    1970   *The Sex Researchers* (London: Andrew Deutsch).
Copley, A.
    1989   *Sexual Moralities in France 1780–1980* (London: Routledge, 1989).
De Rougemont, D.
    1983   *Love in the Western World* (Princeton, NJ: Princeton University Press).
Foucault, M.
    1981   *The History of Sexuality*. I. *An Introduction* (Harmondsworth: Penguin Books).

Freud, S.
  1976 [1900]   *The Interpretation of Dreams* (Harmondsworth: Pelican Books).
  1975 [1901]   *The Psychpathology of Everyday Life* (Harmondsworth: Pelican Books).
  1973 [1915–17] *Introductory Lectures on Psychoanalysis* (Harmondsworth: Pelican Books).
Himmelfarb, G.
  1995   *The De-moralisation of Society* (London: IEA).
Hodder, E.
  1887   *The Life and Works of the Earl of Shaftesbury* (London: Cassell).
Marx, K. and F. Engels
  1967   *The Communist Manifesto* (Harmondsworth: Penguin Books).
Masters, W., V. Johnson and R. Colodny
  1992   *Human Sexuality* (New York: HarperCollins).
Mayhew, H.
  1950   *London's Underworld* (London: Hamlyn).
Pearsall, R.
  1971   *The Worm in the Bud* (Harmondsworth: Pelican Books).
Stopes, M.
  1918   *Married Love: A New Contribution to the Solution of Sex Difficulties* (London: The Hogarth Press).
Storkey, A.
  1994   *The Meanings of Love* (Leicester: Inter-Varsity Press).
Praz, M.
  1970   *The Romantic Agony* (Oxford: Oxford University Press).

SEX IN A WIDER CONTEXT

Linda Woodhead

In John Updike's short story, 'Wildlife', the middle-aged father, Ferris, reflects upon the sexual attitudes and practices of the present generation:

> He had met some of his son's girlfriends. . . Yet, no sooner had Ferris mastered the name of one, and the rudiments of her geographical and educational background, than she was gone. None of them lasted, none of them apparently excited that romantic wish so common to men of Ferris's generation, the wish to marry—to claim in the sight of church and state this female body, to enter into formalized intimacy as if into a territory to be conquered, tamed, sown and harvested. The wife at the kitchen sink, the wife at the cocktail party or the entr'acte buffet, the wife showering to go out or coming back from shopping with sore feet, the wife docile on one's arm or excitingly quarrelsome in the back of a taxi: that romance that, for Ferris, had attached to these images and made him want to marry not once but repeatedly had quite vanished from American culture.[1]

Though we may find some of the details of Ferris's vision of the sexual relationship a little sexist, it is redeemed by its scope. Sex for him is not confined to a narrow context—a night of passion, a few months of intimacy—but opens out to the dimensions of one's whole life. And rather than being confined to one's 'private life', it takes place in the context of state and church, friends and local community.

The contemporary narrowing of perspective on sex which so bewilders Ferris is the subject of this chapter. Its argument is that, such narrowing results in a distortion and diminution of sexual life, and that much recent Christian thought has colluded with this process. Yet, as I also attempt to show, the realities of sex resist this shrinkage and burst out of the artificial confinement of our contemporary narrow-mindedness. I suggest that it takes the resources of an older tradition

---

1. John Updike, *The Afterlife and Other Stories* (Harmondsworth: Penguin Books, 1995), p. 27.

of Christian reflection upon sex to help us see these realities in their true perspective: within the context of friends, families, local community, the state and 'in the sight of God, and in the face of this congregation'.[2] Finally, and by way of conclusion, I explore some of the possible implications of this widening of perspective for sex these days.

Sex in the Context of One: The Privatization of Sex These Days

The narrowest of all contexts in which sex may be conceived is the context of one—the context of the individual person. It is within this context that the habits of thought and practice of the contemporary world encourage us to place sex. This may seem paradoxical: surely sex means sexual *intercourse*, and intercourse demands not one but two? Yet 'sex' these days is just as likely to mean sexuality as sexual intercourse, and sexuality is a fundamentally individualistic notion. Part of a distinctively modern conceptuality, 'sexuality' is understood as an endowment of the individual, a key aspect of individual identity; to say that one is homosexual, heterosexual or bisexual is to say something about who one is quite as much as it is to say something about the other(s) to whom one relates.[3]

The shift towards an understanding of sex in the context of one is shown clearly not just by this shift in the meaning of sex, but also by some of the most characteristic ways in which we direct and evaluate our sexual activity these days. One of the most common guides in this matter is the utilitarian, by which we evaluate sexual activity in terms of the pleasure it affords the individuals concerned. The slogan under which this approach is often manifest today is 'sex is fun': and so long as it is fun it is good. This is certainly the message much youth culture delivers. Adult culture takes the message and reinforces it by giving it a slightly more serious tone: sex is not just fun, it is also one of the major fulfilments of human life. It is fulfilling because it delivers deep and intense pleasure; the person who experiences this pleasure and is able to offer it to his or her partners is the person numerous books and magazine articles promise to help us become.

2.   The first sentence of the Form of Solemnization of Matrimony from the *Book of Common Prayer*.

3.   'Sexuality' is a term that has only recently become current. According to the OED it first appears in 1800 within scientific discourse and in application to lower life forms. It is first applied to a human being in 1879 (*Oxford English Dictionary*, XV [Oxford: Clarendon Press, 2nd edn, 1989], p. 116).

Similarly revealing of the utilitarian perspective is the way we tend to judge our relationships in terms of the intensity of the experience they afford us. Once the 'chemistry' or the 'sexual spark' departs from a relationship its *raison d'être* is thought to be over. And a relationship which promises greater intensity to its participants is thought to count as reason enough to leave an older relationship which has 'gone cold'.

Of course utilitarianism is not our only guide in the sexual life these days. In the evaluation of sexual activity the utilitarian calculus is often supplemented by appeal to liberal values. The freedom as well as the pleasure of the individuals involved in sexual practice is thought to be germane to the evaluation of that practice. Thus we regard relationships in which one partner is coerced as morally reprehensible, as we do those in which an individual is not really in a position to make a rational choice at all (as in paedophilia). As is the case with utilitarianism, however, the liberal habit of thought generally comes into play not so much in the negative evaluation of sexuality as in its positive evaluation and defence. When and where sex takes place between freely consenting adults liberalism views it as sacrosanct *per se*. The freedom from which sexual activity arises is understood as the undisputed ground of its justification and sanctification. This holds good whatever forms such sexual activity may take, and whatever its social consequences.

The individualism inherent in both the utilitarian and liberal perspectives is clear. Even though it is concerned with the 'greatest good', the utilitarian perspective is fundamentally individualistic because its concern is with the pleasure of an amalgam of *individuals*. Social institutions, communities, families and pair-bonds cannot be assessed on their own merits, but only in terms of the pleasure they afford the individuals who participate in them. The individual's happiness remains the only ultimate value. Likewise, liberalism exalts the freedom of the individual over all other values. There is no higher value or greater good which could trump such freedom. Together these perspectives give rise to the idea of a private realm of greater value and significance than any public realm. The private realm is the realm where the individual is truly free and able to give and take pleasure without the interference of others. It is to this realm that sexuality belongs; indeed, sex is perhaps the paradigmatic activity of this realm. By contrast, the public realm is a realm in which the individual is forever in danger of compromise, his or her autonomy forever threatened. On the liberal understanding the public realm exists only to serve the private, and its claims must always respect this order of things. Given the power of the utilitarian and liberal habits of thought and practice in contemporary society it is therefore easy to see how sex becomes privatized. And it is easy to see why this shrinkage into the context of one makes sex appear more sacred to the modern world, not less.

Some of the consequences of this privatization of sex may give us pause and lead us to question the adequacy of the context of one as a context for sexual reflection and sexual activity. Most telling, perhaps, is the fact that reflection which works only within this context can find no reason to condemn practices which many of us feel to be objectionable. Prostitution is a good example. It is hard to condemn prostitution on either libertarian or utilitarian grounds. Participants in prostitution give their free consent to the sexual activity which takes place, and both parties presumably derive pleasure or happiness from it—the one directly from the sexual activity, the other from the financial reward consequent upon it. Likewise, the privatization of sex makes forms of sexual activity like sado-masochism unexceptionable so long as participants consent freely to what takes place and derive pleasure from it. Similarly, moral offences like fornication, adultery and promiscuity cease to be offences at all, with the very words losing meaning and currency in the context of one.

Masturbation is also hard to describe and evaluate adequately if working only within the context of one. Indeed, fluctuating attitudes towards masturbation are interestingly revealing of shifting perspectives on sex. In traditional Roman Catholic moral theology, masturbation has always been regarded as one of the most serious of sexual sins. Yet from the perspective of contemporary individualism it is no longer viewed as a sin at all, the term becoming one of neutral description. Indeed, it may be argued that within the context of one masturbation becomes the paradigmatic form of sexual activity. If sex can only be understood as the individual's free quest for intense pleasure this seems not only to validate masturbation, but to turn all sexual behaviour into a form of masturbation. It becomes impossible to understand sexual activity in terms of anything which transcends the individual—whether that be a relationship or an institution. Sex's sole *telos* becomes the pleasure of the free individual; even when sexual pleasure is brought about by the agency of the other rather than the self, it ceases to have any meaning beyond the pleasure it brings the self.

Sex in the Context of Two: Contemporary and Christian Attempts to Move Beyond Sexual Individualism

Contemporary Christian thinkers tend to be rightly suspicious of the privatization of sex and aware of some of the dangers into which it leads us. Yet in the attempt to develop a sexual ethic for today some unwittingly come dangerously close to advocating the context of one as the proper context for reflection and activity themselves. It is only the employment of a Christian vocabulary and conceptuality in place of that of secular liberalism and utilitarianism that obscures this capitulation to an individualistic perspective.

One of the best examples of this is the tendency of many contemporary Christian theologians and ethicists to take as their starting point for reflection upon sexuality the language of incarnation and bodiliness. Following the lead of thinkers like James Nelson, many Christians now argue that the Christian doctrine of the incarnation of God in Christ should reorient sexual reflection by reminding us of the value and importance of the human body.[4] They maintain that this affirmation of the goodness of the human body is the distinctive Christian affirmation which must inform sexual attitudes. Their argument is that once one realizes that the body is good, then one must realize that sex is also good: therefore a traditional Christian mistrust of the body and sexuality must be rejected as dangerous distortion. A revolutionary Christian re-evaluation of sexuality and its importance is therefore thought to be imperative. Such re-evaluation, it is argued, must bring sexuality and spirituality back into the closest connection. By this means Christians will be freed to view sex for the first time as a proper part of the spiritual life—as a road which leads to the divine rather than away from it.

---

4.   See James Nelson, *Embodiment: An Approach to Sexuality and Christian Theology* (London: SPCK, 1979) and *Body Theology* (Louisville: Westminster/John Knox, 1992). The widespread acceptance of this strategy in sexual ethics is well illustrated by the words with which the editors of a recent collection on Christianity and Sexuality open their introduction to the volume: 'It is ironic that a religion which is grounded in what Weber calls "incarnational consciousness" should have had so much trouble with bodies. . . ' The authors go on to advocate an approach that begins with rehabilitation of the body and of individuals' sexual experience (rather than with traditional theological reflection). Adrian Thatcher and Elizabeth Stuart (eds.), *Christian Perspectives on Sexuality and Gender* (Leominster: Gracewing and Grand Rapids: Eerdmans, 1996), pp. ix-xiv.

But far from moving Christians out of the context of one, it seems that this incarnational and experiential approach to sexuality often acts to keep Christians firmly within it. As will be suggested below, it is very possible for the Christian doctrine of the incarnation to move Christian reflection upon sex out of the context of one by bringing that reflection into proper relation with God, Christ and the church—but this is not what happens in much contemporary incarnational sexual ethics. Rather, the meaning of incarnation is here squeezed and reduced until it comes to speak only of the importance of the bodily nature of the individual and loses connection with Jesus Christ. The exhortation to take an incarnational perspective comes to mean that one should rely on one's own individual experience in sexual reflection rather than that one should bring such reflection under the authority of God's revelation in Christ. Moreover, whereas in traditional Christian reflection the meaning of 'body' is stretched in ways which signal the connection as well as the distinction between human beings (as in language about the body of Christ in which all are one), here the focus upon the body is narrower and tends to emphasize only the individual's physicality, hence that which separates and distinguishes individuals rather than that which unites them. On this understanding the only way in which bodies may achieve some sort of union is through sexual intercourse—hence its tremendous and inflated importance within this scheme of thought. On this understanding, bodies are united not in Christ but only in copulation.

Another notable twentieth-century Christian attempt to draw contemporary reflection upon sex into the context of two in this way was that which drew upon traditional Christian discourse about *love*. Exponents of a more 'positive' Christian attitude to sexuality like Jack Dominian argue that it is love that furnishes the standard by which sex must be understood and evaluated, love which validates sex and makes it a properly Christian activity, and loving relationship rather than the individual fulfilment which must be our guide through the complexities of the sexual life.[5] Augustine's injunction to 'love and do as you like' is often cited in this context as the golden rule for sexual behaviour.

5.   Jack Dominian has written prolifically on the topics of sex, love and marriage. See, for example, J. Dominian, *Proposals for a New Sexual Ethic* (London: Darton Longman & Todd, 1977); J. Dominian and H. Montefiore, *God, Sex and Love* (London: SCM Press, 1989); and J. Dominian, *Passionate and Compassionate Love: A Vision for Christian Marriage* (London: Darton Longman & Todd, 1991).

Sexual activity is justified by the love in which it takes place and which it fosters. The level of sexual involvement in a relationship must therefore be commensurate with the depth of love which characterizes that relationship. So on this account love and sex must always go together: they are natural bedfellows. And this, it is argued, leads to the conclusion that ultimately it is marriage which forms the proper context for sexual activity, for it is here that committed, faithful and exclusive love comes into being.

A more recent development in Christian reflection upon sexuality gives this stress upon the necessary connection between love and sex a new twist by reinterpreting love. Whereas a previous generation of Christian writers often left the term vague or rendered it in terms of *agape*, understood as self-giving, there has recently been a move to render love in terms of *eros*.[6] Feminist writers have been particularly influential in this move, partly spurred by an awareness of how *agape* understood as self-sacrificial love can have deleterious effects on the lives of those Christian women who have tried to live by it.[7] Exponents of an *eros* theology therefore argue that it is in terms of the sovereign standard of *eros* rather than *agape* that sexuality must be evaluated and justified.[8] By contrast with *agape* and with the hierarchical and unequal masculine-heterosexual understandings of sex and love which dominate contemporary understanding, *eros* is said to be a force which undermines any form of domination or submission. It is radically

6.   The influence of Anders Nygren's classic study, *Agape and Eros* (London: SPCK, 1982 [first English edn, 1938–1939]), is evident in all this, for it is Nygren and his followers who draw the sharp distinction between *agape* and *eros* which makes this whole modern debate possible. Even though they reject Nygren's exaltation of *agape* over *eros*, contemporary theorists of *eros* work with the distinction he draws.

7.   I summarize and develop such arguments in my article 'Love and Justice' in *Studies in Christian Ethics*, 5.1 (1992), pp. 44-61.

8.   Exponents of *eros* theology include Carter Heyward and Rita Nakashima Brock. See C. Heyward, *Touching Our Strength: The Erotic as Power and the Love of God* (San Francisco: Harper & Row, 1989); R.N. Brock, *Journeys by Heart: A Christology of Erotic Power* (New York: Crossroad, 1995). Erotic theology takes its rise from Process Theology and from the work of such feminist writers as Mary Daly, Hauuani-Kay Trask, Audre Lourde, and Susan Griffin. For a brief and very sympathetic account of the movement see Sandra Friedman and Alexander Irwin, 'Christian Feminism, Eros and Power in Right Relation', in Thatcher and Stuart (eds.), *Christian Perspectives on Sexuality and Gender*, pp. 152-67.

mutual, passionate, angry, energizing, dynamic, creative and joyous. It is a form of psychic power especially potent for women. It is sexual but more than sexual; it is the empowering creative energy that inspires all relational activity. It is a sacred and unifying life force which seeks to bind all things together in true connectedness. It is, as Rita Nakashima Brock puts it, 'the very foundation of life and the source of energy for human selves that compels us to search for the whole of life'.[9]

While the earlier Christian emphasis upon the necessary relation of sex and love may be credited with trying to move sexual reflection from an individualistic context into the context of two, *eros* theology wishes to move sex into a still wider context by claiming that *eros* undergirds a renewed political vision and the struggle to realize this vision. Eros is thus viewed not just as a force which empowers the individual, nor even as a force which brings two persons into relation, but as a force which engenders a new vision of a mutual and connected society and releases the energies necessary to fight the forces of oppression which hold back its manifestation. Thus *eros* is claimed as a force which breaks down the barriers between private and public, private and political.

In this desire to bring sex into a wider context, *eros* theology may have something to teach us. Yet there are some serious reasons for doubting its ability to move sex into a wider context consistently and convincingly. For, as in incarnational sexual theology, there is much in *eros* theology that seems to hold its reflections on sex firmly within the context of one, despite its claims to the contrary. For is not the *eros* which it sees as foundational to new relationships, a new society and a new religion, an *eros* that is still basically the freely willed pleasure of the individual? As Heyward says, 'Sexual orgasm can be literally a high point, a climax in our capacity to know, ecstatically for a moment, the coming together of self and other, sexuality and other dimensions of our lives'.[10] In other words, *eros* theology buys into the assumptions of modern individualism by making orgasmic experience foundational, the only thing 'thick' enough to ground relationships, society and religion. These latter do not have enough independent value and reality to stand on their own, but must be vivified and ontologised by *eros*. Indeed, in much *eros* theology even God becomes reducible to erotic experience. He is, as Heyward says 'our power in mutual relation'.[11]

9. Brock, *Journeys by Heart*, p. 41.
10. Heyward, *Touching Our Strength*, p. 33.
11. Heyward, *Touching Our Strength*, p. 188.

Far from challenging modern assumptions about sex, the danger of *eros* theology is thus that it merely sanctifies them. Freely willed erotic pleasure becomes the only authentic experience and the basis of all human and divine activity. *Eros* theology baptizes the context of one by taking individual experience as its starting point and by refusing to accept the insight so magnificently demonstrated by Foucault that social, political and cultural institutions are not just the fruit of such experience, but the ground of its possibility.[12] *Eros* theology wishes to erect new forms of just relationship and community upon the erotic experience. By contrast, traditional religion (even before Foucault!) understood the wider context of sexual activity by understanding that the latter is itself the product of social and cultural institutions, and that it is the nurturing and perfection of these institutions which makes possible good behaviour and experience. On a Christian understanding, the entrance into true relationship with God and neighbour is made possible only by entrance into the church, the new community called into being by God. It is the body of Christ which forms the basis of a new society—not the body of the individual.

Despite its insights, *eros* theology seems, then, to deliver sex back to the context of one much too easily. In typically modern fashion it is concerned with individual and state, but has little time for the communities intermediate between them like church, family and marriage. So in the final analysis we may be forced to conclude that the older theologies which tried to bind sex within the context of love and marriage are actually able to move more successfully out of the context of one than is *eros* theology—even if they only move as far as the context of two. And their account is obviously one which harmonizes with deep instincts within our wider society, instincts perhaps left over from Christianity. For the institution of marriage is still one that draws the majority of us through its portals. With or without the help of a theology of the pair-bond, many people today obviously believe that sex should take place in a context wider than that of the individual, and the romantic ideology which supports such a belief is clearly alive and well. The struggle between theologies of love and marriage and *eros* theology seems then to be a reflection of a wider struggle in

12. See M. Foucault, *The History of Sexuality*, published in three volumes: I. *An Introduction* (Harmondsworth: Penguin Books, 1981); II. *The Use of Pleasure* (Harmondsworth: Penguin Books, 1987); III. *Care of the Self* (Harmondsworth: Penguin Books, 1990).

contemporary society: the struggle between ideologies of sex in the context of one and those of sex in the context of two.

Sex in Public:
How Sex Inevitably Leaks Out of the Contexts of One and Two

The attempt to confine sex within the context of one or two seems then to be pervasive within contemporary Christian and secular thought. Yet it is an attempt which is permanently threatened by the realities of sex itself. For sex seems to resist confinement either within the life of the individual or that of the pair-bond. It is forever breaking through the boundaries that our forms of life and thought would erect around it.

The ways in which sex breaks through the context of one are the most obvious. Sex permanently threatens to destabilize the boundaries of individual autonomy and self-contained identity. For while it is undoubtedly possible to control sex in a way that preserves one's full control and self-directedness, fairly serious policing is required in order to ensure this. One must constantly be on one's guard to see that one is never too deeply affected by one's sexual partners, that one does not become too attached to them nor too dependent upon them. For as soon as sex results in the formation of bonds of love or need it threatens to move a person outside the context of one into the context of two.

It is interesting to note in this context that even masturbation, that most individualistic of all sexual activities, generally requires at least the visual presence of the other, a need often supplied by pornographic material. But it is of course in the nature of such material to keep the other firmly an object, unable to threaten the autonomy of the voyeur. The prostitute as an object of desire also tends to be surrounded by similar safeguards, but here the fuller presence of the object of sexual desire to a 'client' makes the possibility of some contact which breaks through the context of one more likely—a likelihood exploited by the imagination of countless novelists and screenplay writers. The context of one, it seems, is a fragile context barely able to contain the fuller reality of sex.

But it is not just the context of one which is threatened and breached by sex: the context of two also suffers the same fate. For, in spite of attempts to confine sex entirely within the bounds of the pair-bond, this confinement too seems hard to sustain. Though less restrictive than the context of one, the context of two seems also to deny the fuller realities of sex and the sexual encounter.

Most importantly, a restriction of sex to the context of two denies
the reality of the wider relationships which surround the sexual
relationship, relationships which both support and flow from the pair-
bond. The most obvious of these is the relationship with children. Sex
is not an activity whose *telos* is entirely immanent—whether in the
individual or the couple. Rather, most heterosexual sex opens up the
possibility of the creation and nurture of children. Sexual bonding
opens up the possibility of the expansion of the intimate community in
this way. Of course, the introduction of contraception has had a huge
impact upon sex, making it possible for us today to think of it solely
within the context of one or two in a way previous generations could
not. Yet no contraception is so perfect that the possibility of procreation
is completely precluded, and every honest sexual encounter should
therefore be entered into in willing acceptance of the possibility that it
may break through the context of two by engendering offspring.[13] The
theologians of love who affirm that sex should tend towards love are
right, but this love must be understood not merely as the love which
joins man and woman together, but as the love which opens itself to
the creation and nurturance of another human being. As Paul Ramsey
puts it, there should not be among men and women, 'any love set out
of the context of responsibility for procreation, any begetting apart
from the sphere of love'.[14]

But it is not just the begetting of children that makes it reductive
and misleading to view sex as having no boundaries wider than that of
the context of two. Sexual relationship also bursts these bounds by
involving those whom it joins in yet wider circles of relationship. For
those who are known to be joined by sexual relationship—those whose
relationship is public and persists over some interval of time—relate
to others by virtue of that relationship and *as* that relationship—not
just as individuals, but as a couple. Through their sexual relationship
each member is thus linked to the friends and family of the other, a
linkage formalized in marriage by the creation of the category of 'in-
laws'. By such means the sexual relationship connects those whom it
joins not only with a future generation, but also with past and present

13. This is powerfully argued by Paul Ramsey in *One Flesh: A Christian View of
Sex Within, Outside and Before Marriage* (Grove Booklets, 8; Nottingham).

14. 'The Covenant of Marriage and Right Means', in William Werpehowski and
Stephen D. Crocco (eds.), *The Essential Paul Ramsey: A Collection* (New Haven:
Yale University Press, 1994), pp. 137-50 (p. 141).

generations. Where the sexual relationship produces children these links are further strengthened, for through one's children one is linked by blood to one's in-laws. Consequently, the breakdown of a sexual relationship means the end—or at least the disruption—not only of that relationship itself, but of the intricate web of other relationships built around it. Thus divorce profoundly affects not just a married couple and their children, but grandparents, aunts and uncles, nephews and nieces, godparents and friends. A whole new realignment of relationships has to be negotiated on the breakdown of a sexual relationship—often at great cost to all concerned.[15]

Marriage has inevitably crept into this discussion of sex, for marriage, far from merely being a means of ratifying and sanctifying the context of two in the way that is sometimes assumed, in fact instantiates the ways in which the sexual relationship must also and inevitably transcend this context. It should by now have become clear that it does so not only by its openness to children, but by its formalization of the relationships it creates between spouses' families. But more than that, marriage moves in a context greater than two precisely because of its nature as public ritual. Marriage takes a significant step beyond private betrothal; it is not merely an optional addition to such betrothal, it is *public* betrothal. As such, marriage does not merely ratify a pre-existing relationship, but establishes this relationship by placing it before the face of God, friends, family, church, and state. It thereby acknowledges and initiates the wider set of relationships which surrounds the pair-bond.

Contrary to what is commonly held today, there is no private realm hermetically sealed from the wider and impersonal public realm. The private is never impermeable to the public nor the public to the private. The sexual relation is not a relation of two upon which all else must be constructed, but is itself constructed within a network of wider relationships. It is only in relation to this wider context that full and

---

15. It is interesting to note that entrance into a sexual relationship establishes relationship not just with one's lovers friends and family, but also with any previous sexual partners one's lover might have had. This can be highly problematic even if such relationships are now in the past. The natural wish of one who is loved sexually to be one flesh with their lover is threatened by knowledge of these previous relationships, and the past may enter the present by undermining or destroying the current relationship. For a hilarious depiction of the ways in which this can happen see Julian Barnes's novel, *Before She Met Me* (London: Picador, 1986), in which a husband enters into obsessive relationships with his wife's former lovers.

enduring sexual relationships flourish. The contexts of one and two are inadequate to the fullness of sexual existence.

Sex in the Church, Sex in Christ: The Wider Context of Sexuality

Though Christians should be open to the wider context of sex formed by children, families, friends and local communities, for Christians sex takes place within a yet wider context: it takes place within the body of Christ. That is to say, it takes place in the presence of God and in the context of the community which God has called into being—the church. For Christians, moreover, these contexts have been and should be the primary contexts of sexual relationship. Remembering this today can help us not only in our understanding of the attitudes towards sex displayed by previous generations of Christians, but in our comprehension of the defects of those contemporary Christian approaches to sexuality which would confine it within the narrow bounds of the individual, the pair-bond or the biological family alone.

An awareness of the new, divine context into which Christians are graciously called dominated the thought and imagination of the first generations of Christians. It was from within this context that early Christian teachers and theologians attempted to reassess the institutions, forms of life and behaviours taken for granted in 'the world'. Not one of these behaviours was excluded from this process of reassessment: all must be judged in the light of Christ. Inevitably there was considerable debate about the outcome of this process, but it was agreed by all concerned that Christianity could not simply take existing forms of sexuality and sexual relationship for granted. Rather, it must consider their appropriateness within the context of the new kingdom God was bringing into being.

The writings of the early Christians are notable for their vivid sense of the nearness of God and the reality of God's presence, a sense fed both by their historical proximity to Jesus Christ and their experience of God active in their lives—the Holy Spirit. Here God has become the most immediate reality of life, and relationship with him the primary relationship. Since relationship with God thus supplants even the primacy and intimacy of the sexual relationship it is unsurprising that many writers use sexual and nuptial images and metaphors to speak of it. Paul provides a good example of this. Several times he speaks about the intimacy of the believer's union with Christ through the Holy Spirit in quasi-physical, quasi-sexual terms.[16] In 1 Cor. 6.13-17, for example, Paul exhorts the Corinthians against sexual immorality in the following terms:

> The body is not for fornication but for the Lord; and the Lord for the body... Do you not know that your bodies are members of Christ? Shall I therefore take the members of Christ and make them members of a prostitute? Never! Do you not know that the person who is joined to a prostitute is one body? For, as it is written, 'the two shall be one flesh'. But the person joined to the Lord is one spirit.

In this extraordinary argument, Paul cites Gen. 2.24 in order to show that those who have sexual intercourse are inevitably bound together by their sexual union. They inevitably move from the context of one into the context of two—or rather, of two-become-one. But, as Paul reminds the Corinthians, the believer is already united with *Christ* in such a context of two-become-one—in a way analogous to sexual union, as 'one flesh'. In immoral sexual union the believer therefore joins not his or her sexual partner to the prostitute, but Christ himself. The conclusion to which the reader is drawn is that Christ himself is defiled by fornication and that fornication is a form of infidelity to Christ.

Interestingly, when Gen. 2.24 is later cited in Eph. 5.30-31 it is again used in a similar way to insist that the one flesh union—the two-become-one—refers not just to the relationship of husband and wife, but to that of Christ and the church: 'This mystery is a profound one and I am saying that it refers to Christ and the church' (Eph. 5.32). Here, however, the relationship of the married (as opposed to the fornicating) couple is understood not as threatening the relationship of Christ and the believer but as illuminated by it: as Christ loves the church, 'even so husbands should love their wives as their own bodies' (5.28). Yet still the relationship of believer with Christ is the one that has priority: it is this relationship that illuminates the relationship of husband and wife, not vice versa. On this account—and contrary to the ideas of *eros* theology—it is not from our erotic relationships that

---

16. This was powerfully demonstrated by Albert Schweitzer in *The Mysticism of Paul the Apostle* (London: A. & C. Black, 1931). As he explains in his discussion of 1 Cor. 6.13-17, 'That what is in view in the Pauline mysticism is an actual physical union between Christ and the Elect is proved by the fact that "being in Christ" corresponds to, and, as a state of existence, takes the place of the physical "being in the flesh"' (p. 127).

we learn about God, but from God's relationship with us that we learn about our erotic relationships.

The immediacy, vitality and priority of our relationship with God in Christ is thus the starting point for much early Christian reflection upon sexuality and sexual relationship. This relationship with God is understood as one of intimate union, and this can lead to one of two conclusions (or possibly to both). First, that the human sexual relationship which is in the image of Christ's relationship to the church is thereby validated. Secondly, that human sexual relationship is at worst a distraction from the more important relationship with God, at best a redundant superfluity; where once the one-flesh union might have been sought with another human, it must now be pursued single-heartedly in relationship with God. A further dimension is added to all this by the fact that Christians understood themselves to be members of Christ's body not just as individuals, but as members of a community, the church. Thus the relationship with Christ spills over into relationship within the new community he has called into being; the priority of this new community may also cast doubt upon the importance of older institutions like marriage. Now one's most important human relationships are within the body of Christ, and again it maybe concluded that marriage serves as a distraction from this more important focus of loyalty, leading inevitably to divided loyalties.

Paul seems to hold all the above conclusions about human sexual relationship together in his epistles (assuming he is the author of Ephesians). On the one hand he validates human sexual relationships by urging that the one-flesh union of Christ and the church must guide married couples in the living out of their calling, and by insisting upon the proper and central place of sex within the marriage relationship. But on the other, Paul views the single life as preferable because offering fewer distractions to single-minded relationship with the Lord. In his simultaneous insistence upon marriage as a valid calling for Christians and upon the superiority of the calling to celibacy or virginity, Paul anticipates most subsequent Christian reflection upon sex and sexuality up to the Reformation. Indeed, Paul tends to be rather more positive about the sexual relationship than some subsequent theologians, many of whom understood marriage not as an intrinsic but an instrumental good and sex likewise as justifiable only in terms of its ends.[17]

17. See Derrick Sherwin Bailey, *The Man–Woman Relation in Christian Thought*

The varied but often negative conclusions about the value of sexual relationship which early Christian writers and teachers reached have recently been explored by the secular historian Peter Brown in *The Body and Society*. Yet what unites those he discusses is the way in which all try to reassess sex and the sexual life within the new context brought about by God through the sending of Christ and the Holy Spirit. Clearly, all conceive this new context in slightly different ways and emphasize different aspects of it. Equally clearly, they often come to different conclusions about its relevance for the sexual life. But upon the broadened perspective within which these issues must now be considered all are agreed. They reflect upon the state of creation as God first intended it, and the place marriage and sex might (or might not) have had within it (appealing to the Genesis narratives). They consider what difference the Fall has made: whether sex comes about as a result of the Fall, or whether it is merely corrupted by the Fall. And they reflect upon the difference that revelation of God's redemptive purposes for us in Jesus Christ may make. They take seriously Jesus' statement that there is no marriage in heaven (Mt. 22.30; cf. Mk 12.25, Lk. 20.34 36), but reflect on the bearing this has on the current age in which old and new age struggle against one another. Can Christians begin to live lives of redeemed sexuality in this time, or should they leave such matters behind and enter the kingdom of heaven proleptically? Different thinkers give different answers, and we may well take issue with some of them; but by contrast with the breadth of their reflections, how confined and sub-Christian our modern musings upon sex and marriage so often seem. And it is a measure of just how far we have moved from the broad mindedness of the church fathers that the one feature of their thought that Brown is most at pains to emphasize is its *strangeness*.[18]

(London: Longmans, Green, 1959). For a clear exposition of the complex history of Catholic Christian thought on the 'ends', 'goods' and 'reasons' of and for marriage, see also Germain Grisez, *The Way of the Lord Jesus*. II. *Living a Christian Life* (Quincy, IL: Franciscan Press, 1993), pp. 553-69.

18. As he says, 'If my book gives back to the Christian men and women of the first five centuries a little of the disturbing strangeness of their most central preoccupations, I will consider that I have achieved my purpose in writing it'; Peter Brown, *The Body and Society: Men, Women and Sexual Renunciation in Early Christianity* (London: Faber and Faber, 1991), p. xv.

Viewing Sex in a Wider Context:
Some Implications for a Sexual Ethic 'These Days'

The importance of viewing sex in a wider context should by now have
become clear. This perspective allows us to take in more of the reality
that discloses itself to us, including our social nature, and the God-
given context within which we find ourselves. Such a perspective is
more truthful to the realities of sex and the sexual condition, and it
can free us from the endemic narrowness and restrictiveness of sexual
attitudes these days. This widening of context will have many important
implications for a contemporary sexual ethic. Here I will mention just
a few of them.

One very important thing that we can learn from this widening of
perspective is that sex is not as important as the modern world assumes.
As I have noted, our age tends to believe that sex is essential to full
maturity, indeed to full personhood. Those who have not been involved
in a sexual relationship have no clear place in our society and are
generally regarded as sad misfits. The wider Christian perspective on
sex should challenge such attitudes and assumptions. As Christ teaches,
we become fully human not through sexual adventure but through
proper relation with God and neighbour: and this may be effected
through and in many different forms of life, including the celibate
life. After all, Christ himself, our model of perfect humanity, was not
involved in a sexual relationship.

Throughout its history, Christianity has been extremely fruitful in
establishing experimental communities of many different forms
designed to enable the living out of a life of love; the variety of these
communities is often obscured by our blanket use of the term 'monastic'
to describe them. It is a sign of the narrowing of our perspective that
such communities have now been eclipsed by the sexual community of
two as the primary context for the living of the Christian life. The
existence of such communities reminded us that there are many ways
in which Christians can live fully human lives, not all of them centred
on sexual activity. The existence of the church has also served to remind
us that even when people choose to live within a sexual relationship,
that relationship itself belongs within a wider context. If our churches
have become peripheral to our lives today, completely subordinate in
significance to our sexual relationships, this is a reflection on our
failing as much as theirs. (And yet it is surely encouraging that our

churches can and do still provide a home for some of the 'misfits' of society, including those who do not, for one reason or another, belong in a sexual relationship.)

If one important implication of the widening of our perspective on sex is thus that it is less important than we tend to think these days, another must be that it is also *more* important. For with broader vision we can see that sex has all sorts of profound effects in all sorts of areas. We can see that sex is not just a bit of harmless fun whose traces can be easily erased. Rather, it shapes and binds individuals in a multitude of ways. It affects character, it affects sexual partner(s), it affects friends and family and local and national community, it affects fellow Christians, church, relationship with God, and it may be fruitful of children. And, in turn, all these interlocking contexts themselves affect sex and the sexual relationship.

Christianity has traditionally kept this sense of the importance of sex alive, though, as we have seen, it has tended to do so in a negative way, stressing the evils of inappropriate forms of sexual practice and relationship rather than the good of appropriate forms. As many modern theologians and church leaders have realized, it is now important that Christianity paint the positive as well as the negative picture (though, as I shall suggest below, the negative must not be wholly abandoned). For some theologians, this desire to paint a positive Christian picture of sex has, as I have suggested above, led to an impoverishing capitulation to the narrowness of contemporary understandings. Others, however, have shown how responsible reflection within church and tradition can serve the task much better, and have drawn attention to important elements in Christian Scripture and tradition which lead us to question the more severely negative assessments of sex made by many earlier theologians. On this, both Protestant and Roman Catholic churches seem to be in agreement.[19]

There are many legitimate starting points for such responsible Christian reflection upon the positive good of sex, reflection which takes place within the context of Bible and tradition. Some twentieth-century theologians have begun with creation and the creation ordinances, placing much weight on what is said about sex (in the broadest sense

---

19. The increasingly positive attitude of the Roman Catholic church towards conjugal love may be traced through a series of official pronouncements, beginning with Pius XI's *Casti connubii* (1930) and culminating with the statements in *Gaudium et spes* on the dignity of marriage and the family.

of the man–woman relationship) in the Genesis narratives. Some have also attempted to reflect upon sex in relation to the internal relations of the Trinity. Another approach that seems to commend itself—and to build on earlier work—is that which begins with reflection on God's love as this is shown in Christ and in the sending of the Holy Spirit, love which is spoken of in terms of the one-flesh union.[20] The relevance of Paul's reflection upon Christ's one-flesh union with the church for understanding marriage has long been recognized by Christian tradition in its reflections upon marriage as sacramental and symbolic of Christ's love. But the full implications of this reflection—including the central and positive role it gives to sex, and the importance of pneumatology in its unfolding—have not always been acknowledged.[21]

In relation to human vocation, Christ's one-flesh relationship with the church has often been understood as most directly applicable to the celibate life, the life of one who dedicates him or herself body and soul to the heavenly bridegroom. Yet its application to the sexual relationship between human beings is in many ways more obvious. If Christ's love is a love which achieves one-flesh union with the beloved, then the one-flesh union between human beings, the sexual union, must surely be amenable to transfiguration by this love and to some degree of transparency to this love. The sexual relation may become a site where those whom it joins learn more of the power and the reality of Christ's love, return that love, and show forth that love to others. Christ, who becomes one flesh with the believer, may thus be known in the one-flesh relationship of human beings, and through believers' bodily union their union within the body of Christ may be strengthened. In becoming one flesh with another we may embody the love of Christ and so obey the commandment to 'love one another; even as I have loved you' (Jn 13.34). Human sexual union may thus serve not as a distraction from a life in Christ, but as a legitimate form of such life, a spiritual path as legitimate as any other. But it may do so only where it takes a Christ-like form. It is not human erotic love that serves as

20. This understanding of Christ's love links up with imagery about Christ as the bridegroom, and feeds into later Christian reflection upon this theme. It also links with Christian interpretation of the Song of Songs, as with Old Testament use of sexual and nuptial imagery to reflect upon God's relation to Israel (see, e.g., Hos. 1–3; Jer. 2–3).

21. In what follows I am deliberately—and somewhat artificially—bracketing out the issue of procreation.

the touchstone of truth and goodness, but Christ the cornerstone, who may illuminate and transform human erotic love so that it becomes true and good. This does not validate all human sexual union, it validates it only when it takes the form of the love Christ reveals for the church.

Reflection upon the love with which Christ loves can therefore be expected to illuminate sex and the sexual relation and reveal their true, God-given, forms. In the post-resurrection age this means reflection upon Christ as present to the church in the *Spirit*. As Paul reflects in Ephesians, one of the most salient features of this love is the *total gift* of God to the beloved; here he is undoubtedly thinking of Christ's gift of his body on the cross, and, by extension, of the gift of his body in the sacraments of bread and wine—and so of the gift of the Spirit. By this total gift the beloved *becomes one* with the lover: 'even so husbands should love their wives as their own bodies. He who loves his wife loves himself' (Eph. 5.28). Christ's love is then an *intimate* love, a love that brings the beloved into a relationship with Christ in which he is as close to believers as they are to themselves. It is Christ in the gift of his Spirit, a Spirit which becomes the basis of the believer's true self as they are indwelt by him. This love does not merely perfect the beloved, it is the ground of their very existence: through it all things were made. It is thus a *creative* love upon which we depend for our very being. It is also a *knowing* love. It searches us out and knows us, and in knowing us reveals us to ourselves. Eventually, we are promised, we will come to know as we are known. Through this love in the gift of the Spirit we become 'members of Christ's body', no longer separated from God but caught up into the divine life.

As we grow in understanding of Christ's love, through the gift of that love itself, we may come to a fuller understanding of some of the ways in which human sexual love may embody it. All the features of Christ's love mentioned above can, it seems, be reflected in human sexual love. As we consider this it is important to note that it is precisely *in* the sexual and bodily nature of this relationship—rather than in spite of it—that this takes place. It is in sexual intercourse, in one-flesh union, that Christ's one-flesh union finds embodiment, not in some more important spiritual union between spouses. Nevertheless, sexual intercourse should not be understood merely in its restricted contemporary sense of coitus; full sexual intercourse, full union and intimacy of persons, means more than the sharing of a bed; it means the sharing of day-to-day life and of the trivial as well as the momentous moments of life—of birthdays and shopping, illnesses and depressions, meals and holidays, triumphs and failures. It means joining one's bodies not just in genital union, but in time—throughout a lifetime— and in space—in simply living together.

It would seem that it is only through such complete intercourse that human beings may give themselves totally to one another, as Christ gives himself for humanity and is poured out in the Spirit. Only thus can humans come to love one another as their own bodies and become incorporate in one another. By their bodies they remain both distinct from one another and incorporate in one another at the same time. The body bestows both unity and difference, just as in the relation to Christ. Through such intercourse the deepest level of human intimacy is made possible, an intimacy which spreads outwards from bodily intimacy to embrace all the common tasks and routines of life. Such love sustains those whom it joins and makes them what they are. It is a creative love on which those whom it joins come to depend for the full-ness of life. In being loved we can become what we truly are; in the withdrawal or denial of such love we may wither and falter. But this love, like Christ's love, it not merely affirming. It is a knowing love, a love which judges, as Christ is both lover and judge. Through it lovers come to know not just the other but themselves better: through seeing oneself through the eyes of the beloved even painful self-knowledge may become possible.

Christ's love may thus validate human sexual union and reveal its true shape. But in the same measure that it does this, pronouncing a 'yes' on sex, it also judges it and pronounces a 'no' to those forms of sexual relationship that take other forms. So a final implication of viewing sex in such a perspective is that not all sex is good. That which is not for Christ is against him, and sex that is not open to his transforming love is distorted, damaging, even demonic. It ceases to feed off Christ's energies and draws on those of a sinful world. This is the danger of sex that the Christian tradition has always pointed out, and that we are in danger of forgetting these days.

A 'no' is thus pronounced on all forms of sex that do not bind lovers together in full union, in which complete self-giving does not or cannot take place. This means that sex that does not take place within a relationship in which the partners are committed to one another for life cannot be good. A relationship that is not open to permanence is a relationship in which love has a limit, in which full self-giving and intimacy are denied. Likewise, a relationship that is not exclusive is a relationship in which limits have been set to full self-giving, a relationship in which the one-flesh union is fractured by union with another. For I cannot become one with two people: to do that would be to divide myself in two as well as to tear my relationship and my partner apart. Further, sexual love must be a forgiving love, for to forgive is to refuse to allow even sin to end a relationship.[22]

But Christ's 'no' is not pronounced only on those forms of sex that are not faithful. It may also fall on forms that *are* faithful and in which there is true intimacy and one-flesh union. For even where there is commitment and permanence in a sexual relationship it may nevertheless be deeply distorting and damaging to those involved. Indeed, it is just because lovers are so opened up and exposed to one another, and just because they receive so much of themselves from one another, that they may do one another so much harm. In some relationships one partner will abuse the other, in others both partners will abuse each other. And in both, the abuse will usually spill over into a wider context. No such sexual relationships are Christlike.

Finally, a 'no' is pronounced on those forms of union which fail to acknowledge the wider context in which they exist. Such relationships may in all other respects seem good: they are not abusive, they are loving, intimate, permanent and committed. But they fail to acknowledge the wider context that sustains them and to which they relate. They are the relationships in which couples retreat into the context of two and batten down the hatches against the wider world and God. Such relationships feed off their own internal energies rather than the power of the Holy Spirit, and they fail to issue in love of others. They become, in other words, a distraction from love of God and neighbour rather than a creative source of such love. They may even become demonic, as the love of Frederick and Rosemary West has recently served to remind us, or as we are shown so vividly in the portrait of the 'marriage' of Micky and Mallory in *Natural Born Killers*.

Love, in short, is not necessarily generated by the sexual relationship, is not exclusive to the sexual relationship, and must not be confined

---

22. From the observation that there should be no end to forgiveness the conclusion that Christian partners should remain in abusive marriages does *not* follow. Full forgiveness depends upon repentance by the abusive partner, and the abused partner may well have to leave the marriage if there is no such repentance, both to save himself or herself and (the soul) of his or her partner.

within the sexual relationship. Yet for many people it will be within this relationship that they will feel Christlike love very directly, and glimpse something of the intimacy and complete faithfulness of the love God bears us. When this happens, it is the work of the Holy Spirit transforming sex, and shaping it into a Christlike form. Where it is genuine, sexual love will therefore flow out in a return of love for God and neighbour. It will be built up by its wider context, and will in turn play its part in building up this context.

Conclusion

Regression from an understanding of sex within a wider context explains the narrowness and impoverishment of much contemporary thought about sex, an impoverishment evident in the church as well as the world. Very often this impoverishment of thought results in the impoverishment of sexual practices and institutions as well. Even where good sexual practices and institutions continue, the absence of ideologies that might support and explain them inevitably cuts away at their foundation.

The rewidening of our perspective upon sex is a vital contribution that Christianity can make to modern society. As in the days of early Christianity, Christianity's different perspective upon sex will undoubtedly be an important factor in distinguishing Christianity from the wider societies in which it now finds itself. Given the wider climate of sexual thought and practice these days, it seems inevitable and necessary that the lines of demarcation become clearer in this way, though the temptation to make such demarcation the driving force of the process must be resisted. Christianity's openness to the world must not be lost in sectarian insularity. But neither must it simply succumb to that narrowness of perspective so ironic in an age that prides itself on its open, broadminded and liberated attitudes to sex.

Part II

NEW FUTURES FOR TODAY

POSTMODERNITY AND CHASTITY

Adrian Thatcher

Introduction

There are millions of unmarried sexually-active Christians in the
churches today. They present a major pastoral problem for the
churches, who are reluctant to modify the official line that all sexual
intercourse outside heterosexual marriage is wrong. In this paper I
argue for a change in the churches' attitude, from the official line
towards a pastoral realism that maintains that Christian marriage is
the right place for procreative sexual intercourse, but that there are
other contexts where non-procreative sex is legitimate. I offer no weak,
liberal capitulation to the sexual mores of a post-Christian, indulgent
age and if my arguments are successful I hope also to show that they
are fully consistent with a developing Christian tradition that is counter-
cultural in the lifestyles it commends and the standards it requires.

There are three parts to the paper. In the first part, I outline the
problem and say what is meant by chastity. The second part takes up a
theme of all the chapters in *Sex These Days*. It locates discussion of
chastity within the major historical shift described as 'postmodernism'.
The third part, the longest part, draws upon the Bible, tradition, *and* the
analysis in the second part in offering a theology of chastity. It may not
look much like chastity, but its adequacy will be for readers to judge.

What is Chastity?

'Chastity', says the Catholic Catechism, is 'the successful integration of
sexuality within the person and thus the inner unity of man [*sic*] in his
[*sic*] bodily and spiritual being'. And sexuality 'in which man's [*sic*]
belonging to the bodily and biological world is expressed, becomes
personal and truly human when it is integrated into the relationship of
one person to another, in the complete and lifelong mutual gift of a

man and a woman'.[1] 'The chaste person maintains the integrity of the powers of life and love placed in him [sic]. This integrity ensures the unity of the person; it is opposed to any behaviour that would impair it.'[2] Chastity, then, is not a characteristic of relationships, however holy they may be, but a particular attention to the individual's own self-preservation before God. Whatever unity the person may have is with himself or herself. It is about refusing to allow the disturbance to the equilibrium of body and spirit that sexual desire constantly threatens. The powers of life and love, the very God-given forces that drive us into relation with others are to be held within the fragile unity of the chaste self.

Three further features of the account of chastity given in the *Catechism* will be noted. There is no space for a more detailed treatment. The first is the deliberate deployment of hierarchical language in the description of how chastity is to be obtained. 'Master' and 'slave', with the corresponding states of domination and subjugation, feature prominently. Drawn from concrete historical relationships between real masters and real slaves, those relationships are relocated reflexively in the inner struggle where the person experiences himself or herself as both master and slave in the heart of their divided being. 'Chastity includes an *apprenticeship in self-mastery* which is a training in human freedom. The alternative is clear: either man [sic] governs his [sic] passions and finds peace, or he [sic] lets himself [sic] be dominated by them and becomes unhappy.'[3] 'Man' [sic] must rid himself 'of all slavery to the passions'. Slavery to the passions suggests a second observation, that the old dualism between reason and passion survives unamended in the Roman Church's official theology. Chastity belongs to 'the cardinal virtue of *temperance*, which seeks to permeate the passions and appetites of the senses with reason'.[4] Priority is clearly given to reason over passion in the contemporary anthropology that informs the analysis, since passions are only to be controlled, and reason provides the means.

A final observation concerns the requirements of the Roman church that are binding on people about to marry. It is unsparing in the view that sexual intercourse is unavailable to them, whatever their circum-

1. *Catechism of the Catholic Church* (London: Geoffrey Chapman, 1994), para. 2337.
2. *Catechism*, para. 2338.
3. *Catechism*, para. 2339 (my emphasis).
4. *Catechism*, para. 2341 (my emphasis).

stances or degree of commitment to each other. Particular efforts at self-mastery are required at certain times, especially during childhood and adolescence.[5] 'Those who are *engaged to marry* are called to live chastity in continence.'[6] If this should prove difficult, it is to be received as a 'time of testing'. Engaged couples 'should reserve for marriage the expressions of affection that belong to married love'. Even masturbation (like rape) is an offence against chastity. It is 'an intrinsically and gravely disordered action'.[7]

Unmarried Sexually Active Christians as a Pastoral Problem

The Anglican bishops' report, *Issues in Human Sexuality*, recognizes that the traditional teaching about sex before marriage is simply not being observed and is unclear what to do about it. Without defining chastity, it says that chastity is 'God's will for married people' before marriage. This is an 'ideal', but (this is where pastoral honesty influences the theology), 'We recognise that it is increasingly hard today for the unmarried generally, and for young people facing peer group pressure in particular, to hold to this ideal, and therefore both the Church and its individual members need to be clearer and stronger in supporting those who are struggling against the tide of changing sexual standards'.[8] This puts pastoral carers in an unresolved dilemma. On the one hand, for the sake of that diminishing number of very faithful Christians who uphold the traditional teaching, such teaching is to be asserted more clearly and strongly. On the other hand, this teaching may be pastorally (and as it will turn out, theologically) unrealistic, and so the more it is affirmed, the more it will alienate Christians who do not live by it and add to the incredulity of those outside the churches.

To their great credit, the bishops recognize this and go halfway towards resolving it. For, they argue, 'if we believe in a Gospel of grace and restoration freely offered to all, we need to give this support in such a way that those who may eventually go with the tide will not feel that in the Church's eyes they are from then on simply failures for whom there is neither place nor love in the Christian community'. This is a godly, typically Anglican, muddle. The bishops are sufficiently

5.   *Catechism*, para. 2342.
6.   *Catechism*, para. 2350.
7.   *Catechism*, para. 2352.
8.   *Issues in Human Sexuality: A Statement by the House of Bishops* (London: Church House Publishing, 1991), para. 3.8.

in tune with the gospel to recognize that it is for sinners, and those who sinfully deviate from the Church's teaching do not place themselves outside the church's care. On the other hand, the *Statement* is clear that swimmers with the tide will have fallen short of an 'ideal' and been swept along by the swirling currents of changing, that is, falling, sexual standards. Dissent from the traditional teaching is allowed, indeed expected, but characterized as a 'falling short'.

The more recent Anglican report, *Something to Celebrate*, gives us important information about this tide of changing standards. The marriage rate for first marriages in England and Wales fell from 82 per thousand bachelors aged 16 and over in 1971 to 37 per thousand in 1992. The most common age for first marriages is 26 for women and 28 for men.[9] The report expects 'about 80 per cent of all women marrying in the 1990s to have cohabited before their first marriage'.[10] *Something to Celebrate* daringly suggests: 'The wisest and most practical way forward... may be for Christians both to hold fast to the centrality of marriage and at the same time to accept that cohabitation is, for many people, a step along the way towards that fuller and more complete commitment'.[11] 'The first step the Church should take is to abandon the phrase "living in sin".'[12] '[We] are aware of the many mature single people in contemporary society who do not feel called to be celibate and yet seek to live creatively and ethically in right relationships with others, with themselves and with God. We believe that one of the tasks facing the Church in the years ahead will be to develop a sexual ethic which embraces a dynamic view of sexual development, which acknowledges the profound cultural changes of the last decades and supports people in their search for commitment, faithfulness and constancy.'[13]

Postmodernity

One church has reaffirmed the traditional view of sexual intercourse within marriage and chastity outside and inside it. Another church upholds the same teaching, but with an uneasy recognition that it is both widely disregarded, and that it must undergo development. It

9. *Something to Celebrate: Valuing Families in Church and Society* (London: Church House Publishing, 1995), p. 33.
10. *Something to Celebrate*, p. 34.
11. *Something to Celebrate*, p. 115.
12. *Something to Celebrate*, p. 117.
13. *Something to Celebrate*, p. 109.

offers little by way of suggestion about how that development might go, and given the rough ride *Something to Celebrate* had in Synod on 31 November 1995, it is not likely to develop at all.

Behind the marriage statistics found in *Something to Celebrate* lie unprecedented social changes. There is now regularly a 15-year gap between the age of puberty and marriage. Higher education, training for jobs, the cost of housing, all contribute to the gap. More importantly, there are many criticisms to be made of the institution of marriage as it has been historically practised. A greater openness about sexuality has allowed sexual minorities to become heard. A growing number of people will not choose marriage at all. And above all, the availability of a range of reliable contraceptives has fundamentally changed the meanings of sexual activity.

The value of the term 'postmodernism' lies in its power to locate these changes within a broader perspective. 'Postmodernity' conveys the sense of 'coming after', and so the sense of both an ending and a beginning, and a broken continuity or even discontinuity between them. What precedes postmodernity is, of course, 'modernity', and this term is also capable of being unpacked in various ways. Whether or not one holds that modernity is gathering speed or that postmodernity represents striking new possibilities, both understandings assume unprecedented social change that will bring in its wake profound consequences for morality and self-understanding. These consequences are well understood by Weeks. He says,

> This sense of change, of indeed being on the edge of time, has been compounded by the weakening of the legitimizing traditions and master discourses of high modernity. The twin processes of a secularization of moral values, and of a gradual liberalization of social attitudes, especially towards what has traditionally been seen as 'the perverse', have begun to dissolve the old verities. The narrative comforts of the Christian tradition have long suffered the corrosive effects of scepticism and critique, creating the space for fundamentalist revival alongside liberation from superstition. Now even the 'Enlightenment project' of the triumph of reason, progress and humanity, the sense that science and history were leading us inexorably to a more glorious future, has been subjected to searching deconstruction, and its roots have been shown to be murky. Reason has been reduced to a rationalization of power, progress has been seen as the tool of white, Western expansionism, and humanity as the cloak for a male-dominated culture which treats women as other.[14]

14. Jeffrey Weeks, *Invented Moralities: Sexual Values in an Age of Uncertainty* (Cambridge: Polity Press, 1995), pp. 25-26.

Weeks has sketched the social context within which Christian sexual ethics and theology are required to operate. Several items of his analysis deserve detailed comment here, but I shall concentrate only on those elements of change that the analysis of postmodernity illuminates. These are the wide commercial availability of reliable contraception together with the separation of heterosexual sexual experience from the fear of, and the reality of conception. Associated with this is a further unprecedented change in the meanings individuals give to sexuality.

Contraception is nothing new.[15] But the sheer extent of its availability in the twentieth century presents a discontinuity with previous centuries. As Giddens notes, after the First World War 'a change in official opinion in the UK, until that date often vehemently hostile, was signalled when Lord Dawson, physician to the King, reluctantly declared in a speech to the Church in 1921: "Birth control is here to stay. It is an established fact and, for good or evil, has to be accepted... No denunciations will abolish it".'[16] The modern movement for birth control began in Britain, where the writings of Malthus stirred interest in the problems of overpopulation. This century has provided for men vasectomy, and for women spermicides, diaphragms, intrauterine devices, 'the pill', contraception by injection or implantation, or sterilization. With other changes effective contraception brought about 'a deep transition in personal life'. Sexuality 'became malleable, open to being shaped in diverse ways'. Sexuality became separated from 'the exigencies of reproduction'.[17]

Giddens has described in detail what is meant by sexuality becoming 'malleable'. The term means 'capable of being shaped or formed', as in a 'malleable metal', or 'able to adjust to changing circumstances'. The point of speaking of a person's sexuality becoming more malleable is to signify that it is now more than ever in his or her control. There are several reasons for this and chief among them is the severance of sexuality and sexual pleasure from the constraints of reproduction. 'Plastic sexuality' is the term given to the freedom of individuals to shape their sexual identities.

15. Uta Ranke-Heinemann, *Eunuchs for the Kingdom of Heaven: The Catholic Church and Sexuality* (Harmondsworth: Penguin Books, 1991), pp. 69-75.

16. Anthony Giddens, *The Transformation of Intimacy: Sex, Love and Eroticism in Modern Societies* (Cambridge: Polity Press, 1992), pp. 26-27.

17. Giddens, *Transformation of Intimacy*, p. 27.

The 'Pure Relationship'

Plastic sexuality is said to give rise to the 'pure relationship'. This has nothing to do with purity in the conventional sense but refers 'to a situation where a social relation is entered into for its own sake, for what can be derived by each person from a sustained association with another; and which is continued only in so far as it is thought by both parties to deliver enough satisfactions for each individual to stay within it'.[18] Marriage is increasingly said to be entered into as a pure relationship. Intimacy is thereby transformed and 'democratized'.[19] Partners no longer accept as natural or given traditional accounts of gender that link men with domination and women with reproduction. Intimacy has become 'a transactional negotiation of personal ties by equals'.[20] Pre-modern and modern marriage was 'always tied to the double standard and therefore to patriarchy. It was a normative demand upon men, but for many honoured only in the breach. In a world of plastic sexuality and pure relationships, however, monogamy has to be "reworked" in the context of commitment and trust. Monogamy refers, not to the relationship itself, but to sexual exclusiveness as a criterion of trust; "fidelity" has no meaning except as an aspect of that integrity which trust in the other presumes.'[21]

How are Christians to respond to analyses of changes in the understanding of sexuality which are influenced by social theory, and in particular those analyses that identify late modernity or postmodernity as epoch-making events in human history? The two official documents discussed earlier are unpromising. The Anglican document is commendable in its attempt to present 'family life' accurately, bleakly even, but it scarcely utilizes social theory (or, it must be said, theology) as a resource for understanding the changes it describes. The *Catechism* sits unperturbed among the certainties of the pre-modern world, providing the perfect target for Weeks's polite jibe about 'the narrative comforts of the Christian tradition'. Sexuality renders in acute form a yet broader problem for theology: how far may socio-cultural change be regarded as a positive source for theological work, and how far has it to be critiqued or resisted in the name of the Christian gospel? In

18. Giddens, *Transformation of Intimacy*, p. 58.
19. Giddens, *Transformation of Intimacy*, ch. 10.
20. Giddens, *Transformation of Intimacy*, p. 3.
21. Giddens, *Transformation of Intimacy*, p. 146.

the rest of this paper, it will be apparent that both recognition and resistance will be offered.

The Magisterium of the Catholic Church now regards contraception as an 'intrinsic evil'[22] and in a recent encyclical Pope John Paul II classifies it with a list of actions that are 'hostile to life itself, such as any kind of homicide, genocide, abortion, euthanasia and voluntary suicide. . . '[23] This is an extreme reaction, akin to a counter-cultural fundamentalism. Weeks's warning that the erosion of Christian tradition creates the space for fundamentalist revival must be taken seriously, even if that space is occasionally occupied by the Roman Pontiff. What is needed instead is a reaffirmation of that tradition that takes seriously the criticisms against it and aims to offer hope, understanding and divine grace in the area of human sexuality. Neither the Orthodox Church[24] nor the Protestant churches have any problem with contraception within marriage: indeed its benefits are manifold. Its uses however, like all God's gifts, are open to sinful purposes.

Christians should also be able to respond positively to the analysis of sexuality that speaks of plastic sexuality and the pure relationship. There is a freedom in plastic sexuality that throws off patriarchal domination and ownership: there is a liberation in the pure relationship that can reintroduce mutuality and equality into partnerships that are unequal. The reworking of monogamy is essential if relationships of domination and submission are to be replaced by reciprocity. The secularization of moral values need not present Christians with dismay. Autonomy in decision-making is the pre-condition for taking charge of one's sexuality and sexual relationships. The general belief in providence allows for a weakening of religious institutions and beliefs, in order, perhaps, for God to show that God will not be confined or hidden by them.

Nonetheless, Christians have their own wisdom to complement that of the pure relationship. They might wish to point out that whatever they become they attempt first to become like Jesus Christ, whose love for God and for his neighbour was coextensive with his earthly life and

22. *Catechism*, para. 2370, p. 508.

23. *Veritatis Splendor* (1993), para. 80, drawing on Pastoral Constitution of the Church in the Modern World, *Gaudium et Spes*, p. 27.

24. For a full discussion see William Basil Zion, *Eros and Transformation: Sexuality and Marriage, An Eastern Orthodox Perspective* (Lanham, MD: University Press of America, 1992), ch. 7.

death. Neighbour-love precludes relationships of domination and exploitation absolutely even if they are legitimized through the institution of marriage. Plastic sexuality is in danger of collapsing into self-preoccupation.[25] A major weakness in all humanist sexual moralities, at least as they are practised by heterosexual partners, is that they too readily discount the possibility that fertile women can become pregnant. Contraception may fail, or be unavailable. The link between sexuality and reproduction proves not to have been completely severed after all. There is a large responsibility on sexual partners not to conceive children who are not wanted. This responsibility is undiminished in any age, whether or not it is postmodern, and the exercise of this responsibility takes us back to the pre-modern preoccupation of Christians with chastity.

Safe Sex

Heterosexual partners who are not ready for, or who do not wish for, sexual intercourse have a broad range of sexual activities available to them that exclude the risk of transmitting sex-related diseases or of becoming pregnant. There is a curious overlap here between Christians seeking chaste forms of sexual behaviour and the wider discussion about what constitutes 'safe sex'. It will be useful to divide these into three categories: (1) sexual contact that stops short of orgasm and excludes penetration; (2) sexual contact that *in*cludes orgasm but that also *ex*cludes penetration; and (3) modern 'safe sex' practices. Sexual contact with penetration but without ejaculation provides no defence against infection or the possibility of pregnancy. There are two forms of this practice discussed in the Roman tradition, *coitus interruptus* and *coitus reservatus*. The former assumes penetration and male ejaculation, but outside the vagina. The latter presupposes penetration and no ejaculation, inside or outside the vagina. It is probably not generally known that the moral teaching of the Catholic Church has supported *coitus reservatus* (provided it was within marriage) at various times (for example, in 1450–1750), and there has been extensive discussion about the matter in the present century (where it has been

25. Weeks, to his credit, recognizes this, and firmly emphasizes the need for 'an ethics of solidarity' within a communitarian framework; see *Invented Moralities*, p. 81 and pp. 75-81.

strongly supported by the Belgian Cardinal Suenens).[26] No attempt will be made to borrow from this discussion, not least because of the assumptions made by it, one of which is the mortal sin of wasting semen. However, the precedent of referring to the minute details of sexual intimacy will be invoked later.

So far two kinds of safe sex practices have been discussed. However, an undoubted association has been made in the popular mind between safe sex and heterosexual or homosexual intercourse with one of the parties wearing a condom. This is the third category. While the condom provides inadequate protection against pregnancy, it is the only protection against infected semen for women having penetrative sex. Oral sex is a low-risk activity, and so is classified as 'safe', though no medical expert has yet declared it risk-free. It hardly needs pointing out that same-sex activity cannot incur the risk of pregnancy, and that lesbian sexual activity (given certain assumptions about the partners' sexual histories) is low-risk. The crucial distinction to be made is between (2) and (3)—between non-penetrative and penetrative sex. From here on, my concern will be confined to (1) and (2).

I suggest that the meaning that people give to sexual activity can be described by reference to one or more of the following four concepts: exploration, recreation, expression and procreation. This is to say, first, that children and young people will want to explore their bodies, and as desire grows, the bodies of others. This is a legitimate meaning of sexual activity. Secondly, people engage in sexual activity because it is intensely pleasurable. Thirdly, since we belong to a species that makes symbolic gestures and actions, it is almost obvious to remark that sexual behaviour is expressive. Intercourse can express a range of meanings from a loving, mutual self-surrender to misogyny and humiliation. And fourthly, the principal meaning given to sexual intercourse by the church for most of its history, is procreation.

The claim to be examined next is that heterosexual routines or repertoires that end up with penetration of a vagina and male orgasm are inessential to having sex. This is where the previous analysis of postmodernity becomes helpful. The case to be made out is that the widespread practice of penetrative sex outside of marriage is the result of a long historical conditioning and routinization that embodied a particular understanding of what it was for, and this understanding rendered unlawful all the others. Sex had to have a purpose, and that purpose,

26. Ranke-Heinemann, *Eunuchs*, pp. 174, 176.

socially legitimized and religiously sanctioned, was procreation. So pervasive did the procreative meaning of sex become that no other meaning was recognizable or available. Now, long after most individuals have removed themselves from the obligations and sanctions of religious teachings, they continue to practice routines or repertoires that may nonetheless be wholly inappropriate to their circumstances.

It is clear enough that any society anxious to maintain its population against the ravages of wars, famines, diseases, and (compared with us) high child mortality rates and short life-expectancy, is going to favour procreation as the basic meaning of sex. I shall call this the 'procreative premise'. Peter Brown says that 'for the population of the Roman Empire to remain even stationary, it appears that each woman would have had to have produced an average of five children'.[27] It is equally clear that strong religious sanctions reinforced and policed the procreative premise. Since having children was the favored result of having sex, procreation became the primary purpose of marriage. All other sexual activity was clearly contrary to the procreative premise. Even sex within marriage after the possibility of conception offended against the procreative premise. Male masturbation (as I have just noted) was a waste of seed because the procreative premise was not served by it. If the procreative premise is true, then lesbian and gay sex is 'unnatural', perverted even, since only those organs that are capable of making babies ought to be brought together. But once the procreative premise is denied, the edifice of compulsory heterosexuality and the dominance of copulation within it as the sole, licensed sexual activity both collapse. The procreative premise then, is unnecessary to the meaning of sex, since many people who have sex do not wish to have babies. This is not to deny that for many partners at some times of their lives, procreation will be both a primary meaning and a dominant desire. Sexual desire and the desire to have children might even be different desires.[28]

Essentialists and Constructionists

The claim that the procreative premise has had, and continues to have, a profound conditioning effect on contemporary sexual behaviour

27. Peter Brown, *The Body and Society: Men, Women and Sexual Renunciation in Early Christianity* (London: Faber & Faber, 1988), p. 6.
28. I am grateful to my colleague Will Large for this point.

derives further support from the current controversy raging between essentialists and constructionists. An essentialist is someone who thinks there are essential, objective facts to be discerned about, say, the purpose of sex, or about the gender roles of men and women, or about sexual orientation. These, as for much traditional Christian morality, are thought to be rooted in nature, or creation, or the will of God. A constructionist is someone who emphasizes that these matters are to a large degree conditioned by the social and cultural histories of peoples; that 'there cannot be an all-embracing history of sexuality. There can only be local histories, contextual meanings, specific analyses.'[29] Women early in this century had to overcome essentialist notions about themselves, for example, that their smaller brains made them incapable of intellectual work, that their weaker bodies made them incapable of playing tennis, running marathons, and so on. What was held against them as essential truths, turned out to be male constructions of femininity that accorded neither with their interests nor with emerging physiological facts.

In terms of this contrast, traditional Christian sexual morality is clearly essentialist. The basic meaning of sexual activity is objective and biologistic. Other affective and secondary meanings may be allowed—it may be expressive of love, and (more daringly) recreational—but its essential purpose is procreative, and so its essential repertoire cannot but include penetrative sex. The constructionist, however, may view penetrative sex as a socially constructed routine which serves a procreative purpose. While at one time such a purpose might be overwhelmingly necessary, at another time it may not be. There will be freedom with regard to the purposes, and so the meanings of sexual activity. Constructionists, unlike essentialists, are able to discern that repertoires need not be fixed, and, if human beings are free, should not be.

The position adopted here is that most heterosexual people, for some part of their lives, will acknowledge the procreative purpose of sexual activity to be essential to their relationship. Having children can be a glorious purpose of sex. But constructionists are in a better position than essentialists to analyse contemporary sexual activity in two respects. They will interpret penetrative sex as a construction serving a purpose that many who engage in it have actually and paradoxically disowned. And they will see, at least if they have read what Christian liberation theologians have written about structural sin, that the

29. Weeks, *Invented Moralities*, p. 6.

overwhelming pressure on contemporary adolescent women and men to engage in penetrative sex, albeit with condoms, and legitimized by the question-begging epithet, 'safe', is itself a social construction with some highly unpalatable ingredients.

The constructionist case derived support from the work of Shere Hite, who reported in 1976 that 70 per cent of women do not have orgasms from intercourse, but do have them from more direct clitoral stimulation.[30] While theologians were discussing *The Myth of God Incarnate*,[31] feminists were discussing the myth of the vaginal orgasm. The assumption that women generally found penetrative sexual inter-course pleasurable was shown to be patriarchal. 'Patriarchal definitions of women's sexuality could not separate reproduction from pleasure.'[32] Hite's analysis was an early 'constructionist' account of heterosexual sexual activity. She showed that 'within the dominant pattern of hetero-sexual interaction male pleasure is primary'.[33] Women run the risks. The sex manuals that had described sexual intercourse as an invariable three-act performance—foreplay, penetration and orgasm (his)—were shown instead to describe a construction that assumed that the pro-creative repertoire, with or without contraception, was the only way to have sex. Real men would settle for nothing less. And it was male pleasure that this repertoire sought to secure.

Essentialists, reeling from this deconstruction of penetrative sex as a 'natural' activity, also found some of the biological facts against them. A penis is not needed for women to enjoy orgasm at all. There are dangers in speaking this way. The mere mention of clitoral orgasm suggests that goal-directed, performance-oriented sex is still on the agenda; that only genital sex is real sex, and so on. The point rather is to indicate that while penetration is necessary for procreative sex (*in vitro* fertilization techniques are, of course, the exception), it is not necessary for pleasurable sex. Hite's analysis actually provides powerful

30. For the significance of this finding, see Naomi Weisstein, speaking of the first Hite Report (1976), in the preface to the third Hite Report, *Women and Love* (London: Penguin/Viking, 1988), p. xxxiv.

31. *The Myth of God Incarnate* was the title of a collection of essays that caused a minor furore in 1977 (ed. John Hick; London: SCM Press).

32. See Adrian Thatcher, *Liberating Sex: A Christian Sexual Theology* (London: SPCK, 1993), p. 101.

33. Rhonda Lottlieb, 'The Political Economy of Sexuality', *Review of Radical Political Economics*, 16.1, pp. 143-65; cited by Weisstein in Hite, *Women and Love*, p. xxxiv.

support for Christians who have insisted all along that casual penetrative sex is wrong. But heterosexual men pursuing sexual pleasure still generally think of penetrative sex as its necessary condition. But what counts as pleasure here is also something that has been culturally constructed. It is as much a matter of expectation as of performance.

Chastity Revisited

Here are five principles that are relevant to the determination of chaste sexual behaviour.

1. *Understanding*. It was suggested earlier that the meanings partners give to sexual activity might be subsumed under the headings of exploration, recreation, expression and procreation. Christians should *understand* better the exploration that adolescents need to undertake in order to experience, express and control their sexuality, and the pleasure that accompanies sexual activity. For adolescents becoming sexually active, the meaning of sex may best be understood as exploratory, and exploration is essential to growing sexual maturity. But exploration is itself intensely pleasurable, and doubtless penetrative sex will be explored sooner rather than later. There has never been such a lengthy period between the onset of the possibility of sexual intercourse and the traditionally sanctioned context to which alone it has been confined. Christian sexual ethics has to deal with this unique situation at a time when secularity is advanced, and openness to revision of traditional teachings is generally discouraged.

2. *Loving Commitment*. The meaning of sex as an expression of love is far from obvious. As two secular commentators observe: 'In the absence of notions like commitment and responsibility, horniness can look an awful lot like "love"'.[34] Christians have worried more about whether sexual intercourse was lawful than whether it was loving. The view that sex and love are related is found in the Song of Songs, and can even be found in Ephesians 5 (where it is intertwined with the acceptance of a gender hierarchy). But for long periods sex had nothing to do with love, only with procreation and the avoidance of sin. It took the emergence of courtly love, and, later, romantic love to remind Christians of their biblical heritage.[35] I have stated the

34. Robert Coles and Geoffrey Stokes, *Sex and the American Teenager* (New York: Harper & Row, 1985), p. 85.
35. See Thatcher, *Liberating Sex*, pp. 49-52; and Vincent Brummer, *The Model*

incarnational and trinitarian grounds for a loving sexuality in *Liberating Sex*,[36] together with the argument that full sexual relations, whether heterosexual or homosexual, may be an expression of mutual commitment and a sign of God's faithfulness. Two people who come to commit themselves exclusively to each other are able to use that shared experience to understand something of God's faithfulness to us in covenant-love, to know something of God incarnate in the flesh, and to reflect on the mystery of the Trinity, which is God as a loving communion of Persons.

3. *The Principle of Proportion*. Western cultures have a highly romanticized understanding of love that is in danger of collapsing into narcissism, into being in love with love. The phrase 'falling in love' gives much away about the experience it describes. Unfortunately, it is as easy and as regular to fall out of it as into it. So romantic love does not and cannot, of itself provide any sort of justification for Christian faith to sanction it as the context (pretext?) for sexual intercourse. Another danger lies in describing love-making as self-giving without first acknowledging that in a gender hierarchy women do most of the giving. For self-giving to be the meaning of sexual intercourse there has to be a recovery of mutuality, reciprocity and equality of giving and receiving. The 'pure relationship' should be seen as a partial realization of this important pre-condition of abiding partnerships. Practitioners of safe sex may be generally assumed not to have reached that point in their relationships where they are ready for exclusive commitment. That point, of course, may never come. In these circumstances, the principle of proportion may serve as a useful rule. According to this principle, 'the level of sexual expression should be commensurate with the level of commitment in the relationship'.[37] The House of Bishops' *Statement* commends it—'the greater the degree of personal intimacy, the greater should be the degree of personal commitment'.[38] Partners may, of course, be mistaken about what level of commitment has been reached, and their understanding of just what activities are commensurate with what levels of commitment are bound

of Love (Cambridge: Cambridge University Press, 1993), pt. 2.

36. Thatcher, *Liberating Sex*, ch. 4.

37. See Karen Lebacqz, 'Appropriate Vulnerability: A Sexual Ethic for Singles', in A. Thatcher and E. Stuart (eds), *Christian Perspectives on Sexuality and Gender* (Leominster: Gracewing; Grand Rapids: Eerdmans, 1996), p. 427.

38. *Issues in Human Sexuality*, para. 3.2, p. 19.

to be influenced by the general promiscuity of the wider culture. But there are other considerations which, taken together, make an appeal to the principle of proportion stronger.

4. *The Practice of Waiting*. It is now time to concede that couples regularly practising non-penetrative sex over time will want to proceed to consummate their love-making with full sexual intercourse, and indeed the desire to do so may become so strong as to be irresistible. This 'pre-penetrative' period in a couple's history can be analysed theologically. In accordance with the general view that sexual intercourse can 'carry' a variety of symbolic meanings, a symbolic meaning can also be found in the intimate but technically unconsummated moment. It is possible to view non-penetrative sex as a failure to reach that point of becoming 'one flesh' that is rightly seen as belonging to another, and a permanent stage of a relationship, if such a point is to be reached at all.

The situation of remaining in waiting for a state of affairs for which one passionately yearns is familiar to Christians. Indeed, one may speak, following the argument of St Paul in Rom. 8.14-30, of a 'theology of waiting'. Christians currently in a state of suffering are said to be waiting for future glory (vv. 17-18) and, indeed, even the 'whole created universe' is groaning 'as if in the pangs of childbirth' (v. 22) for its liberation. Precisely in these circumstances of waiting, the virtue of hope is acquired, eager anticipation is enjoyed, and in the experience of impatience 'the Spirit comes to the aid of our weakness' (v. 26). While there are no references to sexual experience in this passage, there are clear similarities to be found. Anxious for the immediate fulfilment of their desires, Christians are taught to wait, and in waiting to accept frustration, to learn to trust the promises of God, and to be open to the intimation of the Spirit in acquiring hope and patience. This experience of waiting, together with its lack of fulfilment and aching desire, is itself a revelation to the couple of God's own yearning for the redemption of the world. The 'stature of waiting' has recently been attributed to Jesus and elevated to a position of preeminence in Christian life. 'When man [*sic*] waits upon the world... God also waits; and it is in waiting that He invests the world with the possibility and power of meaning.'[39]

5. *The Principle of Exclusion*. St Paul has another convincing argu-

---

39. W.H. Vanstone, *The Stature of Waiting* (London: Darton, Longman & Todd, 1982), p. 109.

ment against the easy or casual surrender of the body in sexual inter-course, developed during his strictures against the casual sex practised in the Corinthian church. At Corinth some Christians celebrated their freedom in Christ by regarding themselves as free from all sexual constraints. Against them St Paul introduced a very positive appraisal of the human body that precludes its casual sexual use. Central to his argument is the claim: 'But the body is not for fornication; it is for the Lord—and the Lord for the body' (1 Cor. 6.13). Later in his argu-ment he introduced a novel distinction between sexual sins and other types of sin. Sexual sin is a sin against one's own body, whereas 'Every other sin that one may commit is outside the body'. The body is then called 'a temple of the indwelling Holy Spirit' (v. 19). On this basis the Corinthians are told their bodies belong to God rather than to them (v. 19), and they are exhorted to 'honour God in your body' (v. 20).

Paul argues that there are consequences for sexual behaviour deriving from the acknowledgement of the holiness of the body. We might speculate that when the body of another is in our arms, we may receive not simply the other, but a profound spiritual experience inseparable from our mutual bodiedness. However, that part of Paul's argument that is about to be redeployed in the present discussion concerns the distinction between sins committed inside and outside the body. The misuse of the body sexually is akin to the misuse of it when it is exposed to tobacco use or alcohol abuse. What makes some sins sins is that they are 'inside' the body, and consequently 'against' it. I suggest that this distinction, forged in the ancient context of sexual promiscuity in the Corinthian church, is able to contribute to contem-porary discussions about sexual promiscuity, and particularly to dis-cussions about safe sex. The contribution it might make concerns the difference between penetrative and non-penetrative sex.

It could hardly be more obvious that penetrative sex is an act com-mitted 'inside the body'. The question is whether the act is also 'against' the body. In many cases the answer must be 'yes', and sexual partners themselves acknowledge this by taking steps to protect themselves against consequences that directly affect their health. Is there not a case for another principle, based on the inside–outside distinction to accompany the principle of proportion? This could be called 'the prin-ciple of exclusion'. According to this principle a penis is to be excluded from a vagina in a heterosexual sexual relationship unless and until that relationship can carry the meanings of mutual self-giving and ongoing commitment that penetrative sexual intercourse conveys. (I have dealt with the complex question of whether this state is 'marriage', elsewhere.[40]) This principle might well be regarded as an expression of the Pauline teaching that the honouring of God with the body and its mutual recognition as incarnate Spirit be regulative for sexual relations involving Christians. I do not argue that Paul is to be taken as advocating safe sex practices, and I may have taken his phrase 'outside the body' too literally. However, when a careful study of the passage and the context it addressed is undertaken in the light of our own contemporary questions about safe sex practices, fruitful and compelling connections are possible.

Betrothal

Little has been said about chastity for post-married and lesbian and gay people. One of the reasons for chastity among fertile heterosexual couples has been the love due to any children born to them. Christians who do not have this reason for chastity nonetheless have other reasons. That would be the subject of another paper.

Given the principal focus in this paper on unmarried heterosexual Christians, it is necessary to mention the lack of any service of official betrothal available to them to mark the point of exclusive lifelong commitment, should it be reached, prior to marriage. This is a pity. Such an arrangement was common in earlier periods. Betrothal was the beginning, not the end, of the entry into marriage. Betrothal, says the historian John Gillis, writing of the sixteenth century, 'constituted the recognized rite of transition from friends to lovers, conferring on the couple the right to sexual as well as social intimacy... Betrothal granted freedom to explore for any personal faults or incompatibilities that had remained hidden during the earlier, more inhibited phases of courtship and could be disastrous if carried into the indissoluble status of marriage.'[41] This practice remains almost entirely forgotten by theologians and bishops alike. It is entirely compatible with the theology of chastity I have outlined above, and in the absence of any official acknowledgement or provision of it by the churches, I expect Christians increasingly to devise betrothals for themselves.

40. Thatcher, *Liberating Sex*, pp. 83-84 and ch. 7.
41. John R. Gillis, *For Better, For Worse: British Marriages, 1600 to the Present* (New York: Oxford University Press, 1985), p. 47.

A Theology of Chastity

Taken cumulatively, the principle of proportion, the theology of waiting, and the principle of exclusion are powerful considerations against hasty sexual experience, whether penetrative or not. The practice of these is what I am calling a 'theology of chastity'. They provide experiential guidance, rather than rational arguments, since it is through the realization of the holiness of one's body, and the experience of the Spirit in patient waiting, that the principle of proportion comes to have meaning. And the experience of the Spirit is primarily the experience of the whole church as the community of faith. Paul's theology of the body makes sense only because he can speak of individuals as members of the society that calls itself 'the body of Christ' (1 Cor. 12.15-16). The church has a responsibility, deliberately and self-consciously to construct sexual relationships so as to give due weight to the holiness of the body, to a theology of waiting, the principle of exclusion and other theological meanings associated with sex.

A comparison between the position now arrived at and the earlier account of chastity is now appropriate. The practice of chastity suggested here is firmly relational, locating it in personal relationships, as a joint responsibility of both parties. The personal unity it embodies is a relational one, involving mutuality, and as an expression of mutuality, joint responsibility for restraint. The language of slavery to passion and its 'conquest' by reason becomes redundant. While the power of desire should never be underestimated, restraint in its expression is best jointly handled, motivated for Christians by the kinds of theological reasons discussed earlier. This is a safer background for the practice of chastity than the battlefield of the autonomous (male) soul beleaguered by longings that it may not comprehend. The analyses of 'plastic sexuality' and the 'pure relationship' may be powerful incentives to holy living among the people of God. For Christians will seek not simply *any* consensual agreement, but will seek also to discern the divine love in all their human loving.

CELIBACY THESE DAYS

Janette Gray, RSM

Not Good News

Celibacy—or 'no sex'—is news these days. Not good news, but the accomplice and presumed cause of scandalous sexual abuse and sadistic exploitation of children and youth, of betrayal of trust and privilege, and of hypocrisy. Celibacy is implicated in this. In news reporting and in the public mind the renunciation of sex appears to implode with horrendous effects. It provides evidence for the long-held assumption that sex is so powerful that its denial only serves to magnify or pervert its inevitable expression. While not excusing the problem of celibacy, it is the failure to live celibately that is represented in these crimes, not celibacy itself. Persons who are not celibate also commit such abuses and violence, and many celibates do not deviate from their public commitment to live positively without sexual relations. Nevertheless, celibacy has come to personify its opposite, the destruction of its purpose.

This so-called 'crisis of celibacy' is not recent, that is, unique to the late twentieth century. Celibacy has always attracted a bad press. Its embodied idealism and extravagant claim to purity and untouchability are invitations to unearth hypocrisy. A superiority produced through self-recommendation and the aloofness of many who live celibately begs to be caught out, found wanting and corruptible. The contrast between the ideal and practice of celibacy has historically provided the source material for great literature and gutter tabloids alike. Celibacy has always grated against the majority's natural urge to heterosexual and/or homosexual union. Celibacy inevitably solicits criticism. Its liminality yet likeness to other lifestyles renders it too ambiguous. Even the terminology associated with celibacy compounds this elusive reputation. Semantically, celibacy merely means 'non-marriage'. Historically it has been distinguished from or coupled with the related terms, 'virginity' and 'chastity'. Virginity is a subset of celibacy, meaning an absolute refraining from genital sex and penetration. Chastity may be celibate but also applies to sexual relations within marriage. Celibacy's contemporary meaning is simply 'no sex' ever, or for some period of time—'no sex these days'.

Celibacy stands outside the pair-bonding and polygamous categories of human relationships. Yet the economy of heterosexual partnership with or without procreation has never been the universal condition of all human beings. It does not exist without the accompanying recurrence throughout history of exceptions—many people living celibately or living homosexually. I would contend, then, that celibacy occurs as a natural but different expression of human sexuality—as natural as sexual bonding. Celibacy may not have been accepted in all human societies, but it does recur in varied non-intentional, circumstantial, and temporary ways. Most societies have members not in partnerships, even if only in preparation for partnering relationships, or as a result of a partner's death. Some cultural and religious traditions have appropriated this recurrence of celibacy and harnessed it with symbolic lifestyles. These culturally distinguished lifestyles represent a range of values including the contrasts of social order and the bodily transcendence of such order, purity of nature and the unnatural flight from nature, personal fulfilment and the overcoming of the self.[1] The Roman Catholic Church and some Hindu and Buddhist traditions produced institutional forms of celibacy, integrating them into their respective socio-cultural menus. But celibate existence has never been limited only to these social constructions, as many other humans have lived celibate lives with the purpose of facilitating other than religious commitments or as a result of a sexual preference or some social inhibition. More recently, some people have taken to describing episodes in their lives, temporary or long term, as living celibately. Sally Cline's *Women, Celibacy and Passion* chronicles and defends the choice of many modern Western women for a celibacy that is neither religious nor a negative denunciation of their sexuality:

> Passionate celibacy is a form of female sexuality. It is the choice to be without a sexual partner for positive reasons of personal, political or spiritual growth, freedom and independence. Passionate celibacy is a sexual

---

1.   Kirsten Hastrup, 'The Semantics of Biology: Virginity' in Shirley Ardeneur (ed.), *Defining Females: The Nature of Women in Society* (London: Croom Helm, 1978), pp. 49-65, particularly pp. 50-56; see also André Guindon, *The Sexual Creators: An Ethical Proposal for Concerned Christians* (Lanham, MD: University Press of America, 1986), p. 207.

singlehood which allows women to define themselves autonomously, whilst still retaining a network of connections, rather than in terms of another person and his or her needs. It is a form of sexual practice without the power struggles of a sexually active relationship, which is neither maintained by nor supports the genital myth.[2]

It is worth noting here Cline's need to apply the adjective 'passionate' to this understanding of celibacy to differentiate it from a traditional Christian view of celibacy that spurns the sexual. She aligns more with what she perceives as the more positive role afforded to sexual denial in ancient Greek male society.[3] This difference, according to Cline, is the celebration of the power of sexuality by controlling it. But it is not obvious that this is so distinct from the purpose of the Christian virtue of celibacy. It is pertinent to observe that not all of the above types of celibate living are so ignominiously associated with the previously mentioned abuses. They are not so loudly blamed as the cause of perverted sexual behaviour. It seems that for religious celibacy and homosexuality alone are reserved the peculiar attribution of uncontrollable sexual depravity and abuse.

This disturbing ambiguity and pervasive suspicion of celibacy has persisted throughout Western history. Early Christian understanding of celibacy had as much in common with the Greek ideals of moral power won by control of the senses and the concentrating of human energies—not dissipating them in sexual activity—as with the spiritual disembodiment of the gnostic theologies. Peter Brown has shown how the understanding of body and sexuality at the origins of Christianity reflected the complexity of views of its cultural contexts. The Christian sexual ethic adopted prevailing civic concerns about family, cohesive stability and sexual restraint at the same time as subverting them.[4] Christianity is not unique in its attitude to unchecked sexual activity. Concern with ritual purity, especially associated with woman's corporeality, is common to religious traditions as widely divergent as Jainism and recent Christian fundamentalist expectations of the sexual probity of American presidents and the accountability of the British Conservative Party's declaration for 'family values'. Similarly, Judaism's emphasis on marital purity has no tolerance for any interference with

2.   Sally Cline, *Women, Celibacy and Passion* (London: André Deutsch, 1993), p. 21.
3.   Cline, *Women, Celibacy and Passion*, pp. 4-5.
4.   Peter Brown, *The Body and Society: Men, Women and Sexual Renunciation in Early Christianity* (New York: Columbia University Press, 1988).

marital co-creation, even celibacy confounds the integrity of human worship of the God of life.

Roman Catholicism has been the Christian tradition that most values the celibate life, as it has also most mobilized the phenomenon in priestly, monastic and other communal forms. Greek and ecumenical Orthodoxy limits the requirement of celibacy only to its bishops, monks and nuns. The reformed Christian traditions, having rejected sixteenth-century clerical and monastic celibacy as distortions of the gospel ethic and complicit in the simony and corruption of the Renaissance church, dissolved its validity as a Christian lifestyle along with the monasteries that housed it. Consequently, celibacy has been almost exclusively defined by Roman Catholic theology in spiritual terms. The biblical warrants for a more socio-political understanding of celibacy, for example, the life of the celibate prophet Jeremiah, lay unexamined for centuries because of Roman Catholic discouragement of biblical studies and Protestant disinterest in celibacy.[5]

It is not surprising to find that the understanding of celibacy in contemporary theologies and ethics of sexuality tends to be negatively couched. Much recent Roman Catholic writing for and by celibates concentrates on the difficulties of celibacy and its psychological pathologies, with very little theological reference. Other Christians, while trying to accommodate celibacy, find difficulty locating it among the usual topics covered under sexuality. Elizabeth Stuart's *Just Good Friends* sympathetically recognizes the efficacy of celibacy and how celibates have as much need for and experience of intimacy as sexually active persons, rather than none at all: 'a person who chooses to be celibate is someone who sacrifices the relationship of passionate radical vulnerability in order to commit themselves completely to the building up of a community of friendship'.[6] Yet her treatment of celibacy in her chapter on 'passion' appears after sections on masturbation, fantasy, disability and old age. Likewise, Adrian Thatcher's *Liberating Sex* places celibacy alongside the controversial topics of masturbation and pornography.[7] These examples highlight the difficulties involved in

5.   Janette Gray, *Neither Escaping Nor Exploiting Sex: Women's Celibacy* (Slough: St Pauls, 1995), pp. 52-60.

6.   Elizabeth Stuart, *Just Good Friends: Towards a Lesbian and Gay Theology of Relationships* (London: Mowbrays, 1995).

7.   Adrian Thatcher, *Liberating Sex: A Christian Sexual Theology* (London: SPCK, 1993), ch. 12, 'Sex and Solitude'.

recognizing that celibacy has some existential validity.

Phases in the Theology of Celibacy

Instead of surveying the widest uses of the term 'celibacy', I prefer to speak of the type I live and know best—religious celibacy in the Roman Catholic Church. This type of celibacy, particularly the discipline of priestly celibacy, is the specific focus of much of the talk about celibacy these days. There are two main representations of this celibacy. The first is the solitary form that eventually developed into monastic celibacy as 'white martyrdom', an adaptation of the hysterical edginess for martyrdom that so characterized early Christianity. The second is the disciplinary requirement of celibacy for entry into the hierarchical caste of priests, that was introduced as a moral reform midway through the history of Christian priesthood. These two expressions combine the domestication of a radical death-wish—replicating the bodily sacrifice of the saviour and the longing of the soul for exclusive union with God—with an eschatological abdication of the social obligation to provide emotionally and economically for partners and progeny into the future. Despite their being inevitably lumped together, priestly celibacy has a very separate theological history and purpose from the more structurally and socially integrated celibacy of vowed religious life.

The theological reasons for the 'no sex' of religious celibacy are historically bound to the Gnostic and Manichean rejection of sex. These religious movements emphasized perfection and an elite discipleship as the superior way of anticipating eschatological perfection by escape from the limitations of the human condition, particularly that of the body. This devaluation of sex can be seen as a product of the 'virulent strain of pelvic anxiety'[8] that is the common misery of the likes of most of the early Christian martyrs, saints Jerome, Gregory of Nyssa, the converted Augustine, Francis of Assisi, Bonaventure, Bernard of Clairvaux and Catherine of Siena, the Flagellants, Jansenists, and Descartes. At the core of this negativity is disbelief in the humanness of sex and the sexuality of being human, despite the central Christian doctrine of creation—that what God creates is good—and the reality of the incarnation, that is, a divine affirmation of the value of humanity. Instead, this view of celibacy denigrates all that is physical and of the senses—

8. Roger Balducelli, OSFS, 'The Decision for Celibacy', *Theological Studies* 36 (1975), p. 235, n.23.

sex, marriage and the world—because it only discerns Godlikeness as spiritual and other-worldly, pure and detached. But *is* God like that?

Theology that rejects the body and sexuality sees the material as inferior to the spiritual, and negatively associates woman, matter, earth, nature and sexuality.[9] This is what I would term the first phase in the development of a Christian understanding of celibacy. This 'white martyrdom' theology of the desert solitaries, the communities of Eastern monasticism and some Celtic recluses, denied the body in order to escape immersion in the material world and assume an 'angelism':

> The monk or nun, purified by fasting and illumined by prayer, learned to live as an 'angel in the body', transcending both the defilement of sex and the limitations of gender to become a passionless, Spirit-filled, miracle-working source of life and holiness for Christians still mired in the flesh.[10]

For men the sexual denial of celibacy allowed their transformation into embodied 'angels', living death through fasting, mortification and prayer. For women this same transformation required two steps. First, by a denial of her sex and her gender a woman achieved spiritual virility, becoming a 'man for Christ': 'when she wishes to serve Christ more than the world, then she will cease to be a woman, and will be called a man'.[11] Then only could she begin to transcend human nature as does the male celibate in one step of renunciation: 'Through chastity the upward pull of grace could neutralize the earthbound gravity of the feminine'.[12]

The next phase of the theology of celibacy imagined an earthly realization of the eschatological city of God. Family, tribal organization and the social and political anarchy of the early Middle Ages were replaced by the communal life of Western monasticism. In these communities a corporate identity was envisaged transcending the individual limitations of human nature and abandoning the corporeality and sinfulness of the personal body for the spiritually enhanced communal body. This was a more social understanding of celibacy, a localized version of the political concept of Christendom within which it thrived

9.   Rosemary Ruether, *Sexism and God Talk: Towards a Feminist Theology* (Boston: Beacon , 1983), p. 80.

10. Barbara Newman, *From Virile Woman to WomanChrist* (Philadelphia: University of Pennsylvania Press, 1995), p. 4

11. Jerome, *Commentarius in Epistolum ad Ephesios*, 3.5, in *Patrologia Latina*, 26.567a.

12. Newman, *From Virile Woman to WomanChrist*, p. 4.

and in turn promoted. The 'white martyrdom' theology of celibacy was not replaced, but built upon. To ethereal angelism was added an intellectual interiority that sublimated the pressure of external socio-political responsibilities and escaped the rule of the senses and subversion of the soul's single-minded response to God. At the same time the structures and responsibilities of monastic community provided some social compensation for familial urges. Despite their critical consciousness of women's difference, nuns like Héloise and Hildegard of Bingen did not effect any modification of this theology's negative evaluation of women's sexuality. Similarly, the urban revolution of the Dominican and Franciscan mendicants contributed less to expanding the understanding of celibacy than to the theology of evangelical poverty.[13]

A further phase in the theology of celibacy shares the dichotomized concerns of early modernism: the privileging of the reasoning self and imagination over and against the body, the seat of sensory illusion. This is evident in the dualist theologies influenced by Jansenism and Alphonsus Liguori:

> Instead of the body and the flesh being construed as requiring discipline, on the grounds that they are prime sites for the defiance of divine injunctions, they are construed as the site for the production of sensory illusion, subverting the epistemological project of establishing truth and certainty, and perhaps undermining faith in reason altogether.[14]

Again, the theology of celibacy that this view represented did not replace the previous theologies but reshaped their suspicion of the body and broadened their reasons for its denial, through the ascendancy of the spiritual over the body and the employment of the reflective intellect in the turn to God away from the flesh and worldly distractions. Even the incarnational exercises of Ignatius of Loyola, with their emphasis on embodied presence in contemplation and material construction by the imagination, could not produce a theology of celibacy that would resist the ascendancy of reason and the separation of the spiritual from bodily experience.

13. Marie-Dominique Chenu OP, *Nature, Man and Society in the Twelfth Century* (Chicago: Chicago University Press, 1968), p. 256.

14. Joanna Hodge, 'Subject Body and the Exclusion of Women from Philosophy', in Morwenna Griffiths and Margaret Whitford (eds.), *Feminist Perspectives in Philosophy* (London: Macmillan, 1988), p. 163; also Michel Foucault, *The History of Sexuality*, I (Harmondsworth: Penguin Books, 1990), pp. 21-23, 116, 120.

These Days

Although this survey may appear to be more about celibacy yesterday
than 'celibacy these days', these negative theologies of celibacy persist
and are conflated in many celibates' understanding of their lives,
despite all the modern biological and psychological understanding of
humanity. Many dissonant behaviours exhibit this dualist theology, for
example, the fascination with 'sex' combined with fear of one's
sexuality, fear of the power of women's sexuality combined with idealization of the church as feminine and obsession with the power of the
Virgin Mary. Worse, such repressive and institutional denial of the
body and sexuality cannot contain or convert unresolved sexual needs
and violence in a destructive personality. Such negative theologies of
celibacy can only restrict the humanity of people, provoke a dissociated view of reality, and confuse personal detachment with a selfish lack
of responsible commitment to anyone. The psychiatrist and former
priest, Richard Sipe, insists in his studies *A Secret World: Sexuality
and the Search for Celibacy* (1990) and the more recent and disturbing
Sex, Priests and Power: Anatomy of a Crisis (1995), that the clerical
power system and its institutional secrecy about infidelities and abuses
by clerical celibates is built on the church's failure to abandon its
inaccurate biology and negative anthropology rather than critically
adopt contemporary insights into human nature and sexuality.

> Fear of women is frequently observed in the attitude of priests and bishops.
> Fear reinforces fixation at immature levels of psychosexual development. . . .
> In some priests the sexual flame of curiosity is actually fanned by their
> fear.[15]

A positive view of human sexuality calls into question the prohibition
of sexual intercourse that is fundamental to religious celibacy. The
inseparability of the body and sexuality from human personhood is
integral to any proper human understanding. If God created humans
as sexual beings, it would appear counter-creational to require some
humans not to engage sexually. A disembodied celibacy is therefore a
caricature of God's creativity, because it confuses the serious relin-
quishing of sexual procreativity and genital intimacy with a total denial
of the human person's sexuality. We have too much disturbing evidence

15. Richard Sipe, *Sex, Priests and Power: Anatomy of a Crisis* (London:
Cassell, 1995), pp. 4, 103.

of how destructive this repression can be. How then can celibacy make sense in a world that does not share such negative views of sex? Ex-Dominican priest, Jacques Pohier, observes:

> Depriving oneself of what is represented by human love and sexuality at the end of the twentieth century cannot have the same significance as depriving oneself of what they represented in the thirteenth century, and such a course of action runs a serious risk of making quite different statements about God and the human condition from what one would want to signify or believe that one was signifying, in such renunciation.[16]

What characterizes a fourth phase in the development of theology about celibacy, 'celibacy these days', is how abstinence from sexual activity can be understood as not devaluing either sex, sexuality or the body. This theology starts from the postmodern privileging of body and engages with current sociological, gender and biological discourses on sexuality. This celibacy is understood in terms of its likeness to other lives as much as in its difference from them. Persons who are celibate are seen as naturally recurring types of humanity. It recognizes that there are many times in the lives of humans other than celibates when they are not sexually engaged, when they live celibately, whether intentionally or not. Sexuality and sexual relationships encompass more than sexual intercourse.

This later phase in the theology of celibacy is still taking form, being consciously embodied within the ranks of the body-denying theologies and the carnage and hatred they have engendered. This understanding is yet to flow through all celibate lives, but it has already been lived by many who have found in celibacy a sexually fulfilling personal and social expression of the life-giving love that is God's gift in us all. It is from their reflection on their experience as celibates for the kingdom (or promise) of God that this theology is being constructed. This phase in the understanding of celibacy is most evident in an attitude to the body as the locus of woman's identity, in the female subject as explored in celibacy, and in celibacy as an experimental praxis of love.

Body and Celibacy

A sexually embodied celibacy is the search for union with God, mediated in human relationships other than sexual partnership. This happens *through* being sexual, not by imagining that sexuality can be abandoned

---

16. Jacques Pohier, *God—In Fragments* (London: SCM Press, 1985), p. 33.

as a zone of sin beyond God's saving action. This celibacy is a way of being sexual. It recognizes the body as constitutive of our being, not merely as a vessel for the spirit. This is the resolution of the dualism so evident in the previous phases of the theology of celibacy, in favour of a more integrated view of humanity, that builds on both modern understanding of the human person and incarnational theology. Men have produced most of the post-Vatican II theological writing on celibacy, abstract and spiritualized accounts that only refer to the body in terms of pastoral 'problems' to do with celibate living or the subject matter of the confessional. Exceptions like André Guindon do resist this dualism and recognize the centrality of the body to any new theological appreciation of celibacy. In his paradoxically entitled chapter, 'Celibate Fecundity', he judges:

> I would contest the genuineness of any such experience that would reveal a fleshless and sexless 'soul', for no living human self is known to be structured that way. No wonder monks who strove to get in touch with only their 'soul' spent the other half of their meditation chasing away the 'devils of the flesh', namely, their exacerbated sexual selves craving attention and care.[17]

Foucault's analysis of the body in modern medical, penitentiary, and social organization concludes that the body has been released from its dualistic subordination and deprecation, becoming the embodied subject, the focus of a proliferation of discourses.[18] In turn this embodied subject becomes enslaved in 'the deployment of sexuality', in another power–knowledge system, that of the 'Faustian pact': 'to exchange life in its entirety for sex itself, for the truth and the sovereignty of sex'.[19] He muses on 'a different economy of bodies and pleasures' where people will wonder at 'how the ruses of sexuality, and the power that sustains its organization, were able to subject us to that austere monarch of sex, so that we became dedicated to the endless task of forcing its secret, of exacting the truest of confessions from a shadow'.[20] An embodied theology of celibacy seeks to model such 'a different economy', one that celebrates sex yet also situates it within the *whole*

17. Guindon, *The Sexual Creators*, p. 211.
18. Michel Foucault, *History of Sexuality* (3 vols.; London: Allen Lane and Penguin, 1981–1988); *Discipline and Punish: The Birth of the Prison* (London: Allen Lane 1977).
19. Foucault, *The History of Sexuality*, I, p. 156.
20. Foucault, *The History of Sexuality*, I, p. 159.

of human life, rather than dominating life as its 'monarch'.

Celibacy does not require a destruction of sexuality, it is a different experience of human sexuality. Embodied celibacy expands our representation of human sexuality beyond its expression in genital sex: 'the body cannot be fully apprehended or represented: it exceeds representation'.[21] It is not 'no sexuality', not a renunciation of being sexual, like the baptismal 'renouncing the devil and all his works'—it is another way of being sexual, of being embodied. Celibate living that positively values sexuality finds that sexual attraction, warmth, and energy permeate all human relationships, all encounters with the 'other who is not one'. This requires consciousness of the diffusion of the sexual in us. As Anglican priest Jim Cotter understands, 'growth in sensuousness is also marked by the diffusion of the erotic throughout the entire body. If the narrowing of sexuality's focus to the genitals is a mark of alienated sexuality, its diffusion throughout the body reflects its sanctification.'[22] Whether God has any particular interest in the celibate's refraining from sex or not, it is the celibate's experience of the reality of God in her life that urges her to embody, outside of partnership and parenting, God's love as surpassing the usual boundaries and limits of our ability to know that we are loved, and are not alone, that we are good as we are, and not the deficient 'other'.

Any differences between women's and men's experiences of celibacy are hidden by the universalizing of the male subject in writing on celibacy. Luce Irigaray judges: 'in order for ethics to be possible, we must constitute a possible place for each sex, body and flesh to inhabit'.[23] Women's experience of an embodied sexuality is the key to any reshaping of theological understanding of celibacy, because the negative concept of woman as sensual, temptress and 'other' has figured as the object of theologies of abjection, of body-denial. As woman's sexuality has been traditionally associated with initiating sin and 'The Fall of Man', celibacy appears to reinforce such negative judgments. This negativity is apparent even in the claim that virginity for women requires 'a far more profound demand for alienation and renunciation

21. Rosi Braidotti, *Nomadic Subjects* (New York: Columbia University Press, 1994), pp. 165-66.

22. Jim Cotter, 'Homosexual and Holy', *The Way* 28 (1988), p. 240.

23. Luce Irigaray, *An Ethics of Sexual Difference* (London: Athlone Press, 1993), pp. 17-18.

of self than any demand for continence on the part of men'.[24] For celibacy not to promote a negative understanding of sexuality requires a revaluation of the implication that God has a particular concern to keep women's bodies under sexual control. This presents a denial of the incarnation. Again, Irigaray questions the fundamental contradiction in this sort of expression of Christianity:

> Why invite the people to a celebration of the Eucharist on Christmas day if not to glorify the felt, the corporeal and fleshly advent of the divine, this coming, all the consequences of which theology seems far from understanding. . . And should most of the clergy refuse to acknowledge the importance of sexuality, it would only be fitting for them to give up on the theology of incarnation.[25]

When celibate women share their understanding of celibacy their accounts of celibate experience disclose bodily and sexually conscious data for the theology of celibacy. Most recent published accounts of secular experience of celibacy have been by women, representing the range from the separatist experience of radical lesbians, through the self-chosen independence and reservation of fashionable celibacy, to the safest 'safe sex' option for worn-out women. Sally Cline concludes that not all experiences of celibacy in women's lives have the intentionality that marks them out as 'passionate celibacy', but those that make a positive decision for celibacy find 'it allows women their own choices about what to do with their bodies' and to explore the complexity of their sexuality beyond performance according to the 'genital myth'.

> Recent research shows that women need affection, desire intimacy, but have little regard for genital penetration. Often they buy it as a part of a media maintained 'package' which they must accept wholesale in order to achieve other goals such as love or companionship.[26]

Women who continue living celibately without damage to themselves report that the meaning of their lives comes through their appreciation of their sexuality and their bodies and not despite them. From the accounts that religious women give of their own experience, celibacy

24. Elizabeth Castelli, 'Virginity and its Meaning for Women's Sexuality in Early Christianity', *Journal of Feminist Studies in Religion* 2 (1986), pp. 85-86.

25. Irigaray, 'Equal to Whom?', *differences* 1.2 (1990), p. 67.

26. Cline, *Women, Celibacy and Passion*, pp. 254, 149.

emerges as something rich, positive and sexual.[27] They bear some like-ness to Irigaray's feminine *jouissance*, 'a specific female representation of the unconscious and of desire, [that] is the non-said of all discourse, and develops a fundamental critique of discourse by trying to inscribe sexual difference in it'.[28] This is despite Irigaray's own disavowal of convents as valid female representation.

Theological reflection on women's experience begins with the celi-bate embodying her sexual and social reality as the locus of her inter-action and contemplation: the place, the meeting-point, the receiver, the giver, the reflector, the valuer of love. This corresponds to Irigaray's description of the first stage in the articulation of the female sex in mimicry: 'One must assume the feminine role deliberately. Which means already to convert a form of subordination into an affirmation, and thus to begin to thwart it.' Ironically, yet as in mimesis, celibate women have needed to reclaim their bodies and sexuality at the same time as other women have needed to transcend biological determinism and patriarchal inscribing of their bodies. An embodied and inter-personal celibacy lived by women channels that bonding and creativity developed in relationships with others, in openness to feelings, genital arousal and sexual needs, and recognition that a woman's body is integral to her female identity. Such a celibate welcomes the constant challenge of her choice about her use of her sexuality and she is vigi-lant about any tendency to body-denial. She is open to opportunities for self-knowledge and actualization through her body, instead of despite it. Alert to her bodily desire for expression, she varies her self-expression according to her needs and rhythms, and to the needs of others. An embodied celibacy would reveal, relate, and reflect another theological understanding of human sexuality.

Celibacy and Woman's Identity

Subjective claiming of their bodies and experience is the common task of all women in search of identity. Women need to redress the power-lessness of definition by others and to find new ways of integrating their embodiment with an identity of their own. Inclusion of celibate women's experience alongside the experience of other women broadens

27. Gray, *Neither Escaping nor Exploiting Sex*, particularly pp. 14-28.
28. Rosi Braidotti, *Patterns of Dissonance* (Cambridge: Polity Press, 1991), p. 248.

this tracing of woman's identity. Celibacy shares the problem of feminist discourse of how to move beyond sexual identities determined
exclusively by the phallus. This parallels Marcelle Marini's view:

> Haven't they [women] been inscribed in it all along as being oppressed,
> accomplices to their oppression, or resistant? Can we not think that a
> 'culture' has subsisted, has sustained itself and transformed itself in the
> course of the centuries: dispersed, fragmented beneath the pressure of the
> dominant culture, but living: although often illegible, it is inscribed in our
> heritage. And this enables women today to struggle (to be) 'subjects',
> even if this term escapes its received definition.[29]

Woman's celibacy, as a deviation from the usual role of being a
sexual partner, also challenges the male-mirroring of itself in woman
as 'other'. Its occurrence as a more popular lifestyle for women than
men points to celibacy's prototypical representation of current feminist
agenda. Such a quest for a different woman's identity, given the gender
consciousness of these celibate women, is not only explained as pre-
critical. Janice Raymond describes such consciousness as historical in

> women who were not attracted to marriage, who were drawn by the
> independence and companionship of women, and who wanted an outlet
> for talents and work not available to them in the secular world, found in
> convents a natural habitat.[30]

Woman's celibacy attempts an understanding of woman not only as
the invisible 'other', but as different. Following Irigaray, woman's
celibacy threatens the male *logos*, by subverting the male definition of
woman as sexual object, through combining the feminist idea of non-
mirrored woman with the male symbolic of female purity:

> To play with mimesis is thus, for a woman, to try to recover the place
> of her exploitation by discourse, without allowing herself to be simply
> reduced to it. . . so as to make 'visible', by an effect of playful repetition,
> what was supposed to remain invisible: the cover-up of a possible opera-
> tion of the feminine in language.[31]

In this sense celibacy acts as an embodied form of the mimesis of
male ideas of what is woman, at the same time as it 'unveils' that

---

29. Cited in Braidotti, *Patterns of Dissonance*, p. 262.
30. Janice Raymond, *A Passion for Friends* (London: Women's Press, 1986),
p. 83.
31. Luce Irigaray, *This Sex Which is Not One* (Ithaca, NY: Cornell University
Press, 1985), p. 76.

performance as demonstrating that woman has a history of being other than the male logic and ideas about woman. The sexual challenge offered by celibate women mimics male control over women's bodies at the same time as subverting it by demonstrating that these women *'also remain elsewhere'*.[32]

Women celibates have explored other identities than those bestowed on them by male patriarchal discourse. They have observed some consciousness and practice of the value of female genealogies of 'mother–daughter', that Irigaray advocates for breaking through the mother's role in supporting the processes of the male imaginary that co-opt the mother into her own non-representation in this universe. At the same time celibate women's genealogies subvert this role by their valuing and revealing of many 'mothers', many sites of 'mother–daughter' love and the power of their lives.[33] Even more, celibacy gives voice to those other women who have been silenced in the male-sexualized universe, where woman is only sex partner and heir-producer—the sisters, grandmothers, granddaughters, aunts, nieces, cousins, nannies, and women friends—different voices of woman's identity. While women religious celibates mimic or perform a variety of roles commensurate with familial female ones, these are too varied and fluid to be reduced to one, such as mother, daughter, or sister. Adrienne Rich commends these subjects for female genealogy: 'for centuries, daughters have been strengthened by *non-biological mothers*, who have combined a care for the practical values of survival with an incitement toward further horizons, a compassion for vulnerability with an insistence on our buried strengths'.[34] Women's celibacy shows how the necessary individuation and subjectivity of the daughters are promoted without committing the symbolic 'matricide' of the usual discourse of the patriarchal family.

32. Irigaray, *This Sex Which is Not One*, p. 76.

33. Irigaray, *je, tu, nous: Toward a Culture of Difference* (New York: Routledge, 1993), pp. 15-22, and *Thinking the Difference: For a Peaceful Revolution* (London: Athlone Press, 1994), pp. 109-12. In a survey of over eighty religious women celibates I was surprised how many referred to their various experiences of mother–daughtering, rather than sistering. Initially I suspected this to be a sign of psychological regression or transferral of patriarchal authority to a matriarchal structure of domination. I now recognize instead the operation of Irigaray's 'bond of the female ancestries' through the freedom of role identity provided by women's celibate communities. I am grateful to Ann Gilroy, RSJ, for alerting me to this.

34. Adrienne Rich, *Of Woman Born* (London: Virago, 1977), p. 252.

Embodied beyond exploitation by others and socialized beyond particularity to one other, woman's celibacy rehearses the biological and
social freedoms possible for all humanity in the fulfilment of the
eschatological promise of God's kingdom (promise). This theological
understanding of celibacy is echoed by Julia Kristeva:

> The sharpest and most subtle point of feminist subversion brought about
> by the new generation will henceforth be situated on the terrain of the
> inseparable conjunction of the sexual and the symbolic, in order to try to
> discover, first, the specificity of the female, and then, in the end, that of
> each individual woman.[35]

An Experimental Praxis

The religious life of celibacy is an experimental praxis. All human
love seeks union, promises mutuality, but is lessened by the fear that
love can be destroyed or can be removed. Celibacy is an experiment
in human love like that Roberto Unger ascribes to the passions:

> experiments to discover the kind and degree of freedom that a person can
> hope for. These experiments, however, are also gambles whose outcomes
> in a concrete life no-one can foresee.[36]

Women's theological understanding of their celibacy in positive sexual
terms links celibacy with the passions. Instead of celibacy being reduced
to an existentially detached lifestyle that is unrelated and only ethereal,
it may be better understood as an experimental lifestyle, not opposed
to marriage and partnership, but an exercise in how love and freedom
are possible for humanity. It rehearses a love where relating can risk,
while it aims for mutuality and yet is respectful of difference in
identity. While celibacy appears to promote a deprived humanity, it
embodies other ways of being human. It appears to devalue love and
sex, yet it seeks other ways to relate sexually than in genital partnerships. Its theological basis is the understanding that desire itself is
already union, a movement of love for union.[37] It is in the desire to be
closer to other humans and to God, that I recognize love in me already

35. Julia Kristeva, 'Woman's Time' in Toril Moi (ed.), *The Kristeva Reader*
(New York: Columbia University Press, 1986), p. 196.
36. Roberto M. Unger, *Passion: An Essay in Personality* (New York: Free
Press, 1984), p. 114.
37. Margaret Farley, RSM, *Personal Commitments: Beginning, Keeping,
Changing* (San Francisco: Harper & Row, 1986), p. 31.

drawing me to other selves that are not like me, or are like me, but not me.

Celibacy relinquishes the fulfilment and satisfaction sought in partnership. It involves attempting to love and be open to the love of more than one person, while not expecting exclusive loving response from any one person. It risks avoidance of being committed to anyone. Like many experiments, it can fail. It will ever be inconclusive, its hypothesis may even be disproved. That love can be more inclusive, that humans can live out the disappointments and limitations of their loves cannot only be hypothesized or preached. Somehow it has to be lived out and embodied to demonstrate the worth and divinity of all loving. Margaret Miles suggests this need in her analysis of 'separateness and relationships':

> Perhaps it is necessary that some people in our culture explore these painful commitments to separateness as a corrective for the total investment of self, of longings, of enjoyment in a relationship that most of us who are in our forties or older received as a model as we grew up.[38]

In the romantic idealization of love, love is equally reciprocated, but in reality love is seldom responded to in the degree it is given. Love is given but not equally returned in human relationships. Many times love is destroyed for lack of an adequate response. Celibate love is no lesser nor greater in intensity and breadth of interaction than many other loves. The celibate intends the type of loving and unloving that most people experience inadvertently in relationships when these freeze, or never grow, or rupture with hatred, or eke out in indifference. The celibate starts out trying to love and, significantly, continues in this love despite its pain and loneliness, its short joys and long waits. While she may be sustained by other experiences of love in experiences of God's presence, or of being loved, a celibate's love, like the *reality* of many other humans' love, is not to love in expectation of being reciprocated. Celibacy is a human experiment in how far humans can go without having particular love returned to us. It is about how much humans can continue loving without being loved in response.

Celibacy experiments with what is the unchosen condition of many humans who love. Celibacy does not ignore the human need for love, but it does not idolize the satisfaction of this need. It is an experiment

---

38. Margaret Miles, 'The Courage To Be Alone—In and Out of Marriage', in M.E. Giles (ed.), *The Feminist Mystic* (New York: Crossroad, 1987), p. 92.

only possible within the hope of God's love. The reality of the cost to humans of love unrequited is too horrifying, too painful to be pretended. Genital intercourse as an escape from lovelessness is therefore impossible for the celibate. It would compromise celibacy's experiment about humanity, because it would admit that the loveless fate of many is too hard to bear. Theologically speaking, humanity would be damned to despair about human ability to sustain life and love in the facelessness of lovelessness. God's experiment in humanly embodying love for us would also appear to fail, as this incarnational act of salvation would seem a deceit unable to reflect the real human experience of the struggle to love and be loved. But the social reality is that many humans do continue to love despite being unloved. The experiment of celibacy acts as a sign pointing out that many people do already live in hope in and out of love. The signs of the kingdom (promise) of God are *there* already among us. The hope–risk of celibacy resists the despair that would overlook the struggle of all loving and loneliness. Celibacy recognizes that while people live and love in silent and loud suffering, they demonstrate that there is hope. Celibacy, then, is a living reminder or amplifier of the hope of love, a joy that can never be taken away (Jn 16.22). God's promise is real, not utopian, already lived out in many lives where love persists even in loneliness.

Conclusion: The God of Celibacy

Who is the God that creates and fosters celibate lives? I have taken Karl Rahner's advice and invoked God sparingly in this chapter because it is especially the experience of celibate existence that God remains a mystery, palpable but indefinable. Celibates learn quickly that there are few appropriate words for God. If they do not, then they tend to compromise their celibacy by turning God into an object of sublimated sexual desire, or projecting onto God a mother or parent attachment.

> God is, therefore, construed as a marvellous surrogate Mother. She represents the fulfilling object *par excellence*. The celibate has Her all to herself or himself. . . God would seem to belong to the vowed celibate in a special way. Thus, the scene is set for a 'particular friendship' with God. Instead of dying and rising with the Lord and allowing all creatures to sing the wonders of Being by delivering them from their inhibitions and their fears, deviant celibates adore their own narcissistic image in Her.[39]

39. Guindon, *The Sexual Creators*, p. 220.

God is sensed more in what is inexpressible in sexual love and in the absences that punctuate all relating, than in the delusion of such spiritualized intercourse. The celibate cannot replace human relationships with a fantasized coupling with God. The incarnation reveals that God is found in the diversity of creation and human encounters, not in narcissism, or exclusively in the isolation of the perfect couple. This revelation through diversity as well as particularity is the challenge and experiment of celibacy. Serene Jones invokes this in her appeal for an understanding of

> a God who is not One but multiple, active, and relational. And if this God is truly to meet humanity in a relationship of mutuality, then this God must also be represented as incommensurably other, as a sign as well as an actual event of true alterity.[40]

'Celibacy these days' is a new dispensation in the theology of celibacy, that values sexuality and women's experience of body as part of the divine intention realized in the creation of humanity. This celibacy is an experiment in Rosi Braidotti's 'process of acquiring a new subjectivity in the love of our own sex', 'defined as a process of "becoming-divine" by women'.[41] Celibacy that refuses denial of sexuality finds that God is love 'abiding' in our sexuality, that God is dynamic in us, is all love, and is all our desire for love and to love. This celibacy imagines that God, union with God, union with all whom we love, are not just ideals or future dreams, but are anticipated and present in our loving, in our human experience of love, no matter how deficient and pain-filled. A celibacy open to human sexuality announces the creator's delight in variety, the saviour's celebration of fullness, and the Spirit's transformation of loneliness.[42]

40. Serene Jones, 'This God Which is Not One: Irigaray and Barth on the Divine' in C.W.M. Kim, S.M. St Ville and S.M. Simonaitis (eds.), *Transfigurations: Theology and the French Feminists* (Philadelphia: Augsburg–Fortress, 1993), p. 141.

41. Braidotti, *Patterns of Dissonance*, p. 261.

42. My thanks to Aune K. Dillon for her comments on this chapter.

CARNAL LOVE AND SPIRITUAL IMAGINATION:
CAN LUCE IRIGARAY AND JOHN PAUL II COME TOGETHER?

Tina Beattie

Is Luce Irigaray a Catholic? Is Pope John Paul II a feminist? Most feminists (and probably most Catholics) might say 'no' to these questions, but I am less certain. The Pope's writings reveal the extent to which the question of women has engaged his thinking. In the encyclical *Evangelium Vitae*, he calls upon women to promote

> a 'new feminism' which rejects the temptation of imitating models of 'male domination', in order to acknowledge and affirm the true genius of women in every aspect of the life of society, and overcome all discrimination, violence and exploitation.[1]

Irigaray, the radical French philosopher of sexual difference, agrees that women's liberation entails more than a campaign for equal rights. She asks, 'What do women want to be equal to? Men? A wage? A public position? Equal to what? Why not to themselves?'[2] She also argues that no feminist attempt to restructure the social order can succeed without addressing the question of religion, saying that

> God is being used by men to oppress women and. . . therefore, God must be questioned and not simply neutered in the current pseudoliberal way. Religion as a social phenomenon cannot be ignored.[3]

However, Irigaray's engagement with the symbols of Catholicism goes beyond a subversive linguistic strategy to offer a glimpse into the latent

1. Pope John Paul II, *Evangelium Vitae* (London: Catholic Truth Society, 1995), p. 176 n. 99.
2. Luce Irigaray, 'Equal or different?' in Margaret Whitford (ed.), *The Irigaray Reader* (Oxford: Basil Blackwell, 1994), pp. 30-33 (p. 32). For ease of reference, I use essay titles when referring to Irigaray's work, since some of the essays appear in several books.
3. Irigaray, *Sexes and Genealogies* (trans. Gillian C. Gill; New York: Columbia University Press, 1993), p. v.

potential of Catholic belief. The Pope puts more intellectual energy into thinking about feminist issues than many women, and Irigaray puts more intellectual energy into thinking about Catholicism than many Catholics.

In this essay, I consider sexual embodiment according to John Paul II and Irigaray, with particular emphasis on women's embodiment.[4] After addressing certain questions that arise in connection with such an unlikely theoretical coupling, I will explore the significance of sexual difference in their work before offering a speculative reclamation of the natural law as it relates to women's sexuality. I engage with Irigaray from the perspective of the Pope's theology of the body as developed in a series of weekly general audiences in 1979 and 1980, published under the title, *Original Unity of Man and Woman: Catechesis on the Book of Genesis*.[5] This text lays the foundations for many of John Paul II's later writings on marriage and sexuality, such as *Mulieris Dignitatem* and his 1994 *Letter to Families*. Although I pose a number of provocative questions to the Pope, I write from within the context of Catholicism and I am not suggesting that Catholic theology should dance to the tune of feminist philosophy. I do, however, ask if perhaps Luce Irigaray and John Paul II are occasionally dancing to the same tune, even if they are not quite dancing cheek to cheek.

This encounter between a radical feminist and a highly conservative Pope might seem contrived. However, this is not a blind date—at least as far as Irigaray is concerned. In 1986, during the Pope's visit to France, she heard one of his homilies and wrote to him expressing her concern.[6] She criticizes him for giving a talk on sexual morality that was lacking in any sense of spiritual sustenance and that failed to

---

4.   I concentrate on the question of sexual difference as it relates to the hetero-sexual encounter, because I am exploring the area of convergence between the thought of Irigaray and John Paul II. This means setting aside important questions regarding relationships between women in Irigaray's work. My focus on hetero-sexuality does not imply an uncritical acceptance of the Catholic Church's present stance on homosexuality.

5.   John Paul II, *Original Unity of Man and Woman: Catechesis on the Book of Genesis* (Boston: St. Paul Books & Media, 1981).

6.   Her letter was rejected for publication by the newspaper to which she first sent it, and was later published in the journal, *Paris-Féministe*. See 'Le Religieux comme droit féminin', followed by 'Le Christianisme, religion de l'incarnation?' in *Paris-Féministe* 31.2 (September, 1986), pp. 37-41. I am grateful to Margaret Whitford for sending me a copy of this letter. Translations from the French are my own.

address the pressing ethical, theological and social concerns of the age. She tells him that 'carnal love is a little more spiritual than you imagine', and argues that the sexual relationship cannot be seen only in terms of procreation but must be seen first and foremost as the means of divinization between the sexes. 'Faced with sexuality, we are all [*toutes et tous*] faced with a dimension of the incarnation to resolve.'

Irigaray clearly wants to be heard by the Pope, but is he listening? It might be far-fetched to suggest that when the Pontiff wants to curl up in bed at night with a good author he chooses Irigaray, but his recent writings indicate that he is at least implicitly aware of some of the questions she raises. He shares her premise that there is a fundamental difference between the sexes, and that recognition of women's rights requires certain changes in the social order in order to accommodate this difference. At times, they have in common a profound pessimism about the present malaise of Western society, allied to a belief that somehow women hold the key to social transformation. The Pope refers to modern society as 'a culture of death'[7] and says that 'a greater presence of women in society... will force systems to be redesigned in a way which favours the processes of humanisation which mark the "civilisation of love"'.[8] I am not implying that Irigaray and John Paul II are like-minded on these issues. Rather, I am asking if it might be possible to create or re-create a world in which the Pope's 'man' and Irigaray's 'woman' might 'at last live together, meet, and sometimes inhabit the same place'.[9]

My engagement with Irigaray is shaped by the Pope's theology, and therefore what follows makes no claim to be a comprehensive representation of her work (nor indeed of his). Irigaray's writing lends itself to many readings, and what we see in her speculum will always depend on the corpus of work into which she is inserted. With this in mind, I turn to an examination of John Paul II's theology of the body.

7.   cf. *Evangelium Vitae*, p. 22 n. 12.

8.   John Paul II, 'A Letter to Women', published in *The Tablet*, 15 July 1995, pp. 917-19 (p. 918). See also John Paul II, *Letter to Families: 1994, Year of the Family* (London: Catholic Truth Society, 1994), pp. 64-65 n. 17; L. Irigaray, 'Civil Rights and Responsibilities for the Two Sexes', in *Thinking the Difference: For a Peaceful Revolution* (trans. Karin Montin; London: The Athlone Press, 1994), pp. 65-87 (pp. 76-77).

9.   L. Irigaray, 'Sexual Difference', in *An Ethics of Sexual Difference* (trans. Carolyn Burke and Gillian C. Gill; London: The Athlone Press, 1993), pp. 5-19 (p. 17).

Significant Bodies and Incarnate Love:
The Genesis of Sexual Difference

In 'Egales à Qui?', an extended critique of Elisabeth Schüssler Fiorenza's book, *In Memory of Her*, Irigaray rejects the idea of Christianity as a religion primarily concerned with issues of socio-economic justice and argues that the fundamental act of exploitation that gives rise to all other injustices is the exploitation of women. She says that Christian concern for the poor must be

> the social consequence of respect for the incarnation of all [*toutes et tous*] as bodies that are potentially divine. Nothing more and nothing less: all men and all women are virtually gods. If the redemption of the world by Christ does not have this significance, I see nothing else about it that is worth so much historical fidelity.[10]

The Pope and Irigaray both affirm the body as the locus of divine revelation, and see the incarnation as requiring a theology that accords central significance to embodiment. To establish in what sense Irigaray is using theological language is beyond the scope of my essay, and I use words such as 'divine revelation' with caution. In their otherwise excellent and nuanced studies, both Margaret Whitford and Elizabeth Grosz take a surprisingly unequivocal stand with regard to Irigaray's use of the word 'God', insisting that it is intended strictly symbolically.[11] Given that Irigaray consistently seeks to subvert the disembodied and abstract symbolism of the linguistic order, I would argue that her language of the divine cannot be comfortably circumscribed. I am inclined to see it as a *via positiva*, a proliferation of language and images that is subversive and destabilizing of any attempt to fix theological meaning too rigidly within conceptual boundaries. This is however a complex question that I leave open.[12]

---

10. Irigaray, 'Egales à Qui?', in *Critique* 480 (May 1987), pp. 420-37 (p. 425). My translation.

11. Cf. Elizabeth Grosz, *Sexual Subversions: Three French Feminists* (St Leonards, NSW: Allen & Unwin, 1989), pp. 151-83, and *idem*, 'Irigaray and the Divine', in C.W. Maggie Kim, Susan M. St. Ville and Susan M. Simonaitis (eds.), *Transfigurations: Theology and The French Feminists* (Minneapolis: Fortress Press, 1993), pp. 199-214; Margaret Whitford, *Luce Irigaray: Philosophy in the Feminine* (London: Routledge, 1991), pp. 140-44.

12. For an interesting appraisal of Irigaray's use of the word 'God', see Serene

In *Original Unity*, the Pope seeks to discover the theological significance of sexual embodiment by revisiting the story of Genesis, on the
grounds that Christ, when questioned by the pharisees about the legitimacy of divorce, refers to the one flesh union of male and female 'in
the beginning' (cf. Mt. 19.3-6 and Mk 10.2-9). The Pope sees Christ's
response as an invitation for every generation to rediscover the
'fundamental and elementary truths about the human being, as man
and woman',[13] by considering the nuptial meaning of the body in the
Genesis account of creation. He says, 'The body, in fact, and it alone,
is capable of making visible what is invisible: the spiritual and the
divine... in his body as male or female, man feels he is a subject of
holiness'.[14] The Pope's reading of Genesis is a complex engagement
with the two creation accounts contained in Gen. 1.26-28 and 2.5-25,
and in many ways it constitutes a profound celebration of the sexual
embodiment of the human being made in the image of God.

   Genesis 1 refers to sexual difference as an integral feature of the
creation of the human being: 'God created man in the image of himself,
in the image of God he created him, male and female he created them'
(Gen. 1.27). Genesis 2 describes the creation of Adam (the Hebrew
'adam refers not to the male but to the generic human being), and the
creation of Eve from the rib of the sleeping Adam. The Pope points
out that at this point in the narrative, *'adam* is replaced by the terms
'man' (*'îsh*) and 'woman' (*'îshshāh*, literally meaning 'from the man').
I presume that the series of talks which constitutes *Original Unity* was
originally delivered in Italian, and it may be that linguistic subtleties
have been lost in translation. However, it is regrettable that the trans-
lators did not use inclusive language when referring to the generic
human. As it is, the use of the word 'man' to signify both humankind
in general and the male in particular, undermines the Pope's point
about the meaning of *'adam* and creates the suspicion that maleness is
still serving as a norm against which femaleness is defined. In other
words, if readers feel uneasy about the use of language in some of the
following quotations, I share their unease.

   According to John Paul II, the two creation accounts of Genesis describe both the original solitude of the human being before God, and

Jones, 'This God Which Is Not One—Irigaray and Barth on the Divine', in C.W.
Maggie Kim *et al.* (eds.), *Transfigurations*, pp. 109-41.
   13. John Paul II, *Original Unity*, p. 173.
   14. John Paul II, *Original Unity*, p. 144-45.

the fulfilment of personhood in the male–female unity of the encounter between the sexes. The man and woman together form a *communio personarum* in which is revealed 'an image of an inscrutable divine communion of Persons'.[15] Original solitude is the condition out of which arises the ability to recognize and celebrate the presence of another person, although there is no temporal distinction between this solitude and the communion of man and woman. I think the term 'original solitude' therefore needs to be understood in conceptual rather than chronological terms. It refers to an ontological dimension of human existence that is prior to, but also inseparable from, sexual difference.

The primal meaning of the body that develops in the solitude of the human being before God, finds fulfilment in the conjugal union. The nakedness of this original state signifies the capacity of the sexes to come to a full awareness of the meaning of embodiment as male and female through one another. The words 'they were not ashamed' (Gen. 2.25) 'do not express a lack, but, on the contrary, serve to indicate a particular fullness of consciousness and experience, above all fullness of understanding of the meaning of the body, bound up with the fact that "they were naked"'.[16] Nakedness therefore denotes the communion of persons who are physically revealed and given to one another, but it also denotes the nakedness of the spirit in the pre-lapsarian fullness of God's presence. In receiving one another as mutual gift, the man and the woman come to possession of their full humanity and personhood:

> Thus man, in the first beatifying meeting, finds the woman, and she finds him. In this way he accepts her interiorly; he accepts her as she is willed 'for her own sake' by the Creator, as she is constituted in the mystery of the image of God through her femininity; and, reciprocally, she accepts him in the same way, as he is willed 'for his own sake' by the Creator, and constituted by him by means of his masculinity. The revelation and the discovery of the 'nuptial' meaning of the body consists in this.[17]

Like John Paul II, Irigaray uses the symbolism of Genesis to suggest a state wherein man, woman and God might co-exist in harmony:

> Once they were 'in god', with man and woman sharing heaven and earth. In the midst of nature. Feeling no need for any shelter but a garden where

15. John Paul II, *Original Unity*, pp. 73-74.
16. John Paul II, *Original Unity*, p. 94.
17. John Paul II, *Original Unity*, p. 116.

they lived naked. . . Then God did not exist in front of or above human
beings. He was in them as they were in him. This 'they'? A man and
a woman, an 'original' couple. Before what is called the fall, or sin, or
banishment.[18]

I will say more about Irigaray's idea of divine immanence later, but
she suggests that God's presence is mediated not by way of a spirituality that is above and beyond the material world, but through the
senses, and particularly through the encounter between sexed human
beings whose difference is mutually recognized and celebrated. She
also sees nakedness as being transformed by sexual innocence:

> Rapture of return to the garden of innocence, where love does not yet
> know, or no longer knows, nudity as profane. . . Face to face encounter
> of two naked lovers in a nudity that is more ancient than and foreign to
> sacrilege. That cannot be perceived as profanation. The threshold of the
> garden, a welcoming cosmic home, remains open. There is no guard but
> love itself, innocent of the knowledge of display and of the fall.[19]

To some extent, it might be said that underlying John Paul II's theology
and Irigaray's philosophy, there is a shared vision of the potential of
the sexual relationship when it is understood in terms of its original
goodness. The Genesis myth provides a storehouse of symbols with
which they seek to reconfigure the man/woman relationship in a way
that accommodates both the significance of sexual difference and the
recognition of the divine presence in the sexual other. How then do
they understand 'fallen' sexuality, bearing in mind my earlier proviso
that theological symbols, including 'the fall', cannot be assumed to have
exactly the same significance for Irigaray as they do for the Pope?

---

18. Irigaray, 'the crucified one—epistle to the last christians', in *Marine Lover of
Friedrich Nietzsche* (trans. Gillian C. Gill; New York: Columbia University Press,
1991), pp. 164-90 (p. 173).

19. Irigaray, 'The Fecundity of the Caress: A Reading of Levinas, *Totality and
Infinity*, "Phenomenology of Eros"', in *An Ethics of Sexual Difference*, pp. 185-217
(p. 201). Both John Paul II and Irigaray are influenced by Emmanuel Levinas, and I
think this explains the similarity in their reclamation of nakedness. In *Totality and
Infinity*, Levinas suggests that the privacy and profanation of the erotic relationship
puts it beyond the threshold of the ethical sphere. He describes the erotic encounter
thus: 'Shame, insurmountable in love, constitutes its pathos. . . The way in which
erotic nudity is produced. . . delineates the original phenomena of shame and profanation' (Emmanuel Levinas, *Totalité et infini: Essai sur l'extériorité* [La Haye:
Martinus Nijhoff, 1961], p. 234, my translation).

'A Great Deportation Camp': The Fall into Sameness

John Paul II understands the fall as bringing about a corruption of the knowledge that allowed man and woman to discover the meaning of the body in nakedness and freedom. Now, the human being seeks knowledge through 'the veil of shame'[20] which complicates the nuptial meaning of the body, and 'the horizon of death extends over the whole perspective of human life on earth'.[21] If nakedness and freedom from shame signify the form of knowledge that belongs to the original righteousness of creation, then, the Pope suggests, shame constitutes 'a "borderline" experience',[22] marking the threshold of the historical experience of sin and a radical change in the way in which the meaning of the body is experienced. With the coming of shame, the human being, who entered the world 'as a subject of truth and love',[23] capable of making a perfect gift of self, becomes instead an object of extortion. The relationship of mutual self-giving becomes 'a reduction of the other to an "object for myself" (object of lust, of misappropriation, etc.)'.[24] The Pope goes on to note that 'this extorting of the gift from the other human being (from the woman by the man and vice versa) and reducing him (her) interiorly to a mere "object for me", should mark precisely the beginning of shame.'[25]

The fall is a cryptic motif that recurs in Irigaray's work, but the pervasive sense of human exile from Eden is encapsulated in her description of the earth as 'a great deportation camp, where men await celestial redemption'.[26] Her use of the word 'men' is significant, since she attributes humanity's alienation from divinity and nature to a patriarchal social order that seeks redemption through sacrifice and denial of the body, rather than through natural fecundity and carnal love, which she associates with women's religion.[27] There is perhaps an

---

20. John Paul II, *Original Unity*, p. 143.
21. John Paul II, *Original Unity*, p. 165.
22. John Paul II, *Original Unity*, p. 94.
23. John Paul II, *Original Unity*, p. 145.
24. John Paul II, *Original Unity*, p. 130.
25. John Paul II, *Original Unity*, p. 131.
26. Irigaray, 'the crucified one', p. 174.
27. For Irigaray's analysis of the social consequences of sacrificial religion, see her engagement with René Girard in 'Women, the Sacred, Money', in *Sexes and Genealogies*, pp. 75-88. See also 'the crucified one'.

analogous relationship between the Catholic idea of original sin, and Irigaray's description of a catastrophic rupture between divinity and humanity, the flesh and the word, nature and culture, and man and woman, perpetuated in a radically disordered symbolic order that dominates culture and language. Like the Pope, Irigaray understands the disruption of the sexual relationship as resulting in a process of objectification. Speaking of the original wonder of the sexual encounter, she says,

> Into this place came attraction, greed, possession, consummation, disgust, and so on. But not that wonder which beholds what it sees always as if for the first time, never taking hold of the other as its object. It does not try to seize, possess, or reduce this object, but leaves it subjective, still free.[28]

However, for Irigaray, the loss of integrity between man and woman is not a mutual process of objectification, but rather entails the near-complete objectification of woman by man within Western culture,[29] originating in the child's Oedipal sacrifice of its desire for the maternal body. This act of 'original matricide'[30] is the primal sacrifice upon which the Western symbolic order is constructed, and it creates a culture of exploitation and hostility towards both women and nature, given that both are closely associated with the body of the mother. The repressed desire for the mother results in the obliteration of women's presence from constructions of meaning and subjectivity within the symbolic order, leading to an economy of the same in which the supposedly neutral, universal subject of philosophy, theology and politics is in fact the male subject, with the system of language and culture being structured around the values of the phallus. Irigaray credits Freud

28. Irigaray, 'Sexual Difference', p. 13. I doubt if Sharon, a prostitute, has read either Irigaray or John Paul II. However, in describing her experience she uses language that is remarkably similar to the ideas they both bring to their discussion of the nature of fallen sexuality: 'Men need to spill their seed; we're just their objects, their things, their means to an end. I tell you this: they almost never look me in the eye. They can't do that, you see. They can't think of me as a woman, a real human being. Cos what would that say about them?' (Quoted in *The Guardian*, G2 tabloid section, 15 May 1996, p. 9).

29. It is important to bear in mind that Irigaray is not seeking to elaborate a universal theory about sexual difference, but rather to analyse the objectification of women in Western culture. Sometimes, this leads to a romanticization of Eastern religion and culture, which she sees as more accommodating of sexual difference (cf. 'Women, the Sacred, Money', p. 77).

30. Irigaray, 'Body against Body: in Relation to the Mother', in *Sexes and Genealogies*, pp. 7-21 (p. 11).

with having unwittingly uncovered '*the sexual indifference that under-
lies the truth of any science, the logic of every discourse*'. She says,

> Freud does not see *two sexes* whose differences are articulated in the act
> of intercourse, and, more generally speaking, in the imaginary and sym-
> bolic processes that regulate the workings of a society and a culture. The
> 'feminine' is always described in terms of deficiency or atrophy, as the
> other side of the sex that alone holds a monopoly on value: the male sex.[31]

The situation as she sees it is therefore bleak indeed, and seems to
accord with the Pope's understanding of sin as the objectification of
the other. So where should we look for the signs of redemption and
regeneration?

'The Future of the Human Ethos': Redeeming Difference

In the Catholic tradition, the fall is not absolute and there are still mani-
festations of grace in the natural world. The Pope recognizes that sin
has the power to blight the sexual relationship and to reduce human
beings to objects for one another's gratification, and therefore the
mutual giving of self must be reconstructed 'with great effort'.[32] Nevertheless, 'the nuptial meaning of [man's] own body, of his own masculinity and femininity...constitutes the future of the human *ethos*'.[33]
There is a sense of optimism in the Pope's theology. The world is
already redeemed, and this redemption holds out to man and woman
the possibility of rediscovering something of the wonder and innocence of the first sexual encounter here and now, within the structures
of this world.

Irigaray is less hopeful about the potential of the existing social
order. She says, 'A revolution in thought and ethics is needed if the
work of sexual difference is to take place'.[34] Only through the disintegration of existing ideas of subjectivity might a new symbolic order
emerge capable of representing both sexes. This leads her to question
if Nietzsche's proclamation of the death of God and the philosophical
lapse into nihilism signals not an end but a parousia, the beginning of

---

31. Irigaray, 'The Power of Discourse and the Subordination of the Feminine', in
This Sex Which Is Not One, pp. 68-85, p. 69. (Italics in these and all quotes are as
given in the text).

32. John Paul II, *Original Unity*, p. 164.

33. John Paul II, *Original Unity*, p. 138.

34. Irigaray, 'Sexual Difference', p. 6.

a new age in which sexual difference would at last acquire its full significance. 'The third era of the West might, at last, be the era of the *couple*: of the spirit and the bride?'[35]

If woman is to be accorded subjective significance in the symbolic order, this will entail finding a way to incorporate woman's embodiment into language so as to create not one but two syntaxes shaped around masculinity and femininity. The Pope refers to masculinity and femininity as being based on 'two different "incarnations", that is, on two ways of "being a body..." '.[36] For Irigaray, full recognition of these two incarnations would radically affect the whole structure of language and meaning. Following Nietzsche, she sees a necessary connection between God and grammar, and therefore she argues that the development of a feminine syntax would also require a feminine God. 'Man is able to exist because God helps him to define his gender [*genre*], helps him orient his finiteness by reference to infinity.' By virtue of the fact that 'man has sought out a <u>unique *male* God</u>',[37] woman has no God to act as the limit to and fulfilment of her gender. 'If she is to become woman, if she is to accomplish her female subjectivity, woman needs a god who is a figure for the perfection of *her* subjectivity.'[38] Feminist theology has exposed the extent to which ideas of God have been dominated by male interpretations and the female imaging of God has been denied, but if Irigaray is correct then the task is far more extensive than merely introducing inclusive language into existing structures. One might even ask if a fully developed theology of the trinity is possible without theology itself being a nuptial venture, a sharing in the intellectual activity of interpreting the male and female experiences of God. The Pope's own understanding of the trinitarian dimension of the sexual encounter seems to imply such a conclusion. In suggesting the possibility of a new sexual order, Irigaray also envisions a trinitarian structure to the relationship between man, woman and God:

> Is it true that Christianity tells us that God is in three persons, three manifestations, and that the third stage of the manifestation occurs as *a wedding between the spirit and the bride*. Is this supposed to inaugurate the divine for, in, with women? The female?[39]

35. Irigaray, 'Love of the Other', in *An Ethics of Sexual Difference*, pp. 133-50 (p. 148).
36. John Paul II, *Original Unity*, p. 62.
37. Irigaray, 'Divine Women', in *Sexes and Genealogies*, 55-72 (p. 61).
38. Irigaray, 'Divine Women', p. 64.
39. Irigaray, 'Divine Women', p. 62.

Perhaps encoded within the Pope's reading of Genesis, there is a prophetic voice that hints at the process necessary for the emergence of
this third stage of the Christian story. The death of God and the death
of the male subject of Western discourse are closely related in post-
Nietzschean philosophy, and Irigaray sees this as creating the possibility for the articulation of the female in culture. In this respect, there
is a poetic resonance with the Pope's description of the creation of Eve.

Gen. 2.21-22 refers to Eve being created out of Adam's sleeping
body. Distinguishing between the Hebrew $h^alôm$, that is, 'dream',
which might lend certain Freudian sexual connotations to the creation
of Eve, and the deep sleep suggested by the word $tard\bar{e}m\bar{a}h$ used to
describe Adam's sleep, the Pope suggests an analogy with

> a specific return to non-being. . . , that is, to the moment preceding the
> creation, in order that, through God's creative initiative, solitary 'man'
> may emerge from it again in his double unity as male and female. . . In
> this way, the circle of the solitude of the man-person is broken, because
> the first 'man' awakens from his sleep as 'male and female'.[40]

Is it possible that Irigaray sees in the disintegration of meaning 'a
specific return to non-being' in the Western cultural order, in order to
allow for a new cultural creation? Might this constitute a deep sleep
from which the 'man' awakens as 'male and female'? With this in
mind, I now consider how Irigaray and John Paul II construe an ethical
encounter between the sexes. What is the 'redemptive' significance of
the relationship between man and woman?

Nuptial Fecundity and Regeneration

Although John Paul II recognizes the temptation to domination and
objectification that blights our fallen sexuality, he sees Christ's reference to the one flesh union of male and female 'in the beginning', as
signifying that the original knowledge of the meaning of embodiment,
sexuality and subjectivity has not been lost. It can be rediscovered
through the union of the husband and wife which perpetuates the image
of God in the creation of the child. Knowledge is therefore intimately
connected with sexuality and procreation, and this adds a new dimension of meaning to the association between sexual intercourse and
knowledge in biblical language. 'Adam knew Eve his wife, and she
conceived and bore. . . saying, "I have gotten a man with the help of

40. John Paul II, *Original Unity*, pp. 64-65; see pp. 67-68 nn. 2 and 3.

the Lord"' (Gen. 4.1). The offer of life that was forfeited with original sin is not withdrawn but 'restricted by the limit of conceptions, births and death'.[41]

> Awareness of the meaning of the body and awareness of its generative meaning come into contact, in man, with awareness of death, the inevitable horizon of which they bear within them, so to speak. Yet there always returns in the history of man the 'knowledge-generation' cycle, in which life struggles, ever anew, with the inexorable perspective of death, and always overcomes it.[42]

Fertile sexual love affords the means by which man and woman together gain insight into the nature of the human being made in the image of God and offered life in perpetuity, which is simultaneously lost through original sin and restored through the cycle of (sexual) knowledge and generation.

Irigaray has little patience with such a literal understanding of the purpose of procreation:

> That 'multiply' might not simply mean 'make children' for the Father, but rather create oneself and grow in the grace of fleshly fulfillment, is sheer blasphemy! That God might be engendered in love, in a fertility that goes beyond and falls short of actual procreation, is an interpretation that the priests of the Messiah still seem unable to hear or make known.[43]

For Irigaray, the oppressive structures of family life and procreation preclude any redemptive understanding of marriage and childbearing within the present social order. Women's sexual and maternal functions have been incorporated into the male economy in a way that obliterates the subjective identity of the woman and reduces her to an object of exchange among men, a commodity valued only for her role in the perpetuation of patriarchy.[44]

When Irigaray explores the relationship between sexuality and fecundity she does so symbolically, seeking to suggest the conditions necessary for the creation of a new symbolic order capable of bringing to birth the fullness of sexual humanity. The third term generated in the sexual encounter is not the child, but an openness to life that is variously described in terms of desire, transcendence, divinity and mediation.

41. John Paul II, *Original Unity*, p. 165.
42. John Paul II, *Original Unity*, p. 167.
43. Irigaray, 'the crucified one', p. 170.
44. cf. Irigaray, 'Body Against Body: In Relation to the Mother', p. 18. See also 'Women on the Market', in *This Sex Which Is Not One*, pp. 170-91.

She speaks of 'a birth into a transcendence, that of the other, still in the world of the senses ("sensible"), still physical and carnal, and already spiritual'.[45] She uses the expression 'the sensible transcendental' to refer to the presence of divinity experienced through the body but also excessive to the material world. This excess is discovered in the encounter between sexual beings who are not assimilable to one another, and who always approach one another anew with a sense of wonder. The creative dimension of sexuality lies not just in reproduction but in the regeneration of culture:

> Sexual difference would constitute the horizon of worlds more fecund than any known to date—at least in the West—and without reducing fecundity to the reproduction of bodies and flesh. For loving partners this would be a fecundity of birth and regeneration, but also the production of a new age of thought, art, poetry, and language: the creation of a new *poetics*.[46]

Irigaray affirms the significance of mothering for women's identity, but she claims that womanhood and motherhood are conflated in such a way that women have no access to symbols of meaning and subjectivity outside the mothering role. She says:

> We also need to discover and declare that we are always mothers just by being women. We bring many things into the world apart from children, we give birth to many other things apart from children: love, desire, language, art, social things, political things, religious things, but this kind of creativity has been forbidden to us for centuries. We must take back this maternal creative dimension that is our birthright as women.[47]

At the same time, she argues that women also need to discover a language that allows them to articulate their identity beyond motherhood. A theme that runs through all her work is the need to avoid setting 'woman' up as mirror image to the existing order, and merely perpetuating that order in reverse. The storehouse of Western ideas about subjectivity and sexuality is a conceptual depository of men's making. If women are to find what authentically belongs to them, they will find it in the detritus and excess, in what men have rejected as inappropriate and superfluous to their social constructs, in the language of the Freudian unconscious and in the hidden layers of materiality and embodiment on which the Western order has been constructed. To quote her:

45. L. Irigaray, 'Wonder: A Reading of Descartes, *The Passions of the Soul*' in *An Ethics of Sexual Difference*, pp. 72-82 (p. 82).

46. Irigaray, 'Sexual Difference', p. 5.

47. Irigaray, 'Body Against Body: In Relation to the Mother', p. 18.

> The rejection, the exclusion of a female imaginary certainly puts woman in
> the position of experiencing herself only fragmentarily, in the little-
> structured margins of a dominant ideology, as waste, or excess, what is
> left of a mirror invested by the (masculine) 'subject' to reflect himself, to
> copy himself.[48]

The maternal dimension constitutes one such area of repression and
denial. Retrieving it is a necessary but not a sufficient condition for
the elaboration of a syntax and a culture that can give expression to
the reality of women's embodiment. With this in mind, I return to the
Pope's nuptial theology of the body in order to ask if it allows for a
genuinely liberating vision of an alternative sexual order. Is it capable
of expressing the mutual subjectivity of men and women, or does it
perpetuate the objectification of women and the eradication of sexual
difference?

The Body that Speaks her Desire: Woman as Theological Subject

From the perspective of women's embodiment, there are at least two
major flaws in the argument put forward in *Original Unity*. First, the
Pope pays insufficient attention to the fact that biblical references to
parenthood are post-lapsarian, apart from the call to 'multiply and fill
the earth' in Gen. 1.28. The fact that parenthood is only referred to
after the fall, including Eve's designation as 'mother of all the living',
necessitates a theology that accommodates the suffering and ambiva-
lence of parenthood, even while celebrating its joy and its love. If
motherhood symbolizes the promise of life, it also symbolizes the threat
of death for the mother and the inevitability of death for the child. (It
is an old truism that death is the only certainty in life.) For women,
fertility has the power to blight the joy of sex and therefore to disrupt
the nuptial relationship, whether through the infertile woman's longing
for children, or the fertile woman's dread of unwanted pregnancy. In
its identification of women's sexuality with maternity, the church is
perpetuating not only Eve's blessing but also her curse.

Secondly, John Paul II fails to recognize that his rich and liberating
vision of the mutual subjectivity of men and women as two incarnations calls into question the very possibility of an exclusively male
hierarchy generating a nuptial theology of the body. The relationship

48. Irigaray, 'This Sex Which Is Not One', in *This Sex Which Is Not One*,
pp. 23-33 (p. 30).

between experience and revelation, one of the foundations of feminist theology, finds cautious affirmation in the Pope's text. 'In the interpretation of the revelation about man, and especially about the body, we must, for understandable reasons, refer to experience, since corporeal man is perceived by us mainly by experience.'[49]

If this is the case, then the schema that the Pope sets out in *Original Unity* makes it essential that a theology of the body should include the full participation of women. Any interpretation of revelation derived from the significance of women's bodies must be done primarily by women themselves, and only derivatively by men. A woman might assent to the Pope's assertion that

> The constitution of the woman is different, as compared with the man; we know, in fact, today that it is different even in the deepest bio-physical determinants. It is manifested externally only to a certain extent, in the construction and form of her body.

But given this, one might ask on whose authority he surmises that

> Maternity manifests this constitution internally, as the particular potentiality of the female organism, which with creative peculiarity serves for the conception and begetting of the human being, with the help of man. 'Knowledge' conditions begetting.[50]

Implicit in the task the Pope sets himself by writing a nuptial theology of the body is a sense that he is not guilty of objectifying woman but is capable of representing her in all her embodied subjectivity. However, as a man drawing upon a theological and cultural tradition which has systematically and often violently silenced women, one wonders where he finds the resources to construct a theology of woman's embodiment. And if he lacks such resources, then his theology of the body is not nuptial but male. The woman in this scenario would not be 'constituted in the mystery of the image of God through her femininity',[51] but would rather be a projection of the image of man through his masculinity.[52] So how might a woman's contribution to a nuptial

---

49. John Paul II, *Original Unity*, p. 40.
50. John Paul II, *Original Unity*, p. 155-6.
51. John Paul II, *Original Unity*, p. 116.
52. This is not to deny that the Pope, at least prior to his papacy, appears to have made a genuine attempt to understand female sexuality. Referring to his 1960 treatise, *Love and Responsibility*, Carl Bernstein and Marco Politi write that it 'would cause a sensation in Church circles because no one had ever heard of a bishop dealing

theology of the body destabilize the Pope's theory?

It is helpful at this point to refer to the Pope's retrieval of Aquinas's theory of natural law in the encyclical letter, *Veritatis Splendor*. Rejecting any 'physicalism or biologism' which would treat the human body as 'a raw datum', the Pope argues instead for '*the unity of the human person*, whose rational soul is *per se et essentialiter* the form of his body'. He goes on, 'The person, by light of reason and the support of virtue, discovers in the body the anticipatory signs, the expression and the promise of the gift of self, in conformity with the wise plan of the Creator'.[53]

If Irigaray is right in arguing that women have an identity that is excessive to motherhood, there might be some way in which the natural law reveals the possible locus of such an identity. If, as the Pope suggests, the rational soul is the form of the body, perhaps woman's soul has a uniqueness of its own that is revealed through her non-maternal body and that might add new dimensions to the theological meaning of sexual embodiment. This would be an aspect of sexuality that is known only by the woman herself, and is therefore inaccessible to the man who knows her as a projection of his own sexuality. What is it about woman that man cannot know unless he knows her in the biblical sense, that is, in the sense of understanding and relating to her in terms of the naked sexuality that she reveals to him? Is it true to say that 'the mystery of femininity is manifest and revealed completely by means of motherhood?'[54] 'Has something been held in reserve within the silence of history in the feminine: an energy, a morphology, a growth and flourishing still to come from the female realm?'[55]

During a raucous conversation recently, I learned from my husband and sons that men leaving a pub after a snowfall sometimes write their names in the snow while urinating. Theology might not be as inviting a *tabula rasa* as a fresh snowfall, but this scenario seems to suggest an analogy with the way in which Augustine has signed his name to

in print with subjects like sexual excitement, unsatisfied wives who faked orgasms, or the fundamental importance of a man's making sure that his mate climaxed.' (Carl Bernstein and Marco Politi, *His Holiness: John Paul II and the Hidden History of Our Time* [New York: Doubleday, 1996], p. 82, referring to Karol Wojtyla, *Love and Responsibility* [San Francisco: Ignatius Press, 1993]).

53. John Paul II, *Veritatis Splendor* (London: Catholic Truth Society, 1993), p. 76 n. 48.

54. John Paul II, *Original Unity*, p. 155.

55. Irigaray, 'Sexual Difference', p. 19.

Christian ideas about sexuality. For Augustine, the association between sex and original sin can be demonstrated by the fact that the sex organs, unlike all the other organs of the body, are not controlled by the will. Considering various ways in which people and animals have control over their bodies, he says that

> man himself also may have once received from his lower members an obedience which he lost by his own disobedience. It would not have been difficult for God to fashion him in such a way that even what is now set in motion in his flesh only by lust should have been moved only by his will.[56]

Women's lust might not be more controllable than men's, but Augustine's phallic model is irrelevant for a theology of women's embodiment. The erect penis makes men's desire difficult to conceal, and no doubt has considerable power to focus the mind. The penis is a multi-purpose organ, and it is understandable that men concerned to know the mind of God by observation of their own bodies come to the conclusion that in physiological terms, sexual desire is inseparable from the capacity to procreate (which is not, of course, to say that men are only capable of procreative sex). But if the nuptial significance of the body entails close attention to the female body as well as the male, this requires a more nuanced interpretation of the function of pleasure and desire, particularly as far as the clitoris is concerned. The men of the church have never been shy about reading theological significance into women's bodies, and not just the breasts and the womb—Mary's hymen has also been made to bear intense theological meaning, particularly in debates about her virginity prior to, during and after childbirth. To attach symbolic meaning to the clitoris is quite faithful to tradition, although it might shock those who have only ever considered sex from a masculine perspective.

In what follows, I take seriously the Pope's theological understanding of the body as the privileged locus of revelation. I am not advocating a reductive biologism nor a naive celebration of sexuality that ignores the ethical and emotional quagmire that surrounds us as sexual beings. I am, however, suggesting that women and men are asymmetrical in their sexual embodiment—unknown and unknowable to the other except in a state of naked mutuality in which each is permitted to speak, to reveal, to name his or her loving desire, without any need to reduce it or assimilate it to that of the other.

56. Augustine, *City of God* (Harmondsworth: Penguin Books, 1981), p. 588.

In his analysis of female sexuality, Freud designated the clitoris as 'a little penis'[57] and said that childhood sexuality was masculine for girls as well as for boys. In order to become sexually mature, a woman must transfer her sexual sensitivity from the clitoris to the vagina. Ever since Freud, the clitoris has been a point of debate for psychoanalysts, Darwinians, feminists and others interested in the function and development of the female body, but it has yet to attract much theological attention.[58] Several studies of women's sexuality have challenged Freud's findings and suggested that the clitoris continues to be the primary locus of sexual stimulation and orgasm for women.[59]

The Pope interprets the purpose of women's sex organs as being uniquely designed for and fulfilled by the function of motherhood. 'The whole exterior constitution of woman's body. . . [is] in close union with motherhood.'[60] I do not want to deny the close relationship between a woman's sexual and maternal embodiment—a woman's breasts are sexual and maternal, her vagina is birth-canal and sex organ. However, the clitoris invites the woman to a non-maternal understanding of desire, and suggests that her sexuality is not reducible to maternity. This is an organ created purely for a woman's delight, mercifully protected from the wounds of childbirth. Susan Ross says, 'Unlike the penis, the clitoris has one function only: exquisite female sexual pleasure'.[61] What does it say to the woman who recognizes in her own embodiment 'the anticipatory signs, the expression and the promise of the gift

57. Cf. Sigmund Freud, 'The Sexual Theories of Children', in *On Sexuality: Three Theories on the Theory of Sexuality and Other Works* (Harmondsworth: Penguin Books, 1991), pp. 187-204 (p. 195).

58. Two recent essays that explore the theological significance of the clitoris and the female orgasm are Mary D. Pellauer, 'The Moral Significance of Female Orgasm' in James B. Nelson and Sandra P. Longfellow (eds.), *Sexuality and the Sacred: Sources for Theological Reflection* (Louisville: Westminster/John Knox Press, 1994), pp. 149-68, and Susan A. Ross, 'Extravagant Affections: Women's Sexuality and Theological Anthropology', in Ann O'Hara Graff (ed.), *In the Embrace of God: Feminist Approaches to Theological Anthropology* (Maryknoll: Orbis Books, 1995), pp. 105-21.

59. Cf. Shere Hite, *The Hite Report* (London: Talmy Franklin, 1977), pp. 99-107; Alfred C. Kinsey *et al.*, *Sexual Behaviour in the Human Female* (Philadelphia and London: W.B. Saunders Co., 1953), pp. 582-84; June M. Reinisch and Ruth Beasley, *The Kinsey Institute New Report on Sex: What You Must Know to be Sexually Literate* (London: Penguin Books, 1990), pp. 201-203.

60. John Paul II, *Original Unity*, p. 157.

61. Ross, 'Extravagant Affections', p. 114.

of self?'[62] Does it represent the vestige of her original innocence, her capacity to experience virginal desire that is free from penetration and the reproductive function, affirmation that the original purpose of Eve's existence as woman is still good in the eyes of God beyond the blessing and curse of motherhood? For the man who has the patience to know her, it offers a new insight into the meaning and purpose of sexuality that he cannot learn from his own body. For him, orgasm and the means of fertilization are physically inseparable. For her, there is a more complex relationship between orgasm, sexual intercourse and conception. Unlike the man, she can reproduce without orgasm, and her orgasm has no reproductive function. The clitoris symbolizes this otherness and difference, woman's *jouissance*,[63] that requires its own language. To quote Gayatri Spivak:

> Male and female sexuality are asymmetrical. Male orgasmic pleasure 'normally' entails the male reproductive act—semination. Female orgasmic pleasure (it is not, of course, the 'same' pleasure, only called by the same name) does not entail any one component of the heterogeneous female reproductive scenario: ovulation, fertilization, conception, gestation, birthing. The clitoris escapes reproductive framing.[64]

The gift that woman discovers within her own body and might offer to man, irrespective of motherhood, is that of her gratuitous pleasure that escapes all functional explanations. Moreover, the clitoris signifies the disruption of men's exploitation of women's bodies. Contrary to centuries of Catholic teaching, it whispers to woman that God smiles on her autoeroticism, if she dares to attend to that quiet whisper through the din of the church's prohibition. If a woman decides to share her clitoral sexuality with a man, she offers him nothing apart from some share in her pleasure, and if he is to know this pleasure of pleasuring her, his approach to sex must consist of generosity and loving attentiveness. One woman describes what this means for her:

> That my pleasure was important to him, this was hard to accept, to let in. That he would refuse his own release till I had mine, that he was willing

62. John Paul II, *Veritatis Splendor*, p. 76 n. 48.

63. The word 'jouissance', which features frequently in Irigaray's work, is difficult to translate. It refers to a quality of embodied delight that has sexual connotations, but implies an abundance that cannot be reduced to genitality.

64. Gayatri Chakravorty Spivak, 'French Feminism in an International Frame', in *In Other Worlds: Essays in Cultural Politics* (New York and London: Methuen, 1987), pp. 134-53 (p. 151).

to persist in trying to bring my release/ecstasy, that he reveled in it: this shook me very deeply. It was so very unexpected. My surprise about this says more about me than it does about him. I did not expect to be loved. I did not expect him to have the capacity to put me before himself. I expected only to be secondary.[65]

The theological 'discovery' of the clitoris might lead to a new appreciation of non-reproductive sexual pleasure as part of the goodness of creation. It would be enough simply to construe this in terms of a more positive attitude towards sex, but if the phallus can symbolize a culture of domination, aggression and power, the clitoris might even symbolize a culture that celebrates playfulness and nurtures small delights in the loving and patient encounters of daily life. If this seems to overstate the symbolic power of the body, perhaps we should ask why so many women in the world suffer from physical or psychological clitoridectomy.[66] If women's sexual pleasure were not profoundly subversive of men's need to dominate, it is hard to understand why so much energy has been devoted to its cultural and physical eradication.

Irigaray suggests that woman's embodiment provides the clue for a new 'morphology', a new language in which the pluriformity of the female subject might be constructed in a way that is neither dependent upon nor reflective of the phallic subject of Western discourse. She says,

> As for woman, she touches herself in and of herself without any need for mediation, and before there is any way to distinguish activity from passivity. Woman 'touches herself' all the time, and moreover no one can forbid her to do so, for her genitals are formed of two lips in continuous contact. Thus, within herself, she is already two—but not divisible into one(s)—that caress each other.[67]

---

65. Pellauer, 'The Moral Significance of Female Orgasm', p. 157. In a footnote which explains her use of male pronouns rather than inclusive language in this passage, Pellauer invites the reader to try substituting these with female pronouns. She suggests that this changes the moral structure of the argument, and says, 'His maleness was the fundamental reason that I expected to be secondary in our sexual relationship' (p. 167 n. 27).

66. The term 'female circumcision' seems to perpetuate the mirror-imaging of male and female sexuality in a particularly cruel way. Whatever the demerits of male circumcision, only if something goes catastrophically wrong does it blight a man's sexuality in the way that infibulation and clitoridectomy are intentionally used to destroy a woman's capacity for sexual pleasure.

67. Irigaray, 'This Sex Which Is Not One', p. 24.

The foregoing makes no claim to be a developed theology of women's embodiment, but rather constitutes a gesture in the direction of a path that has yet to be explored. The Pope's theology of the body is a remarkable contribution to Catholic teaching, but it is still the product of a church that accords man the right to speak on behalf of all humanity, and therefore it denies the Pope's own fundamental insight about the nature of the mutual subjectivity and reciprocal knowledge of man and woman.

In my concluding section, I want to draw together some of the questions that arise out of this encounter between Irigaray and John Paul II.

An Open-Ended Beginning

Irigaray's philosophy constitutes a sustained critique of the disembodied metaphysics of Western thought, and some of her most stringent criticisms are levelled against theology in general and the Catholic Church in particular. The last chapter of *Marine Lover*, entitled 'the crucified one—epistle to the last christians', is a lyrical and moving dialectic between the Nietzschean critique of Christianity and the potential of an incarnational theology. But Irigaray's work is itself located in the symbolic topography of postmodernist philosophy and Lacanian psychoanalysis. She subverts this world from within by pitting symbol against symbol, idea against idea, but is she trapped within the disembodied discourse that she seeks to escape?

In Irigaray's exploration of the sexual encounter, biological fertility, sex and procreation are displaced to make way for a disembodied ideal to do with culture, language and divinity.

> Sexual difference represents one of the great hopes for the future. It is not to be found in reproduction (whether natural or artificial) but in the access the two sexes have to culture. Childbearing is just one effect of this.[68]

She lifts the symbolism of Catholicism out of its 'embodied' context of lived belief and practice in order to bring it into play with other systems of language and belief, but in the process she is perhaps at risk of setting up a disincarnate discourse in place of incarnational theology. In her philosophy, the idealized symbols of sexual difference take the place of men and women grappling with the painful realities of embodied living. In articulating her vision of a potentially better order, she appeals to the symbols of Greek mythology and to those of Catholic

68. Irigaray, *Sexes and Genealogies*, p. vi.

Christianity. She acknowledges that although there is much to learn from mythology, it cannot be recaptured as part of the lived reality of modern life,[69] but the symbols of the Catholic faith constitute the spiritual dynamism of a living tradition. However justified Irigaray is in her criticism of the institutional church, the question remains: if the church had not been so diligent in her vocation, would the symbols of Christ, Mary, the Spirit and the Bride that Irigaray engages with so creatively be available to her at all? She criticizes Christianity for what she sees as its over-emphasis on sacrifice, but in her near-wholesale rejection of social institutions such as marriage, the family and the church, she herself risks sacrificing living worlds of value, joy and sexual love on the altar of a vision that she acknowledges is precarious and possibly unattainable.[70]

For all its emphasis on sin, Catholicism has consistently affirmed the goodness of the created world. Embodied within the present sinful reality of our human relationships there are signs of grace making possible authentic loving communion between persons. These are the signs that the Pope is looking for in his vision of redemptive sexuality. However, he risks impoverishing the symbolism of the church by identifying it too closely with the social institutions of marriage and the family. When the writers of the New Testament speak of marriage, they are referring first and foremost to the relationship between Christ and the church (cf. Eph. 5.32, Rev. 21.2). Perhaps it is not coincidental that the increasing glorification of marriage and motherhood has come at a time of the increasing demystification of the nuptial and maternal symbolism of the Church. The third party in marriage is not the child but God, and in this, perhaps, Irigaray alludes to a forgotten truth of the Catholic faith. If she is wrong to reduce the significance of sexual intercourse primarily to a play of symbols, the Pope is surely no less wrong to reduce it to its reproductive function. Somewhere, between these two visionaries, there is a conception yet to be achieved.

69. Cf. Irigaray, 'Divine Women', p. 60.

70. Julia Kristeva warns of the risks inherent in radical feminism (with, I think, an implicit reference to Irigaray), in her essay 'Women's Time'. She speaks of 'a revolt which they see as a resurrection but which society as a whole understands as murder. This attempt can lead us to a not less and sometimes more deadly violence. Or to a cultural innovation. Probably to both at once. But that is precisely where the stakes are, and they are of epochal significance' (Julia Kristeva, 'Women's Time' in Toril Moi (ed.), *The Kristeva Reader* [Oxford: Basil Blackwell, 1986], pp. 187-213 [p. 200]).

I would suggest that in any theoretical coupling of Irigaray and John Paul II, it would be the Pope who would provide the carnal love and Irigaray who would provide the spiritual imagination.

In the process of reading and engaging with these two thinkers, one glimpses a dramatic enactment of the rupture in sexual knowledge to which the Pope refers. Irigaray speaks from the margins, neither defined by nor free of the system that the Pope represents. Her voice is dislocated, subversive, fluid in relationship to the boundaries of faith. More effectively than the sober analyses of feminist theology, her wayward faith puts into play the ambiguities and tensions as well as the possibilities and promises that the Catholic church symbolizes for women today. The Pope speaks out of a world that for him already exists, because he belongs within the male community of interpretation. Irigaray speaks out a world that for her might come into being, if women's voices begin to be heard. Then perhaps the two of them might come together, in a joyful celebration of sexual difference.

Could Irigaray's voice ever find expression within the doctrinal framework of Catholic belief? To say that Catholicism has no place for the woman's voice would be wrong. Woman speaks from the no-man's land that borders the church. It is the space where theological language breaks down and speaks the language of the mystic and sometimes of the heretic.[71] But this does not represent the community of equals hinted at in the Gospels and described in the Pope's theology of the body. If Irigaray is Catholic woman to John Paul II's Catholic man, then within the limited symbols available she would have to be seen as an Eve-figure rather than a Mary-figure. She tempts with a strange form of knowledge. She invites the man out of his solitude to a new experience of life that must also risk death. She suggests that we have nothing to lose—we have already fallen so far. Yet she also uses the symbols of Christian redemption to describe her hope and her vision. This is why ultimately I believe her voice does not seduce the Church into death so much as whisper its potential for life. Wisdom has always spoken with a woman's voice. Do the men of the church dare to discover the wisdom that rests between the lips of women?[72]

---

71. For Irigaray's extensive play on the idea of the mystic as mimic, see 'La mystérique', in *Speculum of the Other Woman* (New York: Cornell University Press, 1985), pp. 191-202.

72. I am grateful to friends and colleagues who have read and commented on drafts of this chapter. This does not implicate them in its indiscretions.

SEX IN HEAVEN:
THE QUEERING OF THEOLOGICAL DISCOURSE ON SEXUALITY

Elizabeth Stuart

Sitting on the Fence

> Sitting on a fence can be an exciting pastime. Perched, half in comfort and half scared you'll tip over, not quite sure which way to look, but with unique vantage points, it has a lot going for it. Precarious yet creatively safe. But fence-sitting suffers a bad reputation—if you don't take sides you're accused of woolly mindedness. . . For me it affords time for listening, time for exploration, time for letting something unwind and reveal more than is there at first sight. It gives space for uncertainty.[1]

Like the lesbian feminist writer Sue O'Sullivan there are times when I want to sit on the fence rather than sell my soul to a particular theory. Postmodernism is a case in point. There is much within it that 'rings true' to me, particularly in matters of religion and sexuality, as this paper will demonstrate. But postmodernism also carries the seeds of its own destruction. Like a wooden idol, its cracks have become increasingly obvious over time. It is rent asunder by its inbuilt irony. For, as has often been remarked upon, the narrative that proclaims the end of the metanarrative is itself a metanarrative. The system that collapses transcendence into the 'reality' of the localized and contextual offers an objective, universal diagnosis of the human condition, while being itself severely localized amongst the first world intelligentsia. Whilst proclaiming liberty to those of us, including women and gay men, who have been held in bondage by the autonomous self and hegemonic discourse, it dissolves the universal of freedom and emancipation and leaves room for groups to claim that their contextual, local knowledge includes the oppression or marginalization of particular groups of people.

1. Sue O'Sullivan, *I Used to be Nice: Sexual Affairs* (London: Cassell, 1996), p. 112.

So, like many feminist theologians, I choose to sit on the fence, 'playing' with postmodernism as it encourages us to 'play' with other metanarratives, using it as a tool to make sense of the current Western preoccupation with 'homosexuality', recognizing with Rebecca Chopp that the disruption that postmodernism wreaks upon the dominant discourses of Christian theology has a family resemblance with the disruptive behaviour of the Holy Spirit in the Christian tradition that gives to the silenced or unheard the power to speak.[2] But since postmodernism sows the seeds of its own destruction I do not wish to dive headlong into it. It has done a good job in deconstructing oppressive universals but it is apt to leave us sitting among the ruins talking to ourselves, unable even to imagine how to carry on. With Sharon Welch I want to suggest that at the moment the only ethical strategy in the face of postmodernist deconstruction is solidarity. Unlike her, however, I want, from a lesbian feminist perspective, to reclaim eschatological vision and utopian dreams as a method for both subverting current theological discourse on sexuality and creating a surface upon which a tapestry of common value might be built.[3]

Diagnosing the Disruption

The issue of 'homosexuality' appears to preoccupy almost every mainstream Christian denomination in the West as the twentieth century draws to a close. Yet it is a preoccupation caught in the quicksand of complete stalemate and despair. The issue is not resolved but endlessly debated, a debate that is now overlaid with rigorous condemnations of homophobia from all sides. This stalemate is at least in part the result of the interaction of liberal theology with the post-enlightenment sexualization of the human self, represented most clearly in the work of Freud, and the resulting social construction of the pathological homosexual suffering from displaced 'normal' (that is heterosexual) desire. People who found themselves 'created' out of this classification used it both to develop a sense of self and a defined community through which they were able to challenge the pathological construction of their sexuality and present themselves to society as a distinct social and

2. Rebecca Chopp, *The Power to Speak: Feminism, Language, God* (New York: Crossroad, 1989).
3. Sharon D. Welch, *A Feminist Ethic of Risk* (Minneapolis: Fortress Press, 1990).

cultural minority. The creation of the homosexual, indeed the creation of sexual personhood, created a fissure within Western theological discourse that had precious few resources to draw upon in the face of a new anthropology that centralized sexual desire and held it in positive terms. The response from Christian theology was threefold. First, to partially accept the new anthropology, that is, to affirm that sexuality is at the heart of our personhood, but with the caveat that it is hetero-sexual sexuality that is given to humanity in the grace of creation: aberrations from this are the result of deliberate perversion that must be condemned. This view was bolstered by the unprecedented biblical literalism that took hold in the modern era. Secondly, liberal theology, having surrendered the right to describe and analyse the world and humanity to science, bought into the new anthropology more deeply but still partially, affirming that sexuality is at the heart of our personhood and also accepting the post-Stonewall[4] claim that homo-sexuality is not a pathological condition, while at the same time main-taining that it falls short of the ideal of heterosexuality that Scripture, tradition and natural law demonstrate to be God's normative will. Lesbian and gay people, therefore, while not being responsible for their inadequacy, must acknowledge it, either (in the most generous option) by recognizing that any intimate relationships they have could never live up to a heterosexual marriage or by refraining from sexual relations altogether.[5] The third approach is adopted by people whom the lesbian theologian Alison Webster has labelled 'pseudo-radicals':[6] people (generally, it has to be said, heterosexual men) who buy most heavily of all into the new anthropology and upon this basis declare the equality of heterosexuality and homosexuality and argue that there-fore lesbian and gay people should be welcomed into the previously heterosexual institutions of marriage, family and clergy.[7] Webster

4. The Stonewall Riots that took place in New York in June 1969 have become the symbol of the birth of the lesbian and gay community, namely the point at which lesbian and gay people began to become subjects rather than objects of history and claim the right to interpret their own experience.

5. The clearest example of this line of argument in recent times is found in the House of Bishops of the General Synod of the Church of England, *Issues in Human Sexuality* (London: Church House Publishing, 1991).

6. Alison Webster, *Found Wanting: Women, Christianity and Sexuality* (London: Cassell, 1995), p. 13.

7. Among contemporary theologians taking this stance are Adrian Thatcher, *Liberating Sex: A Christian Sexual Theology* (London: SPCK) and J.S. Spong,

calls these people 'pseudo-radicals' because, while they go further than most in the churches are currently prepared to go in affirming the equality of lesbian and gay people and their relationships, at exactly the same time they are affirming heterosexual normativity. For the prize that lesbian and gay people win is heterosexuality, incorporation into its already existing systems and they win this prize by behaving heterosexually, by mirroring heterosexual relations and aspiring to heterosexual dreams. Pseudo-radicals have no interest in non-monogamous, flamboyant, lesbian, gay and bisexual people.

The debate about homosexuality in the churches is so stale and repetitious because it is not really about homosexuality. It is about heterosexuality and how far the mantle of heterosexuality can be flung—what are its borders? Certainly, homosexuality triggered the debate, but discussion of lesbian and gay lives masks what is actually going, namely the assumption and preservation of heterosexual normativity, by inclusion rather than exclusion. This is why it is homophobia—irrational fear of homosexual persons—that is named as the sin in theological discourse and not heterosexism—the assumption of heterosexual superiority. Hence, church leaders can constantly condemn homophobia while supporting or condoning legislation that discriminates against lesbian and gay people and do absolutely nothing about the violence, discrimination and marginalization lesbian and gay people encounter inside and outside the churches. The fissure that opened up in theological discourse as a result of the sexualizing of personhood initially caused only minimal disruption, although that disruption was of course painful and taxing, but it resulted in the shoring up of theo-patriarchal gender constructions as the foundations of heterosexuality, or, as it is represented in current hierarchical discourse on sexuality, 'complementarity'.

However, there are signs, rumblings, jerks on the theological seismograph, that a much greater disruption/eruption is on its way and the cause and source is the lesbian and gay voice. One of the features of the most recent ecclesiastical statements on sexuality (with the exception of Roman Catholic documents) is the professed desire to listen to the 'queer'[8] voice. Lesbian and gay people are invited to fill in question-

Living in Sin: A Bishop Rethinks Human Sexuality (San Francisco: Harper & Row, 1988).

8.   Unless otherwise stated I use 'queer' as a self-designated shorthand for lesbian, gay, bisexual and transsexual persons.

naires, appear before panels, come to tea. Usually hand-picked, these lesbian and gay people give a 'package holiday' insight into lesbian and gay lives. As Charles Winquist has noted, when we go on package holidays we know that, although we may be exposed to challenging, perhaps even terrifying difference during the day, we can retreat to comfortable, secure and familiar surroundings at night. We remain safe. He points out that we often desire the same of philosophy and theology, that they have 'made all of the arrangements for meaning prior to [their] thinking the world'.[9] This is particularly obvious in the conscious or unconscious clinging to heterosexual normativity in the three chief responses to the creation of the homosexual person, set out above, but it is also evident in the packaging of lesbian and gay experience. It is a taste of the difference in the context of ultimate safety; the lesbian and gay people—often chosen for their ability to look and sound 'just like us'—go home. Winquist goes on to note that 'the problem with strategies of containment to ordinariness is that the world remains ordinary. The price of safety is a loss of interest and intensity. This price ironically endangers the system because in its extreme realization we lose interest in the system.'[10] Anthony Giddens has argued that the rigid and routinized ordering of sexual relations under hetero-patriarchy has effectively exiled passion by containing it within the privatized sexual realm: 'yet who can live without passion, if we see it as the motive-power of conviction'?[11] It can be no accident that many of those who now seek to recentre passion (encompassing but also reaching far wider than the sexual realm) at the centre of theological discourse and practice, and who also recognize within it a wild and warm divine presence, are lesbian theologians.[12]

If Monique Wittig is right that lesbians are the greatest threat to the 'straight mind' because we subvert the content of the signifier 'woman' by being women unrelated to men, then it is to be expected that the

    9.   Charles E. Winquist, *Desiring Theology* (Chicago and London: University of Chicago Press, 1995), p. 11.

    10. Winquist, *Desiring Theology*, p. 11.

    11. Anthony Giddens, *The Transformation of Intimacy: Sexuality, Love and Eroticism in Modern Societies* (Cambridge: Polity Press, 1992), pp. 210-12.

    12. See Carter Heyward, *Our Passion for Justice: Images of Power, Sexuality and Liberation* (New York: The Pilgrim Press, 1984) and *Touching Our Strength: The Erotic as Power and Love of God* (San Francisco: Harper & Row, 1989) and Elizabeth Stuart, *Just Good Friends: Towards a Lesbian and Gay Theology of Relationships* (London: Mowbray, 1995).

most disruptive, challenging and frightening theology should erupt from that quarter.[13] And erupting it is. Lesbian theology and gay theology is beginning to disrupt the theological surface, a minor literature disrupting the dominant discourse. These are voices of frustration but also voices of play and creativity. The frustration arises out of the inability of our experience to fit into the theo-heterosexual system, despite the best efforts of well-meaning heterosexuals who seek to adopt us into it. The play and creativity comes from the recognition that it is a system and not a divinely created 'reality', that it is possible not to escape it but to subvert and transform it through 'play', by taking theological language and images and conjuring up new meanings and significance that are true to our own experience of life. In my work I have sought to do this with the concept of friendship, using it as a paradigm for sexual relationships. If this is perceived by others to contain within it the threat to end life as they know it, they may be right. Winquist has identified as a characteristic of a system under terminal attack a defence strategy based upon 'a debilitating smallness'.[14] This smallness is evident in the current ecclesiastical debates upon sexuality, which generally take no consideration whatsoever of women's experience, of diversity within heterosexual or homosexual experience, of bisexuality or of violence and abuse. In particular, there is no examination or even acknowledgement of heterosexuality as a construction. To use an image beloved of feminist theologians, we are weaving ourselves into the rich texture of theological discourse and in that weaving we may unravel other threads, creating holes that will only be mended by a different pattern of weave.

Lesbian and gay people queer the pitch on which the dominant theological discourse on sexuality has been built. Thanks to Foucault and others we are now aware of ourselves as socially constructed beings. In recognizing and embracing this historical reality (though not all of us do) we unglue what the lesbian poet Caroline Claxton has called the 'sticky, sticky lies'[15] about heterosexual normativity and the divinely ordered world of sexual relations. We make up a subculture in Europe and North America, created largely in response to the emergence of

13. Monique Wittig, *The Straight Mind and Other Essays* (Boston: Beacon Press, 1992).

14. Winquist, *Desiring Theology*, p. 11.

15. Caroline Claxton, 'Lesbian' in Christine McEwan (ed.) *Naming the Waves: Contemporary Lesbian Poetry* (London: Virago Press, 1988), p. 31.

modern heterosexuality, the latter characterized by its 'debilitating smallness', its narrowing and domesticating of passion and affection to the family, and its construction of maleness and femaleness in terms that lock both into diminishing and restrictive roles.[16]

One postmodern insight is that 'it is the culture that contains the most comprehensive available truth at any one time and place, and the culture is the creative matrix par excellence in which advance is possible, and since this is equally true at the religio-moral dimension, all theology must be of and for the culture in the first instance'.[17] Adding to this a postmodern understanding of the incarnation as the embeddedness of the word in a signifying play enables lesbian and gay theologians to find a voice through which to play in the theological field and nurture theologies that bear strong family resemblances to the dominant theological discourses in the language and rootedness of their God-talk, but which also deconstruct those dominant discourses to reveal their cultural embeddedness.

Lesbian and gay theology also ruptures the texture of ecclesiastical discourse in another way—by destabilizing the notion of 'Christian'. The recent failed attempt to try the retired Episcopalian bishop, William Righter, for heresy for ordaining an openly gay man demonstrates the extent to which sexual orthodoxy has become linked in most churches to theological orthodoxy and the notion of what constitutes a Christian has been destabilized by the outbreak of different theological tongues in recent years. Alison Webster brings queer theory to bear on this issue. She uses Judith Butler's analysis of gender and sexual identity to queer—that is, 'disrupt what is otherwise considered to be. . . self-evident and natural'—not simply the realm of sexuality and gender but the 'doctrine-belief-expression' triad of Christianity. Just as Butler understands gender and sexual orientation in terms of performance, so Webster wants to argue that Christian faith is no longer something you have but something you perform and create.

> Or, to put it another way. . . how and where will I 'play' at 'being Christian'? As [Butler] might have written, 'To say I "play" at being Christian is not to say that I am not one "really"; rather, how and where I

16. For an excellent account of this process (but from a purely male perspective), see Michael Vasey, *Strangers and Friends: A New Exploration of Homosexuality and the Bible* (London: Hodder & Stoughton, 1995), pp. 69-113.

17. James P. Mackey, 'Christianity and Cultures: Theology, Science and the Science of Religion', *Studies in World Christianity*, 2.1 (1996), p. 18.

play at being one is the way in which the "being" gets established, instituted, circulated and confirmed. . . it is through repeated play of this
religious identity that the "I" is insistently reconstituted as the Christian
"I".'. . . These possibilities for religious agency bring with them,
however, questions of accountability. What kind of Christian 'I' do I
want to constitute and reconstitute through accountability.[18]

Christianity therefore becomes a matter of orthopraxis rather than
orthodoxy because orthodoxy has been exposed as historically and
culturally conditioned. How are we to perform Christianity in a postmodern world, in a way that honours our recognition of cultural
diversity, of theological construction and sexual diversity? How is it
possible to be a Christian in a context which recognizes that Christianity
is in fact a bunch of Christianities, a sexual Christianity in a context
that recognizes homosexualities and heterosexualities? How dare we
speak at all? A clear answer to these questions has yet to emerge,
largely because so many are still clinging to the old metanarratives of
Christianity and sexuality.

Sharon Welch has produced a postmodernist feminist theo-ethic of
risk that seems to me both to honour the diagnosis of postmodernism
and to ground itself in the language and imagery of Christianity. Welch
rejects any notion of absolute truth or a theistic God who guarantees it
on the grounds that these concepts simply legitimate the quest for absolute power. She also rejects the quest for universal consensus because
it too is in reality a 'continuation of the dream of domination'.[19] What
we need, rather, is a quest for solidarity, a willingness to listen to the
voices of otherseven when agreement cannot be reached. Solidarity is
born out of 'dangerous memories', a concept that Welch receives from
liberation theology. These are memories that include the 'history of
salvation' of conflict, hope, freedom and resistance. These memories,
which to some degree make up the deposit of faith inherited by every
Christian, challenge all of us to 'take a stand' with those who perform
those memories in acts of resistance and solidarity. Memories of oppression and resistance spark together and ignite a fire of resistance and
solidarity and they also give rise to a new kind of power, an empowerment that is based not upon competition or domination but upon
solidarity—which is embracing of others, healing and uniting. It is

18. Alison Webster, 'Queer to be Religious: Lesbian Adventures Beyond the
Christian/Post-Christian Dichotomy', unpublished address given at Lancaster
University, 13 March 1996, p. 7.
19. Welch, *A Feminist Ethic of Risk*, p. 133.

experienced when people take the risk of acting in community, in solidarity, even though they may make mistakes. Nihilism and despair may
be the ultimate reality, but they choose to act as if they were not. The
great grace of realizing the non-existence of absolute truth is that it is
possible to risk making mistakes, you just learn from them and carry on.

The ethic of risk is made up of three elements: grounding in community, strategic risk-taking and responsible action. Responsible action
is creative action, it keeps the ball rolling towards a desired goal by
making further action possible, even if the goal may be out of sight and
ultimately unobtainable. It is responsible because it is done in community and in solidarity, including the transfer of power from the powerful to the powerless. This theo-ethic of risk is being carried out amongst
communities of lesbian, gay and feminist theologians, black and Asian
theologians, disabled theologians and all those doing theology from the
underside of the tradition. They take the risk of appropriating the
dangerous memories of their faith history. For lesbian and gay theology
such stories as those of the Exodus or of Jesus' subversion of the family
and its replacement by friendship, resonate with recent memories, such
as the Stonewall Riots and the resistance of Greenham Common, and
inspire the risk of doing theology out of our diverse experience. They
are also learning the necessity of solidarity, of building coalitions theologically and practically, of learning from one another. And it is no
accident that it is lesbian theologians who have been at the forefront of
theologizing around this ethic of risk, developing what I have called
'theologies of humility' and Carter Heyward has called 'not knowing
for sure'.[20] Humility is, of course, a Christian virtue, but it has been
grossly disordered by hetero-patriarchal theologizing into an intro-
verted, self-obsessed attempt to be non-self-obsessed. As Heyward has
pointed out, such an approach assumes a radical disconnection between
oneself and others and God. It presumes, 'that if I am for myself, I
cannot be for you; that if we are for ourselves, we cannot be for others;
and that if we are for one another, as human and creaturely sisters and
brothers, we cannot be for God'.[21] Yet as Micah (6.8) knew, and those
doing theology from the underside have discovered, being for God
necessarily involves being for ourselves and one another. Humility is
then fundamentally relational because it involves experiencing ourselves

20. Carter Heyward, *Staying Power: Reflections on Gender, Justice and
Compassion* (Cleveland: Pilgrim Press, 1995), pp. 3-11.
    21. Heyward, *Staying Power*, p. 7.

as related, as bonded in solidarity with one another. Therefore humility will be grounded in mutual exchange and willingness to be changed but also the willingness to wrestle and struggle with one another.

There are two sides to theological humility. One is the recognition that 'we never know for sure', we may be wrong, we will sometimes be wrong. The recognition that there is no certainty in the realm of theology, that we play with metaphors, analogies, words, music to capture something of the elusive presence of the divine whose shadows may fall across our experience, creates a space (provided everyone is willing to take part in this recognition) for genuine openness and mutual encounter. The other side of humility is a confidence, a delight in a theology that rings true with the community of resistance from which it springs, it is faith in the deepest and most intense sense of that word, a risking of commitment and confidence in the face of the real prospect of misguidance and wrongness. It is only in the context of a theology of humility that ethics, sexual or otherwise, is possible. For, as Philip Davies has pointed out, to be obedient to Bible, or church, is not to act ethically, for it can lead to non-ethical acts. In a post-Holocaust, post-Bosnia world, we no longer accept the 'excuse' that 'I was only following orders' as an ethical justification. Interestingly, from the point of view of homosexuality, Davies believes that the book of Leviticus 'represents the values of that least ethical community, the totalitarian state'.[22] To act ethically requires moral autonomy and discernment, neither of which the churches are very ready to concede to gay and lesbian persons, but which they are claiming for themselves. It also requires, as is clear in the narratives of the Jesus-event, active solidarity. Having explored something of the nature of the 'problem' of homosexuality within Christianity I want to go on in the spirit of humility just described to do some theology from a lesbian and gay perspective.

Sex in Heaven

Whatever happened to life after death? Christian theologies (with one or two notable exceptions, such as Moltmann) certainly in our culture have ceased to talk about 'life after', either life after death or life after the coming of the kingdom. Liberal theology, with its slavish addiction

22. Philip R. Davies, 'Ethics and the Old Testament', in John W. Rogerson, Margaret Davies and M. Daniel Carrol R. (eds.), *The Bible in Ethics: The Second Sheffield Colloquium* (Sheffield: Sheffield Academic Press, 1995), p. 170.

to the rational and great forgetting of the metaphorical, analogical and symbolic nature of all theological language, and still stinging from the Marxist exposure of the oppressive use of 'pie in the sky when you die' theology, tends to avoid the issue altogether or employs the vaguest and most useless of terms. (A classic example of this is the recent Church of England report, *The Mystery of Salvation*, in which the final chapter, 'Ending the Story', which is about life after death, is the shortest in the report and contains only the vaguest and therefore distinctly unattractive vision of what it will be like.[23]) This is deeply ironic considering the fact that one of the most important theological remembrances of this century has been that Christian theology must begin in eschatology. Yet even among those who have been at the fore-front of driving this point home, liberation theologians, for all their important theologizing around hope and utopia, have never really fleshed out that hope into a textured, colourful picture. We are embarrassed to talk about the future because, since Schleiermacher, theologians have told us that it is impossible and therefore pointless for finite minds to reach beyond finitude. Rationalism, as Dennis Nineham noted as far back as 1977, has starved our theological brains of imagination.[24] Just as the church signed away its anthropological rights to science in the wake of the Enlightenment, so it handed over its rights over death. Death became a natural bodily function to be dispensed with and got over as quickly, hygienically and unemotionally as possible and the Church was recruited to be part of that process. Also gone are the poetic speculations about life in the kingdom. It has to be said that this is not a gaping hole that the new theologies have rushed to fill. On the contrary, feminist theology has identified concern with immortality as male-gendered and responsible for the perpetuation of dualism and the independent, autonomous self, resulting in injustice and ecological apathy. Women, they claim, are generally more concerned with creating right relationships in this life and ensuring that those who come after will be able to live well and this is how it should be.[25] Similarly,

23. The Doctrine Commission of the Church of England, *The Mystery of Salvation: The Story of God's Gift* (London: Church House Publishing, 1995).

24. Dennis Nineham, 'Epilogue' in John Hick, *The Myth of God Incarnate* (London: SCM Press, 1977), p. 201.

25. For a classic statement of this approach, see Rosemary Radford Ruether, *Sexism and God-Talk: Towards a Feminist Theology* (Boston: Beacon Press; London: SCM Press, 1983), p. 258.

apocalyptic determinism has been rejected by feminist theology as encouraging a lack of responsibility for the present world. Yet, as Catherine Keller has pointed out, feminist theology stands firmly within the tradition of dissident millennialism. 'Indeed, whether or not they use the term *eschatological*, feminist theologians return persistently to the prophetic themes of collective hope for the disenfranchised, for bodily, social and cosmic renewal.'[26] And so do lesbian and gay theologians. Postmodernism has with a strange irony sought to uphold one absolute, that of death, for death stands as the spotlight that illuminates our 'realities' as fictions. All these points are perfectly legitimate, particularly in view of the fact that within our store of dangerous memories are horrific reminders of what happens when we create an absolute that resides beyond death. But while being aware of this we must avoid falling into the mortal sin of taking ourselves and our theology too seriously. Of course, any talk about life after death or life in the kingdom tells us absolutely nothing about life after death or life in the kingdom, but they tell us a great deal about our current values and aspirations. Such discourses function both as mirrors and as critiques of the present, as a flurry of recent historical studies have demonstrated.[27] They are the spaces where we dare to dream impossible dreams, where language cracks and the divine presence may seep through.

> Eschatological symbols strain what we ordinarily mean by meaning by placing severe demands on the text. 'Ultimate revelation' and 'ultimate salvation' are ineffable within familiar discourses. In this sense, they defamiliarize and pressure a text of ordinary meanings.[28]

Like Jesus' parables, which were eschatological in content, eschatological discourse makes room for God by cracking 'the deep structure of our accepted world'.[29] So much Christian theology is conducted not in the present but in the company of the past. This is particularly evident

---

26. Catherine Keller, 'Eschatology' in Letty M. Russell and J. Shannon Clarkson (eds.), *Dictionary of Feminist Theologies* (Louisville: Westminster/John Knox Press; London: Mowbrays, 1996), p. 87.

27. See, for example, Colleen McDannell and Bernhard Lang, *Heaven: A History* (New Haven and London: Yale University Press, 1988) and Caroline Walker Bynum, *The Resurrection of the Body in Western Christianity, 200–1336* (New York: Columbia University Press, 1995).

28. Winquist, *Desiring Theology*, p. 76.

29. John Dominic Crossan, *The Dark Interval: Towards a Theology of Story* (Niles: Argus Communications, 1975), pp. 121-22.

in Christian sexual discourse, which tends to revolve around trying to find a way of reconciling contemporary understandings of sexuality and gender with the tradition. No one has yet attempted to do sexual theology from an eschatological perspective. A trinitarian model of theology done in the present in the company of past and future is desperately needed in our churches because without it liberating praxis is impossible.

Without some vision of what equality, justice, mutuality, community and so on are going to mean in concrete terms, even though they may have no ultimate value, how can we begin to endeavour to restructure our worlds and learn to stand in solidarity with one another? One of the most interesting aspects of modern gay and lesbian culture is the fact that there is a strong strain of eschatological vision within it. In part (but only in part) this is due to the AIDS pandemic, which Michael Vasey believes has the potential to produce a 'rearticulation of death' in British culture, as gay men living with the virus, their partners and lesbian friends demand the right to live and die with dignity and with some control over their treatment, and make it very clear that a twenty-minute send-off at the crematorium just will not do. As Vasey points out, the extraordinary response to the funeral scene in the film *Four Weddings and a Funeral* may indicate both a desire on the part of our culture as a whole to resume the awkward dance with death and a recognition that gay people are ahead of the rest of British society on this one.[30]

The AIDS pandemic has inspired some extremely moving visions of 'life after' from people affected by the virus themselves: from a re-reading (or re-singing) of Judy Garland's 'Somewhere Over the Rainbow' as an anthem of pride and hope for life beyond the rainbow flag (a symbol of lesbian and gay liberation), which quickly became popular, to a re-singing of the Village People's 'classic', 'Go West', which was originally written as a celebration of the freedom for lesbian and gay people found on the west coast of the United States (rather naughtily borrowing the tune from a Christian chorus). But in the shadow of AIDS it became a vision of life beyond the virus and disease (*sic*), a life of solidarity and mutuality, of teaching and learning and of basking in the glory of the sun. Perhaps most moving of all is the scene at the end of one of the earliest films about the pandemic, *Long-Time Companion*, in which three characters, the sole survivors

30. Michael Vasey, *Strangers and Friends*, pp. 238-44.

from a massive network of friends, activists and acquaintances, imagine what it will be like the day they find a cure for AIDS. Suddenly, the people you have watched fade and die throughout the film come back to life (emaciated bodies exchanged for robust and filled out ones) to enjoy a picnic on a beach with the friends they have left behind. It is not that AIDS has not happened, but that it has been conquered. On the day that the virus that has caused the disintegration of bodies and of friendships is conquered, when this entropic force is defeated, then friendships even with the dead are resumed, the power of solidarity triumphs. Every time I watch it I think of John's resurrection encounter between Jesus and his friends on a beach for breakfast (John 21). 'I just want to be there' says one of the characters; it is the sustaining and empowering vision of those who remain.

Several points are worth noting here. The ultimate value of embodiment, relationship and community are affirmed in these visions of 'life after'. This community dimension is also evident in the practice of creating panels either of yourself or for a loved one to be attached to the AIDS quilt. People seek to commemorate themselves in the context of community: individuality in relationship.

Images of 'life after' also abound in the considerable body of literature that makes up the genre of lesbian science fiction. The feminist science-fiction writer, Ursula Le Guin, has noted that most science fiction is trapped in the capitalist, patriarchal myth of constant progress and is 'bright, dry, clear, strong firm, active, aggressive, lineal, progressive, creative, expanding, advancing and hot'. (We might note in passing how much Christian eschatological vision fits into this pattern.) She suggests that a feminist image of utopia will be 'dark, wet, obscure, weak, yielding, passive, participationary, circular, cyclical, nurturant, retreating, contracting, and cold'.[31] To a large extent this is borne out in lesbian science fiction, which demonstrates remarkably similar concerns and visions: communal, tribal societies; no formal, central government; living in harmony with nature; lack of urban or industrial conurbations; war and violence existing only outside of the community; people rejecting 'normal' means of power in order to become all-powerful, acquiring supernatural gifts; the abolition of all gender and sexual categories, while embracing sexual permissiveness, with sexual love depicted as 'non-exploitative, non-possessive, non-monogamous, and

31. Ursula Le Guin, 'A Non-Euclidean View of California as a Cold Place', in *Dancing at the Edge of the World* (London: Gollancz, 1989), p. 90.

strongly combined with friendship'.[32] But this is usually very fragile, threatened and non-perfect. Lesbians who have been forced to live in the twilight zone, the non-place (Monique Wittig, in her mischievous rewriting of Dante's *Inferno*, finds rest during her journey in limbo, which consists of lesbian bars![33]) have imagined a different type of non-place, a utopia, a 'life after' which is and isn't life now, and like the end of *Long-Time Companion*, the vision is of friendship, embodiment and right relationship.

What lesbian and gay people in their envisioning of 'life after' have done is to reconnect unconsciously and precariously the severed relationship between desire and immortality. Present experiences of embodiment, desire, and love, fractured though they are, both contain and anticipate some future fulfilment.[34] What I want to suggest is that these lesbian and gay visions of 'life after' resonate with and stir up some dangerous memories from the Christian tradition which together challenge so much theo-sexual orthodoxy.

The affirmation of the ultimate value of friendship and community is reflected in Christian eschatological discourse throughout its history. Lang and McDannell, in their study of the history of heaven, note that while there were always those who advocated a purely theocentric heaven, in which the individual exists solely in relationship to God, they were generally outweighed by the numbers of people who advocated a social heaven. Aquinas changed his mind on this issue and moved from a theocentric to a more social vision.[35] This social vision became stronger as love and friendship became in the late medieval world an essential part of humanness. However, this social life was envisaged in extremely hierarchical terms, even when the envisioned hierarchy was subversive of earthly hierarchies—for example, in Mechtild of Magdeburg's insistence that only women could enter the third level of heaven where God alone dwells.[36] This is a vision

---

32. Sarah Lefanu, *In the Chinks of the World Machine: Feminism and Science Fiction* (London: The Women's Press, 1988), p. 76. For further critical studies of women's science fiction see Lucie Armitt, *Where No Man Has Gone Before: Women and Science Fiction* (London and New York: Routledge, 1991) and Gabriele Griffin, *Heavenly Love? Lesbian Images in Twentieth Century Women's Thought* (Manchester: Manchester University Press, 1993).

33. Monique Wittig, *Across the Acheron* (London: The Women's Press, 1988).

34. Vasey, *Strangers and Friends*, pp. 244-49.

35. McDannell and Lang, *Heaven*, pp. 89-93.

36. McDannell and Lang, *Heaven*, pp. 101-106.

displaced in lesbian and gay reflection, which places ultimate value on equality and mutuality. Embodiment is also a vital element in both sets of reflections, which focus on a body redeemed from decay and disease, continuous with the previous body yet transformed. Disabled theologians like Nancy Eiesland have some difficult questions to ask of those who make the 'perfect' body the eschatological goal, pointing out how this grates against the gospel representation of the resurrected Christ as the disabled God and rebounds upon the disabled.[37] This is a voice to which all Christian theologians, including lesbian and gay ones, need to pay heed. For most of Christian history the reality of embodied resurrection was affirmed as a means of insisting that gender hierarchies have ultimate, divinely grounded significance. In lesbian visions of utopia embodiment is rigorously affirmed, but the body becomes the location of fluid possibilities in terms of gender and sexual orientation—reflecting the deconstruction of gender that has taken place within feminism and the deconstruction of sexual orientation that has taken place in the wake of Foucault. The body has been queered[38] in this utopian vision. There may be resonances here with Paul's deconstruction of social hierarchies in the body of Christ (Gal. 3.28) and the polymorphous desire of Milton's angels.[39] The sexualized person is regarded as having ultimate value, to be human is to be sexual, but the performances or categories of sexuality are dispensable, historical and social constructions that restrict rather than empower our loving. Human beings are created sexual and relational. These are gifts of grace that have yet to be brought to fulfilment.

We might ask (tongue in cheek) whether this is why there will be no marriage in heaven (Mk 12.18-27)? Is there no marriage in heaven because in heaven we are all made queer? Analysing the answers to the question put by the Sadducees that have been offered down the centuries is a fascinating enterprise. While sexual desire was equated with God-denying lust there could be no marriage in heaven. Sex in

---

37. Nancy L. Eiesland, *The Disabled God: Toward a Liberatory Theology of Disability* (Nashville: Abingdon Press, 1994).

38. ' "Queer". . . includes all whose sexual identities and practices fall beyond the parameters of "Hetero-patriarchy". . . It also implies that sexualities can and will change over a lifetime and that ethical reflections need to take these matters into account' (Mary Hunt, 'Queer Theology' in Russell and Clarkson, *Dictionary of Feminist Theologies*, p. 298).

39. McDannell and Lang, *Heaven*, p. 232.

heaven was also associated in the medieval period with the Islamic heresy. As romantic love entered the scene sexual fulfilment was often projected as finding ultimate fulfilment in intense absolute union with the divine—Bernard of Clairvaux, Mechthild of Magdeburg and Gertrude of Helfta are among those celibates who chose to use vivid sexual imagery to describe the somatomorphic soul's union with God. As romantic love became the property of the middle classes and the modern family emerged, the ecclesiastical, urban images of heaven, which themselves had replaced the garden paradise, now gave way to a domesticated heaven. Heaven became the family home writ large (as graves became family homes writ small). Families were thought to stay together (although some of the more radical speculators allowed people to choose a new spouse if their earthly one had been unsatisfactory). In other words, Jesus' words on marriage were ignored or rationalized. Among those who did this were William Blake and Charles Kingsley. In one of Blake's engravings, 'The Meeting of a Family in Heaven', husband and wife embrace with physical intensity, children gather around them and two angels hover above them, looking on with admiration, their wings meeting to form a Gothic arch 'over the sacred scene'.[40] Certainly, for Blake, this scene served several symbolic purposes: male and female symbolized the union of soul and body, but the literal was also true. Passion was not something to jettison in order to get into heaven, but to cultivate, for passion, along with friendship, is like a 'Glass of Eternal Diamond' in Blake's Platonic universe.[41]

Kingsley's biographer explains that he thought heaven 'would consist of one perpetual copulation in a literal, physical sense'[42] with his wife, Fanny, and he left several drawings illustrating his belief. In Kingsley's extraordinary reflections upon the afterlife we see reflections of a wider idolization of marriage that the churches (even eventually the Roman Catholic) bought into without much critical reflection. For Kingsley, Jesus only ruled out 'marrying' in heaven, and this suggested to him that earthly marriage continued. Indeed, marriage was essential because it was 'the highest state... through and in which men can know most of God, and work most for God'.[43] In his insistence that marriage

40. McDannell and Lang, *Heaven*, p. 242.
41. McDannell and Lang, *Heaven*, p. 240.
42. Susan Chitty, *The Beast and the Monk: The Life of Charles Kingsley* (London: Hodder & Stoughton, 1975), p. 17.
43. McDannell and Lang, *Heaven*, p. 262.

was essential to his personhood and that therefore resurrection and eternal life made no sense without it, Kingsley touched upon an idea that would later bear partial fruit in the theory of complementarity now used by most British churches as a theological strategy to reinforce heterosexism. Human beings, male and female, can only fully image God in marriage. This collapsing of heaven into the eternal nuclear family persists in popular Christianity even while the nuclear family itself is breaking up.[44] But sex in heaven is not a topic much discussed. The House of Bishops of the General Synod of the Church of England in their report, *Issues in Human Sexuality*, take their cue from Mark 12 to look wistfully towards the time when 'the physical expression of sexuality, which is required now because of our mortality in order that human life may continue', will no longer be needed and we will be able to enjoy 'the fullest possible relationships with all, being no longer restricted by the particularity of the flesh'.[45] The bishops appear to be saying that sexuality is primarily about reproduction and once we are liberated from that burden and the burden of mortality, bodies and sex will no longer be needed and we will be free to love all to the fullest possible degree, but this will not involve bodies. Love can then be disembodied—a notion which I think the doctrine of the incarnation, if nothing else, calls into question. The queer vision of 'life after' does not fit into any of these pre-existing Christian models— there is certainly sex, sexuality, relationship, embodiment, but not marriage, no nuclear family, no enforced coupledom. Ironically, the queer heaven resonates more deeply with the heaven of the Jesus of the synoptics than that of past or contemporary mainstream Christian visions. Jesus' clear rejection of the idea that marriage persists in heaven was but part of his overturning of the familial structures of his society. Marriage and family seem to have had no place in his vision of the kingdom of God as represented by the gospel writers and indeed were regarded by him as antithetical to it, possibly because they bound people in relations that prevented them enjoying the radical equality of the reign of God, systems of exclusion and privatized love. A new kinship was proclaimed, based not upon blood-ties, but upon inclusive

44. Christopher Lewis, 'Beyond the Crematorium: Popular Belief', in Dan Cohn-Sherbok and Christopher Lewis (eds.), *Beyond Death: Theological and Philosophical Reflections on Life After Death* (Basingstoke: Macmillan Press, 1995), pp. 199-206.

45. House of Bishops of the General Synod of the Church of England, *Issues in Human Sexuality*, para. 3.26, p. 30.

friendship. In this 'kindom' (to use Ada María Isasi-Díaz's translation of *basilea*) hetero-patriarchal structures such as marriage (as so far constructed socially and theologically) and the nuclear family can have no place. Lesbian and gay people as resident aliens within societies and churches that revolve around these institutions experience their oppressive power and this brings them (largely unconsciously) very close to the kin(g)dom of God. Michael Vasey believes that the loss of the biblical vision of heaven is at least partially responsible for modern evangelical antipathy towards homosexuality:

> While modern evangelical Christianity struggles to gain a hearing in society and to make an impact on issues that it regards as close to the heart of the gospel, it is largely ignorant of the extent to which it has bought into the modern project. Its recurrent anxiety over 'family issues' is a measure of how deeply it has sold its soul to the destructive idols of Western culture: the reduction of a sense of beauty to 'heterosexual love' and the elimination of bonds of affection in the search of prosperity through the market. Its hostility to gay people is not so much a sign of its loyalty to scripture as a mark of the extent to which it has not heeded St John's advice, 'Little children, keep yourselves from idols' (Jn 5.21).[46]

Vasey suggests that the images of heaven found in the early and medieval Christian tradition will appeal to lesbian and gay people because the descriptions 'are so preoccupied with style and public celebration as to be almost camp. While relentlessly political, they have more in common with a Gay Pride event than with the sobriety of English political life or the leisurewear informality of evangelical life.'[47] Oppression, suffering, discontent with injustice, breed not only camp, but also visions of the afterlife radically different from the present. The fact that Western Christianity can only bother at present to envisage 'life after' as an extension of this world with some of the unpleasantness removed is a massive indictment of its insularity.

Lesbians and gay men are not the only people to voice a hope beyond marriage and family. The Scottish theologian, Elizabeth Templeton, writing as someone who is happily married, still hopes that Jesus or the person who put words into his mouth was right that there will be no marriage in heaven: 'For it seems to me that, however we envisage the state of redeemed co-existence, in or out of time, it cannot be properly envisaged as a place of excluding relationships'.[48] She regards

46. Vasey, *Strangers and Friends*, pp. 248-49.
47. Vasey, *Strangers and Friends*, p. 248.
48. Elizabeth Templeton, 'Towards a Theology of Marriage', in Susan Durber,

marriage as a manifestation of our sinfulness because it reveals our 'embeddedness in a limitation of love'.

The reluctance to envisage sex in heaven is closely related to Jesus' declaration that there will be no marriage there, for to take these words seriously and yet to posit the existence of sex is to be led to the conclusion that in heaven non-monogamy is okay. This is clearly the case in the lesbian visions of 'life after'. In many respects monogamy is a greater Christian idol than marriage and it is one that many lesbians and gay men support. Yet it is an idol because it has come to us through the systems of patriarchy and very few Christian theologians are prepared to break it open and even question it. The only theologians who have been prepared to do so are lesbian and gay theologians. Carter Heyward notes that monogamy was constructed on the basis of ownership and as such cannot just be absorbed unreconstructed into a Christian life. Similarly, though exclusive sexual relations can be a place in which mutuality, reciprocity, justice and passion thrive for both persons, they can also be 'a smokescreen behind which partners, or spouses, shield their real feelings, fears, yearnings, and relational questions... An unexamined, static commitment to monogamy can become a canopy for unspoken hurt, lies, and, in time, the dissolution of a relationship.'[49] To be non-monogamous, she argues, is not necessarily to be promiscuous, that is, unthinkingly and uncaringly indiscriminate. It is possible, she argues, to embody faithfulness within more than one sexual relational commitment:

> To be sexually faithful is to experience and express ourselves relationally in such a way that both we and others are empowered, and empowering, as co-creators, liberators, and bearers of blessing to one another and to the world. To be faithful lovers is to touch and be touched... with a depth and quality of tenderness that actually helps create life where there is death, comfort where there is despair. To be faithful in our sexualities is to live a commitment to mutuality. Reciprocal relations between and among ourselves in which no one owns, possesses, dominates, or controls the other but rather in which the lover participates with the beloved in living together in a home, a society, and/or a world in which each gives and receives.[50]

Faithfulness is not about the obligations of ownership or being owned but about taking responsibility for our own and our partner's well-

As Man and Woman Made: Theological Reflections on Marriage (London: United Reformed Church, 1994), p. 17.

   49. Heyward, *Touching Our Strength*, p. 136.
   50. Heyward, *Our Passion for Justice*, p. 192.

being, empowerment and fulfilment in ways that are just. When the concept of fidelity is redeemed from its patriarchal roots the possibility for faithful non-monogamous relations becomes real. Another lesbian theologian, Kathy Rudy, has also recently dared to suggest that the type of sexual activity that is usually the least acceptable to anyone—public, communal sex—is compatible with the Christian vision because it can be communal and unitive (though often it is not), part of the process of building and sustaining a safe community in which the bonds of individualism are broken.[51] How does the Christian vision of an all-loving, almost defiantly promiscuously loving God (who is not two but three persons in mutual relation) square with the idolization of monogamy? In any case, the reluctance of most theologians even to consider the possibility that monogamy may be a hetero-patriarchal construction means that exclusive sexual commitments are not being given the theological defence they may deserve.

Communities of resistance and solidarity create eschatological visions of 'life after' in order to provide some common content to the hope and struggle for liberation. At the same time they seek to subvert this dreaming by 'deliteralizing [their] own utopias, returning the future possibility to the present community'.[52] In so doing they follow the early Christian paradigm. Eschatological reflection does create a safe space to dream impossible dreams, to discuss in the context of playfulness what is ultimate and essential to humanity and to divine life. Because it is the realm of the impossible, only the foolish or the insane would claim to be able to speak with or of absolute truth, and so within this discourse it may be possible for representatives of various Christianities and sexualities to engage in genuinely productive debate on sexuality. We have tried with little success to meet each other in the past and present. Perhaps the time has come to focus less on sex in those days and sex these days and more on sex in the next days, which is a profoundly Christian methodology. Christianity is as much about dangerous futures as it is about dangerous memories. Perhaps the discussion about sexuality could be the place where Western Christianity relearns this truth.

---

51. Kathy Rudy, '"Where Two or More are Gathered": Using Gay Communities as a Model for Christian Sexual Ethics', *Theology and Sexuality* 4 (1996), pp. 81-99.

52. Keller, 'Eschatology', p. 87.

ENDING SEX

Gerard Loughlin

My first theme is the 'ending' of sex: the point, purpose or *telos*, the final cause or end of sex; that which calls it, to which it moves, for and by which it is given. My second theme—to which I will, I am afraid, give somewhat less attention, but which should be borne in mind throughout—is the question of sexual difference. Is it possible today to really think the difference of sex, the difference of man from woman, of gay from straight, of one sexed body from another, in such a way that one body—the straight male body—does not colonize the others, inventing them as the feared alien of itself, so that the body of the woman and the homosexual is always caught within the imaginary of the man and the heterosexual, always finally devoured for fear that it will devour? And my text is the first of two remarkable films by the director David Fincher: the horror science-fiction film, *Alien3* (USA, 1992) and the neo-noir detective story, *Seven* (USA, 1995), both of which describe descents into the circles of hell, into the decay and ending that is the body, which, even as it harbours life, destroys and is destroyed.

Fincher's films are remarkable not least because, as products of a culture that trades in the want of the body beautiful, they dwell upon the desperation of the body *in extremis*. Both films take lustrous Hollywood 'stars'—Sigourney Weaver and Brad Pitt—and not merely bring them down to earth, but subject them to earth's powers of corruption, their bodies visibly collapsing before our gaze: Pitt increasingly covered in cuts and bruises, Weaver—her head shaven because of lice—reduced to the appearance of a death-camp inmate. Far from celebrating the plastic body of desire, of fulfilment through physical intimacy and sexual coup-ling, Fincher's films articulate the dreadful fear that sex finds its ending —its *telos*—not in life, in the body enhanced, renewed and burgeoning; but in death, in the defilement, decay, and destruction of the body.[1]

---

1. See further, Amy Taubin, 'The Allure of Decay', *Sight and Sound* 6.1 (January 1996), pp. 22-24.

One might think of David Fincher's films as neo-medieval texts, not just because *Alien3* dresses its prisoners in monk-like garb and alludes to Augustine, while *Seven* refers to Aquinas and Dante, but because both films concentrate on a central medieval concern: the decrepitude and corruption of the body. The camera lingers on rotting, gouged or otherwise mutilated flesh, or, in startling close-ups, shows us body-parts variously invaded or caressed. These films look with a certain tenderness on the perishability and defeat of the body: on the presence of death in life.

The third of the seven victims in *Seven* is discovered lying on his back, bound to a bed, where he has been cruelly cosseted so as to prolong his dying. In the process he has become a figure of death, a sore-ridden emaciated corpse, the skin so shrunken upon his face that it hardly remains more than a skull, ligaments contorted into a frozen visage of agony. It might be a *transi*, a cadaver tomb,[2] or a vision of the dead Christ, as shown to Mother Julian of Norwich, with his nostrils shrivelling and drying before her eyes, his body turning black and brown. His 'dear body was so discoloured and dry, so shrivelled, deathly, and pitiful, that he might well have been seven nights in dying'.[3] The poor soul in *Seven* has been a year about it, though even as the detectives talk over him—taking samples of blood and faeces—some life still remains, and the cadaver suddenly jolts and coughs, unexpectedly and grotesquely animated, become a mobile *memento mori*. Julian and Fincher well understand that putrefaction is a truth of the body, in life as in death. It is the ending to which all bodies tend; the *telos* that awaits every engendering.

Images of descent and fall recur throughout Fincher's two films, so dominating the second that even its end-titles go down rather than up the screen. *Alien3* opens with the sudden descent of its heroine, warrant officer Ripley (Sigourney Weaver), into hell. Sleeping soundly in cryogenic suspension, homeward bound from her adventures in the preceding film of the Alien trilogy, *Aliens* (James Cameron, USA, 1986), an onboard fire leads to her and her fellow crew members—Newt and Hicks—being placed in an evacuation craft and sent

2.   See Philippe Ariès, *Western Attitudes Toward Death: From the Middle Ages to the Present* (trans. Patricia M. Ranum; London: Marion Boyars, 1976 [1974]), pp. 39-46.

3.   Julian of Norwich, *Revelations of Divine Love* (trans. Clifton Wolters; Harmondsworth: Penguin Books, 1966), ch. 16 (pp. 87-88).

hurtling to the nearest planet, Fiorina 161.

Ripley awakens to find herself the sole survivor, rescued by the planet's only inhabitants, the inmates of an isolated penal colony. From then on her journey is forever downwards, descending to ever deeper levels of what is quite literally an inferno, since the prison is also a mineral ore refinery and foundry, capable of making lead sheeting for nuclear waste containers. But this hell into which she has fallen is also our world, in which that more primal fall of the first man and woman has already occurred. And she comes to it as a reminder of that first couple and their fallen, lustful coupling by which their degradation was passed to each of their offspring, down the long line of years, and across the deserts of the universe.

The men of Fiorina or Fury 161 are not only criminal recipients of society's punishment, but the subjects of a self-imposed bodily discipline, which serves to control their fleshly desires, while orienting them to the ultimate void—the *nihil*—that encompasses their captivity. Five years before the story opens, Dillon (Charles S. Dutton) and other 'alternative people' among the prisoners, embraced an 'apocalyptic, millenarian, Christian-fundamentalist' kind of religion. It is these 'brothers' who now comprise the inhabitants of the prison foundry, together with two 'minders' and a 'medical officer'. The 'brothers' have taken a vow of celibacy and bound themselves into a semi-monastic community, seeking spiritual solace through self-regulation in the midst of damnation. They know that sin enters through the eye; the disruption of proper order following upon the elicitation of bodily desire through sight of forbidden fruit: the flesh of the other. On being told of Ripley's arrival, one of their fellows reminds them that they have all taken a vow of celibacy, which includes women. To the order of the male penal body—each member of which is a YY chromosome multiple murderer—Ripley appears as a new Eve, bearing forbidden and—as it transpires—rotten fruit. She is warned not to go unaccompanied among the men, and at one point in the story—when in an isolated part of the prison—she is set upon by a group of prisoners who, forgetting their vow of celibacy, are intent upon raping her. She is saved by Dillon, who had, on first meeting her, described himself as a 'murderer and rapist of women', and who now lays about her attackers with an iron bar, while informing her that he has to 're-educate some of the brothers'. They have to discuss 'some matters of the spirit'.

In this way Fincher's film evokes the Augustinian thematic of lust, which for Augustine is the 'general name for desiring of every kind',[4] though most particularly that desire that 'excites the indecent parts of the body',[5] overcoming the control and regulation of the will. After the fall, Adam and Eve had to sew together fig leaves and make aprons to cover their *pudenda*, in order that each might hide from the gaze of the other those organs that had become the site of an instinct beyond their control.[6] It is as if their 'genital organs' had become 'the private property of lust, which has brought them so completely under its sway that they have no power of movement if this passion fails'.[7] For Augustine the sexual organs have become an alien within the body; the very sign of that disobedience which constitutes our fallen world.

Augustine, writing at the end of his life, but perhaps remembering his own youthful ardour for the embrace and excitement of flesh, both evokes the pleasure of fallen sex—the intensity of which can breach the city-walls of body and mind from without and within[8]—and imagines the possibility of a sexual act without lust; an embrace without passion. He admits the difficulty of conceiving such an act, since we have no example of such obedient members as the sexual organs would then be; not even Adam and Eve, for whom such sex was available, experienced it, since 'their sin happened first'.[9] But if they had embraced and coupled before their disobedience, the 'man would have sowed the seed and the woman would have conceived the child when their sexual organs had been aroused by the will, at the appropriate time and in the necessary degree'.[10]

> Then, without feeling the allurement of passion goading him on, the husband would have relaxed on his wife's bosom in tranquillity of mind and with no impairment of his body's integrity. Moreover. . . when those

4.   Augustine, *The City of God* (trans. Henry Bettenson; Harmondsworth: Penguin Books, 1972), Bk XIV, ch. 15 (p. 576).

5.   Augustine, *The City of God*, Bk XIV, ch. 16 (p. 577).

6.   Augustine, *The City of God*, Bk XIV, ch. 17 (p. 579).

7.   Augustine, *The City of God*, Bk XIV, ch. 19 (p. 581).

8.   'This lust assumes power not only over the whole body, and not only from the outside, but also internally; it disturbs the whole man, when the mental emotion combines and mingles with the physical craving, resulting in a pleasure surpassing all physical delights. So intense is the pleasure that when it reaches its climax there is an almost total extinction of mental alertness; the intellectual sentries, as it were, are overwhelmed' (Augustine, *The City of God*, Bk XIV, ch. 16 [p. 577]).

9.   Augustine, *The City of God*, Bk XIV, ch. 26 (p. 591).

10.   Augustine, *The City of God*, Bk XIV, ch. 24 (p. 587).

parts of the body were not activated by the turbulent heat of passion but brought into service by deliberate use of power when the need arose, the male seed could have been dispatched into the womb, with no loss of the wife's integrity, just as the menstrual flux can now be produced from the womb of a virgin without loss of maidenhead. For the seed could be injected through the same passage by which the flux is ejected. . . so the two sexes might have been united for impregnation and conception by an act of will, instead of by a lustful craving.[11]

Such a sexual scene must seem strange to us, who are now so deeply fallen into disobedience that we cannot imagine such a calm integrity of mind and body. To us it will seem like alien sex; like the sex that— in a hideous parody of Augustine's paradisal and lustless coupling— opens David Fincher's *Alien3*. The main titles of the film are intercut with the primal scene of sexual penetration that sets the story of the film in motion. As Ripley lies passively upon her back, asleep and unaware that the security of her 'cryotube' has been breached—a hapless Eve, a sleeping princess[12]—the hand of an alien sex covers her face and places its seed within the earth of her breast.

The reproductive cycle of the alien is the central fascination and horror of all three Alien films. First appearing as a face-hugging, mucous-dripping and bony-fingered creature, in Ripley Scott's *Alien* (USA, 1979), it jumps from a plant-like pod onto the face of its victim, rendering him insensible while secretly laying its seed within his chest, through his mouth: patient of alien oral-rape. Only later will the growing alien child suddenly and terribly rip through the chest of its host-mother, killing the latter in the very moment of birth.[13] That

11. Augustine, *The City of God*, Bk XIV, ch. 26 (p. 591).

12. The version of the story of the sleeping beauty in Basile's *Pentamerone* (1636) makes explicit what is at most implicit in Perrault's latter telling of the tale in *Histoires ou contes du temps passé* (1697). The 'beauty' is found by a prince who 'cannot rouse her, yet falls in love with the insensible body as did the prince who came upon Snow White laid out in her coffin; but being less courteous, he rapes her, and forgets her'. It is only when one of the two children to whom she gives birth nine months later sucks the poisoned splinter from her finger that she is restored to life. See Iona and Peter Opie, *The Classic Fairy Tales* (London: Oxford University Press, 1974), p. 81. The Opies find an earlier version of the story in a fourteenth-century prose romance, *Perceforest*, and locate its origin in the story of Brynhild in the *Volunsunga Saga* (p. 83).

13. In *Aliens* the otherwise unexplained seed-pods of the first film are revealed to be the eggs of an alien 'queen', capable of lying dormant until a suitable host-victim comes into proximity with them.

this alien biology—so carefully and explicitly rendered in the film—represents a male-identified fear of penetration, gestation and birth, is a commonplace of commentary on the film, not least because the rape victim is a man. For Amy Taubin, the film plays on 'anxieties set loose by a decade of feminist and gay activism', embodying the 'return of repressed infantile fears and confusions about where babies come from and the anatomical differences between the sexes'.

> [The alien's] toothy, dripping mouth was hermaphroditic: while the double jaws represented the inner and outer labia of the vagina dentata, the projectile movement of the inner jaw was a phallic threat. Granted that the terror of being raped and devoured by the monster loomed large for both sexes, *Alien* was a basically male anxiety fantasy: that a man could be impregnated was the ultimate outrage.[14]

This thematic is played down in Cameron's *Aliens*, where we witness a woman rather than a man giving 'birth' to an alien, and where an egg-laying alien 'queen' is introduced, a mother every bit as protective of her offspring as is Ripley of her adopted child, Newt. As Taubin notes, the climactic fight between Ripley and the alien queen is 'structured as a cat fight between the good mother and the bad'.[15] Thus in the film sexual difference is properly ordered and the audience invited to side with the good against the bad mother, who is, of course, a single parent.[16] Its object of fear is woman out of place, rather than the body of woman as such. It is the latter fear that *Alien3* again thematizes, with renewed force.

For Taubin, *Alien3* is 'all about the AIDS crisis and the threat to women's reproductive rights',[17] which is to say, perhaps, sexuality

---

14. Amy Taubin, 'Invading Bodies', *Sight and Sound* 2.3 (July, 1992), pp. 8-10 (p. 9). On the 'vagina dentata' see Barbara Creed, *The Monstrous-Feminine: Film, Feminism and Psychoanalysis* (London: Routledge, 1993), ch. 8.

15. Taubin, 'Invading Bodies', p. 9.

16. Taubin suggests that as well as representing the 'monstrous feminine', the alien queen 'bears a suspicious resemblance to a favourite scapegoat of the Reagan–Bush era—the black welfare mother, that parasite on the economy whose uncurbed reproductive drive reduced hard-working taxpayers to bankruptcy' ('Invading Bodies', p. 9).

17. Taubin, 'Invading Bodies', p. 9. 'Aids is everywhere in the film. It's in the danger surrounding sex and drugs. It's in the metaphor of a mysterious deadly organism attacking an all-male community. It's in the iconography of the shaven heads. Exhorting the prisoners to defy The Company, Ripley shouts, "They think we're scum and they don't give a fuck about one friend of yours who's died", an Aids activism line if ever there was one' ('Invading Bodies', p. 10).

and death. Of course the film is about AIDS, graphically playing on the fear of an invisible enemy within the individual and social body: the alien embryo within Ripley, herself an alien within the penal colony, a woman among men. Of course the film is about bodily control and its loss, the body given over to another life, another body. Life grows within Ripley and she seeks its abortion. But she can do so only at the cost of her own life. At the end of the film, the 'pro-life' representative of The Company—which desires the alien for military research purposes (as the ultimate phallic aggressor)—urges her to save the 'child', and herself. But in the inverted world of *Alien3* such an act would be to give death and not life. Here we touch upon the themes of redemption and salvation that figure prominently in the film, and to which I shall return. But for the moment I want to consider how the film, as well as being about AIDS and 'reproductive rights', is also about sex more generally, and about the fear that to engage in sexual congress is to engage death, to inaugurate the end of your own life, even as the life of another begins within or from you: that to conceive is to die. In Fincher's film, death is the end of sex; the *telos* to which it moves.

At the same time there is life in death; but what sort of life it is, is to say the least, ambiguous. This is most clearly—even didactically—expressed in the scene of the funeral service that is held for Ripley's ship-mates, Hicks and Newt, in which the words of the service are ironically counterpoised with the birth of an alien out of the body of a prisoner's dog, elsewhere in the prison. First, the prison superintendent, Andrews (Brian Glover), commits the dead child and man to the keeping of the Lord. They have been 'taken from the shadow of our night, they have been released from all darkness and pain'. They 'have gone beyond our world, they are forever eternal and everlasting. Ashes to ashes, dust to dust.' But then Dillon, the leader of the 'brothers', comes forward to make his own, more impassioned and questioning speech. 'Why? Why are the innocent punished? Why the sacrifice? Why the pain? There aren't any promises. Nothing is certain, only that some get called, some get saved.' Then he also commits the bodies, but this time to the void, and does so with a glad heart, 'for within each seed there is a promise of a flower, and within each death, no matter how small, there is always a new life, a new beginning'. It is this last expression of faith in the natural cycle of birth and death—to which all the 'brothers' respond 'Amen'—which is intercut with the scene of

a hideous alien life emerging from the small death of the dog. Neither
Andrews nor Dillon expound a theology of resurrection.

As I have already indicated, *Alien3* is replete with religious resonance. The story of Ripley's descent into hell, which is also the story of
a birth, can be read as a horribly inverted Christian nativity play, with
Ripley taking the part of the Virgin Mary. As already noted, she comes
among the men of Fury 161 as Eve the temptress, but she also appears
as the second Eve, bearing their destiny within her. The conception
she bears has left her 'virginal', conceived among the stars, through the
mouth, by an alien being. Her child has no human father. Furthermore,
her child, like that of the earlier virginal conception, will bring the men
of Fury 161 a genuine—though pagan—redemption through heroic
struggle with the monster; a parody of the Christian hope of life
through death with Christ. Against the common enemy each man must
risk his own life in the hope that he may thereby save it.

But what is the common enemy that at one and the same time destroys and makes possible a certain moral heroism? There are two
aliens in the film: the one that emerges from the prisoner Murphy's
dog—the ravaging beast—and the one that secretly grows unseen within
Ripley. Indeed, one can read the first as a prolepsis of the second, an
extrapolation of the gestating embryo, enacting the horror that is the
secret of pregnancy: the fear that in sex is death. These themes and
others are complexly brought together in a central scene of the film,
that concludes its first part and inaugurates its second.

The scene is set in the prison hospital, to which Ripley has been confined by superintendent Andrews, who does not believe her story about
the alien creature she believes responsible for the violent deaths that
have occurred among the prisoners. She is being tended by Clemens
(Charles Dance), the medical officer, with whom she has established a
(sexual) relationship. Tied to a bed beside Ripley's is the now deranged
prisoner, Golic (Paul McGann), who has witnessed a 'dragon' des-
patching the prisoners he is suspected of killing. While Clemens gives
Ripley an injection of pain-killer, he explains the crime that first
brought him to Fury 161, not as a doctor, but as a prisoner: a morphine
addict, he killed eleven patients with the 'wrong dosage' of pain-killer.
This is the most tender and, as Amy Taubin notes, erotic scene in the
film, with Clemens taking Ripley's arm and carefully injecting her
with one of his own 'special cocktails'. It is, as it were, the missing
scene from an earlier sequence in which we saw them together, before

and after sex. Then the scene of their sexual coupling was replaced with one showing the first slaying of a prisoner by the alien. Death was already present at their union.

As Clemens prepares to give Ripley her injection, Golic suddenly asks her if she is married. He tells her that she should be, that she should have children. Then he tells her that she is going to die. Clemens draws a curtain between the beds, shutting Golic out, but repeats Golic's question to Ripley: is she married? She responds by asking about his past, which he explains, and then he administers the injection; his fluid passing into her body. It is at this moment that the alien strikes; looming behind the rubber curtain, it grasps Clemens and lifts him away before puncturing his skull. It then approaches Ripley, cowering on the floor; while all the time, Golic, strapped to his bed, watches terrified, as do we. What we see is the annunciation of an impending birth.

The alien approaches to within an inch of Ripley's face, opening its hermaphroditic jaw and projecting its inner phallic mouth towards her. But then it shuts its mouth and leaves her, as swiftly as it came. It has sensed the presence of the alien embryo, silently growing within Ripley. She is with child.

Sigourney Weaver is both star and co-producer of *Alien3*, and Amy Taubin suggests that we should not underestimate Weaver's 'contribution to its authorship'.[18] Does it then present us with a woman's view of sex—of the fear, as Taubin suggests, of 'being pregnant with a monster, or being forced to carry a foetus you don't want to term, or never being able to have a baby though you desperately want one'?[19] Or is it a masculine view of sex—a (heterosexual) man's fear of what he thinks sex means for women: an impregnation, gestation and birth that destroys the body? Or is it the fear that to engage in sexual congress is to court death: the very fate that befalls Clemens?[20]

Let me suggest that though the film may, in certain respects, be viewed as feminist—in the sense of claiming equality for women—it nevertheless remains within a patriarchal imaginary—in the sense that

18. Taubin, 'Invading Bodies', p. 10.

19. Taubin, 'Invading Bodies', p. 9.

20. This is, of course, the teaching of Darwinism, in which the purpose of sex is viciously reproductive; the rhetoric of the 'selfish gene' being a particularly manic version of the theory. Needless to say, such ideas are the antithesis of the Christian gospel.

the equality claimed for women is an equality with men. All three *Alien* films make a woman—Warrant Officer Ripley—their central character; and there is little doubt that her success lies in being more resolute, resilient and courageous than any of the other—largely male—characters. In short, one could argue that Ripley survives because she is more of a man than are the men. In Cameron's *Aliens*, Ripley and the other women among the soldiers are the equal of their male counterparts in handling the massive phallic armoury with which they are supplied. In *Alien3*, Ripley's masculinization is further marked by her clothing and shaven head. The difference of her sex is not marked by bodily adornment. Yet she remains sexually different: the men, despite everything, insist upon it. They mark her out as not one of them; all that is, except Clemens, who seems to have more in common with her than he does with any of his fellow males. It is with him that she establishes a sexual relationship. In this way, perhaps, one can read the film as contesting the price of masculinization that Ripley has to pay in order to survive in the fraternal society of the penal colony. It would then be this tension—of the feminine body within a masculine economy, and the question of female identity within such an economy—that is complexly articulated and disturbingly explored at the level of the film's sexual symbolic: the biology of alien sex. Before suggesting how complex and disturbing this is, I want to return to some of the film's religious themes.

As I have already suggested, Ripley comes to Fury 161 as Eve, and as Mary, but she also comes as Christ or Christa, descending into the maw of hell in order to announce the possibility of life in the very place of death itself. But she descends, not as Christ risen in glory, but as Christ fallen, headlong, into an underworld whose gates she cannot unlock. Growing within her is the alien, whose import is proleptically announced by the adult alien that devours the prisoners, as a foretaste of the death to which she will give birth; but at the same time she will, in leading the men to fight the alien, give their lives a purpose in the possibility of a heroic, sacrificial death for the good of the fraternity, and indeed of the world. And even before that comes to pass, she comes among them as someone who accepts them as they are: someone who—like Christ—eats with sinners. Her act—which is not without challenge to the men—is perhaps more radical than that of any in the gospel stories: for she is a woman who sits down to eat with rapists.

The scene of Ripley's eschatological meal with the prisoners opens with her coming to stand in front of a cross-shaped structure, which is on the wall behind her. This allusion to her eventual sacrificial death, and to the death of Christ, is picked up as she crosses the room by the prisoner in the foreground who covertly makes the sign of the cross on his chest, while at the same time he places his long fingers on his neck. Why does he cross himself? Perhaps against the temptation of the flesh that has just entered the room. Perhaps because he dimly senses the alien life within her—the presence of death—that even now comes to eat (with) them. Perhaps because he obscurely recognizes the Christic import of the newcomer?

The alien growing inside Ripley is, we are told, a 'queen', capable of producing thousands of alien eggs. The Company's man, Bishop (Lance Henriksen), offers to release Ripley from her predicament. The alien child will be removed from her body, saving both it and her. But if the alien child lives and grows, people will die. Thus Ripley, at the very end of the film, having, with Dillon, destroyed the adult alien that was devouring the prisoners, chooses to sacrifice her life, as has Dillon sacrificed his. Before the Company's men can get to her, Ripley falls backwards into the furnace, her arms outstretched, as if on the cross of Christ. And as she falls, the alien bursts out of her chest; and she holds it, as if holding a child to her breast. Mother and baby disappear into the all-consuming fire of death itself.

There are at least two senses in which this climactic moment, to which the whole film labours, is a scene of life in death. The alien queen comes to birth in the very moment that she and her host-mother are consumed by the fire; and Ripley's death gives life to all those who will not now be devoured by the alien body she has harboured within her. But these mythic and religious themes are crossed by a more disturbing symbolic, suggested by the image of the alien birth itself.

What, if anything, has Ripley gained by the end of the film? Has she secured an identity as a woman over against the 'brothers' or the Company? Or is she, at the end as at the beginning, possessed rather than possessing, invaded by an alien life that makes her its own, from without and within? The phallic nature of the alien has been noted by most commentators on the Alien films, and it is at its most penis-like when still an 'alien baby (or as one 42nd Street moviehouse denizen exclaimed, "little-dick-with-teeth")'[21]—bursting from the chest of

21. Taubin, 'Invading Bodies', p. 9.

John Hurt in *Alien* and from the chest of Sigourney Weaver in *Alien3*. What is at one level a scene of birth in *Alien* is also a scene of castration, since the penile alien rips away from Hurt's body and disappears into the dark labyrinth of the spaceship. Could it then be that in the last birth scene in *Alien3*, Ripley does not lose but gains a penis; so that what we witness is her complete masculinization by an ultimate phallic aggressor? Might it even be that this most feared event is what she has most secretly desired? If this, or something like it, is a plausible reading of the film, then we must suppose that at the last Ripley remains within patriarchy, within the Freudian imaginary;[22] and so once more Hollywood, in its myth-making, has been unable to imagine an identity for woman that is not given by man.

However we may decide to read this final scene, one thing of which we can be certain is that it is not a scene of resurrection. Fincher's films do not release us from hell, or suggest that there is any possibility of a radical remaking of the body, individually or socially. At best, there is the struggle.[23]

So, in my closing remarks I want to describe a scene of resurrection in which sexual difference is preserved, in which, possibly, women can become women, in and for themselves, and not as a body colonized by the male, but in which, at the same time, sex is transcended and ended. This is a scene of resurrection as imagined by Augustine.

In the last book of the *City of God*, Augustine appropriately turns to the question of resurrection, and to the questions by which pagans seek to ridicule the idea: Will abortions rise? Will all bodies be the same height and size? Will all our hair be restored, including that which the barber has cut off throughout our life? Will the same happen with our nail-clippings?[24] But the most difficult question, for Augustine, concerns cannibalism.

> 'When someone's body has been eaten by another man, who turns to cannibalism on the compulsion of hunger, into whose body will it return?' For it has been converted into the flesh of the man who has been nourished

---

22. See Sigmund Freud, 'On Transformations of Instinct as Exemplified in Anal Erotism' (1917), in *The Penguin Freud Library* (15 vols.; Harmondsworth: Penguin Books, 1977), VII: *On Sexuality*, pp. 294-302.

23. However there is 'resurrection' in Hollywood. 1997 sees the release of a fourth Alien film, Jean-Pierre Jeunet's *Alien Resurrection*, in which Ripley is 'reborn'.

24. Augustine, *The City of God*, Bk XXII, ch. 12 (pp. 1052-53).

by such food, and it has supplied the losses which the emaciation of hunger had produced. Is it then to be returned to the man whose body it had been originally? Or to the man whose flesh it became?[25]

But among the other questions that Augustine considers is this one: Will women keep their sex in the resurrection, for some say that 'they will all rise again as men, since God made man out of clay, and woman out of man'? Augustine has no doubt that women will rise as women, in their essential nature; a nature that is not defined in terms of motherhood, of sex and birth.

A woman's sex is not a defect; it is natural. And in the resurrection it will be free of the necessity of intercourse and childbirth. However, the female organs will not subserve their former use; they will be part of a new beauty, which will not excite the lust of the beholder—there will be no lust in that life—but will arouse the praises of God for his wisdom and compassion, in that he not only created out of nothing but freed from corruption that which he had created.[26]

For Augustine, the making of woman out of the rib of man, is not an indication that the former is but a part of the latter, to which she is destined to (re)turn, but an allegory of the relation between the church and Christ, emphasizing the 'idea of the unity between them'. The woman-church is born in the flow of blood and water out of the side of the man-Christ. This symbolic reversal of the sexual roles in biological birth is certainly problematic, but it is clear that in contemplating the resurrection, Augustine, despite his cultural circumstances, begins to imagine men and women not as they stand in relation to one another in the contingencies of this life, but as they stand in relation to the divine 'wisdom and compassion', and thus beyond the social symbolics of a fallen world.

In the resurrection we will 'enjoy one another's beauty for itself alone, without any lust'.[27] We will not desire the other to meet our

25. Augustine, *The City of God*, Bk XXII, ch. 12 (p. 1054). Nothing, of course, is impossible for God. 'Any flesh that starvation stripped from the hungry man evidently exhaled in to the air, and the Creator. . . has power to bring it back from the air. And so that other flesh will be restored to the man in whom it first began to be human flesh. We must reckon the other to have borrowed it; and like borrowed money, it has to be given back to the place from which it was taken' (Augustine, *The City of God*, Bk XXII, ch. 20 [p. 1063]).

26. Augustine, *The City of God*, Bk XXII, ch. 17 (p. 1057).

27. Augustine, *The City of God*, Bk XXII, ch. 24 (p. 1074).

need, but desire him for himself, her for herself, as herself, as himself, in her or his own beauty. In this imagining of the resurrection there is no more lusting after the flesh, as Augustine understood it, and so an end to lustful sex; but sexuation, our difference from one another as sexed bodies is maintained, enhanced and celebrated. We will be more ourselves as sexual beings than we are now.

If we think of heavenly bodies as in a sense beyond sex, yet with their essential sexual difference—a nature which is not one—preserved and enhanced, so that the eschaton represents not a denial, but an intensification, a sublation, that both preserves and overcomes our sexuate nature, the church may even now begin to allow this future body to inform its present practice, just insofar as the church is that community which shapes bodies fit for heavenly fulfilment. The church is therefore right to insist on sexual difference, and to mark, enhance and celebrate this difference, while resisting those tendencies in modernity that would deny sexual difference in the name of a neuter or egalitarian sex, which is, as Luce Irigaray argues, always finally a male sex. Yet at the same time the church must also seek to enact that heavenly 'family' or 'household' in which all are equally different or differently equal in virtue of their relationship to the one who has called them to the heavenly banquet, as sisters, as brothers.[28]

Over against the myths of our time—which find in the body and its sex the seeds of death, and which resonate so powerfully with the ancient vision of a world fallen into corruption as we find it in Augustine—the church must still strive to tell the latter part of Augustine's tale, which modernity denies, but which for Augustine is the point and purpose of the story, its *telos* and ending. With Augustine the church may still say: 'Behold what will be, in the end, without end! For what is our end but to reach that kingdom which has no end?'[29]

28. On the heavenly 'family' see further, Gerard Loughlin, 'The Want of Family in Postmodernity', in *The Family in Theological Perspective* (ed. Stephen Barton; Edinburgh: T. & T. Clark, 1996), pp. 307-27.

29. Augustine, *The City of God*, Bk XXII, ch. 30 (p. 1091).

INDEXES

INDEX OF REFERENCES

INDEX OF AUTHORS